I0840902

How States Can Outlaw Abortion in a Way that Survives Courts

Court-recognized fact finders have unanimously established what Roe said would end legal abortion.
A strategy for presenting that evidence in court and forcing courts to address it.
A vision of victory both in courts of law and in the "court of public opinion": legal arguments that are irresistible not only to judges, but to the public.
Not just maybe, but for certain.
Not just after another Supreme Court Justice dies, or a constitutional amendment is passed, and not just in a few states, but in every state, in a year or two of whenever prolifers act.

By Dave Leach, The Partnership Machine, Inc.
ISBN: 9781730767579

This edition January 13, 2020. First published November 16, 2018. Corrections & criticisms sent to SLIC@Saltshaker.US will be addressed in future editions if the author finds them valid *or* interesting.

Part One explains the political as well as the legal strategy for getting this challenge before courts in a way that forces them to agree that abortion can't stay legal.

Part Two is a model legal brief showing how a complete abortion ban could be defended in court. Legal terms are explained in maroon text, to enable anyone to read it.

Part Three is about the author, the Rhetoric Wars, and the spiritual battles.

Contents

Contents of the Legal Brief – Part 2
A legal defense of a law fundamentally outlawing abortion
(Easy-to-read highlights: Complete contents are on page LXV)

The Question that Silences Hell

Appeals to SCOTUS (Supreme Court Of The United States) must begin with a question or two which summarizes what the appellant is asking the Court to answer. We need to ask SCOTUS this question.

Do the unanimous, uncontested rulings of court-recognized finders of facts – juries, expert witnesses, state legislatures, individual judges, and Congress* – that all unborn babies are humans/persons sufficiently invoke *Roe's* ruling that when that is established, legislatures and courts must protect their 14th Amendment rights?

* To soften the resistance of Democrats in Congress in 2004, prolife leaders promised that passing 18 USC 1841(d) would not create the legal power to stop abortion. This book explains why that was an empty promise. Now, 16 years later, let's apologize, cite it in court, and stop the slaughter.

Successfully ending legal abortion in all states, in a year, requires a law that:

** includes evidence that babies are people which no judge can squarely address and keep abortion legal;*

** lacks complexity in which judges can hide from evidence (see p. LXII);*

** addresses myths about abortion precedents;*

** **substantially** reduces abortion, denying that murder must be protected from any "undue burden";*

** orders courts to "expedite" any review, "because lives are lost with each day that courts delay", and/or that enacts the measures on page XXXIII.*

The Enforcement Section.

All laws have an enforcement section, with definitions of criminal actions and penalties for committing them. Many, like this bill, have an additional "findings" section.

The following paragraphs are an example of a bill (a proposed law) that would achieve a "substantial burden" on legal abortion without adding fatal complexity. (See p. LXII)

(*Underlining indicates additions. Strikethroughs indicate deletions.*)

> Feticide. Iowa Code 707.7 Any person who intentionally terminates a human pregnancy <u>at any stage of gestation,</u> with the knowledge and voluntary consent of the pregnant person, ~~after the end of the second trimester of the pregnancy~~ where death of the fetus results commits feticide. Feticide is a class "C" felony. (The next three paragraphs would be altered similarly.)....
>
> <u>Any court review of this law must be expedited, since lives are lost with each day that courts delay.</u>

Why the restriction must be "substantial". No state appearing before SCOTUS has substantially restricted abortion, but has instead claimed some other "compelling government interest" than saving lives. (Such as a 3 month murder season ("heartbeat law"), sanitizing the murder rooms ("medical standards"), or making sure moms know they are murderers ("informed consent").

Why? Because *Casey,* 1992, said no law can be an "undue burden" on or a "substantial restriction" of abortion, or can have the reduction of abortion for its purpose.

That ruling was actually slightly logical, in the vacuum of evidence submitted to SCOTUS by any state that babies are people whose right to live outweighs their mother's right to stay skinny. That ruling cannot survive the overwhelming, court-recognized evidence that abortion is legally recognizable as murder. SCOTUS has never said the factual evidence doesn't matter. It matters.

But as long as restrictions of abortion are minor, the normal defense will still be that they are not substantial, or an "undue burden" on the right to murder your very own baby, and their purpose is *not* to save lives.

That defense is incompatible with the evidence, and is an unsound platform for challenging legal abortion. In order to spare defense attorneys from the temptation to fall back on it, and judges from the temptation to rule on that instead of on Life, the enforcement section needs to (1) substantially reduce abortion, and (2) have penalties covering the unique circumstances of abortion (ie. the absence of a body, the shipment of pills from abroad) so courts won't have to guess how prosecutors will proceed.

Why the law must demand Expedited Review. Legislatures can require courts to rule quickly to avoid "irreparable harm",. See page XXXVII for examples of grounds for expedited review in various jurisdictions.

Expedited Review can do more than speed up the review from a few years to a few months. If the judges comply and expedite without objection, they imply their acceptance of the premise for expedited review, that it saves lives, [meaning, in law, *human* lives].

But on what ground could judges object? No court-recognized legal authority, or expert medical or genetics witness, will affirm that protectable human life begins any *later* than fertilization. Judges couldn't just say, as *Roe* did, "the judiciary...is in no position to speculate". Judges would have to have *evidence* that babies of humans are *not* humans. Evidence which does not, and never can exist.

They couldn't invoke protection of a woman's rights: the only issue would be a judge's right to drag his feet.

Expedited Review "because lives are lost with each day that courts delay" makes evidence of Life the subject of the review even before the case begins. The judgment that "lives are lost with each day that courts delay" interrupts the illusion of detachment of judges from personal responsibility from the horrors they visit upon the unborn.

The "Findings" Section. (The part which has no penalties, but instead contains principles, facts, or arguments to help judges apply the Enforcement Section.)

This section of the bill is sometimes called "Findings of Facts", "Legislative Findings", "Preamble", etc. Sometimes, as here, it contains facts or legal arguments designed to help the law survive courts.

Unlike the Enforcement Section which, in our case, must be free of distractions, the Findings Section must contain the evidence and argument which no judge will be able to squarely address and keep abortion legal.

It needs to untangle several false assumptions that have confused judges and prolifers, and have prevented prolife lawmakers from directly challenging legal abortion.

In other words the same arguments which need to be in the law so judges can't overturn it, need to be in the bill so lawmakers will pass it. Ideally the arguments will satisfy lawyers and yet be understandable to all, *and as persuasive in the "Court of Public Opinion" as in courts of law.*

Proposed Finding of Fact: Evidence of Life

> **Finding #1**: This state must "of course" outlaw abortion, *Roe v. Wade* ruled, when the fact is "established" that "life begins" at fertilization. No fact could be more legally established, being the consensus of all American legal authorities who have taken a position, in every category of court-recognized finders of facts – juries, expert witnesses, state legislatures, individual judges, and Congress. No legal authority has affirmed that any unborn baby of a human is *not* in fact a human/person, or that protectable "life begins" any *later* than fertilization, including *Roe* which said "the judiciary...is not in a position to speculate". (98 words)

JURIES: When prolifers blocked abortionists' doors until 1993, the only seriously disputed issue at trial was whether human lives were saved. The earliest juries ruled that they were, and acquitted, until judges stopped allowing defendants to present their defense to juries. A law school journal reports: "After the court ruled that it would allow the Defense to go to the jury, the ... Clinic dropped the prosecution." (Necessity as a Defense to a Charge of Criminal Trespass in an Abortion Clinic, 48 U.Cin.L.Rev. 501, 502 (1979).

EXPERT WITNESSES: "If the defense is permitted, evidence is introduced that life begins at conception. This evidence [from doctors, geneticists, or scientists] is rarely contradicted by the prosecution...." Ibid.

INDIVIDUAL JUDGES: For example, Judge Clark, who ruled for a defendant who flew in a world renowned geneticist from France to testify. Clark was overruled with zero mention of the evidence in City of Wichita v. Tilson, 253 Kan. 285 (1993).

STATE LEGISLATURES: "At least 38 states have enacted fetal-homicide statutes, and 28 of those statutes protect life from conception." Hamilton v. Scott, 97 So. 3d 728 (Ala. 2012)

CONGRESS: "'unborn child' means a child in utero, and the term 'child in utero' or 'child, who is in utero' means a member of the species Homo Sapiens, at any stage of development, who is carried in the womb", 18 U.S.C. § 1841(d). Clause (c) doesn't diminish this *fact*.

That's the defense that will court-proof the law.

How much simpler can a defense get? It is easy enough for a child to understand, and hard for any adult to explain how any judge could squarely address that defense, and keep abortion legal.

But why have these facts established by court-recognized fact-finders not been thought helpful by prolife lawmakers and attorneys?

Why were they not mentioned by any state appearing before SCOTUS?

More assumption untangling is needed.

*Next: The Overlooked Power of
Court-Recognized Facts*

Finding #2: Lower courts said *Roe* ruled that unborn babies are *non-persons* *"as a matter of law"*, which makes irrelevant the *fact* that they are fully human so that killing them is murder. That is absurd, and the opposite of what *Roe* said.

Roe treated "when life begins" as a question whose answer can only be "established" by *fact* finders. Had *Roe* thought the issue a *matter of law,* it would not have said "the judiciary…is not in a position to speculate" about such a "difficult question" because "those trained in…medicine…and theology are unable to [agree]".

Nor would *Roe* have described "establishment" of this fact as a possibility despite the inability of any judge to "speculate", which infers superior ability in *other* authorities: *"[Texas argues] that the 'fetus' is a person. If this suggestion of personhood is established, the case* [for legal abortion], *of course, collapses, for the right to life would then be guaranteed specifically by the [14th] Amendment."* Nor did SCOTUS later say "when life [in fact] begins" no longer matters.

If the *fact* that we are people could be made irrelevant because "as a matter of law" "the judiciary is in no position to speculate" whether we are people "within the language and meaning of the 14th Amendment", (phrases from *Roe*) slavery would still be legal. The Amendment protects those who are *in fact* people – what is irrelevant is whether babies are people *as a matter of law.*

"To say that the test of equal protection should be the 'legal' rather than the biological relationship is to avoid the issue. For the Equal Protection Clause necessarily limits the authority of a State [or its judges] to draw such 'legal' lines as it chooses." *Glona,* 391 U.S. 73, 75 (1968)

#2 responds to the excuse that judges made up to

dodge evidence of Life: that Roe made "when life [in fact] begins" irrelevant by ruling "as a matter of law" that babies are not real people. It began in 1973 with *Doe v. Israel*, 358 F. Supp. 1193: "To me the United States Supreme Court made it unmistakably clear that the question of when life [in fact] begins needed no resolution by the judiciary as it was not a question of fact. ... I find it all irrelevant...." This became the excuse for judges to not even let juries hear evidence of Life in hundreds of abortion prevention trials - see *City of Wichita v. Tilson*, 253 Kan. 285 (1993).

SCOTUS said no such thing – but not that SCOTUS is anxious to hear evidence. From *Casey* (1992) to *Hellerstedt* (2016), SCOTUS has not allowed abortion restrictions that are "substantial" enough to be an "undue burden" on a woman's choice, and SCOTUS has dodged many cases raising evidence of unborn humanity.

But the states reviewed did not raise it. In the absence of any challenge before the Supreme Court to Roe's claim that judges are "unable to speculate" about "when life begins", it has been logical for SCOTUS to overturn restrictions "substantial" enough to be an "undue burden" on "a woman's choice".

Rather than challenge SCOTUS' premise that no one knows if babies are people, states have dodged the "undue burden" standard by thinking of restrictions that aren't "substantial", and that don't "intend" to restrict abortion. In other words they have invented other "compelling government interests" than "saving human lives". For example, sanitizing the murder rooms, a 3 month murder season, or making sure moms know they are murderers.

SCOTUS never said even if babies are humans, murder is a mother's right. Now that we know, it is whether the unborn are "persons" *as a matter of law* that is irrelevant.

Finding #3: SCOTUS must accept legislative findings of facts that are not obviously irrational. "..the existence of facts supporting the legislative judgment is to be presumed...not to be pronounced unconstitutional unless in the light of the facts made known or generally assumed it is of such a character as to preclude the assumption that it rests upon some rational basis within the knowledge and experience of the legislators...." *U.S. v. Carolene Products,* 304 U.S. 144, 152 (1938).

Aside from court-recognized fact finding authority of legislatures, courts must conform their rulings to laws until such time as courts declare laws unconstitutional. No court has declared 18 U.S.C. § 1841 or the many similar state laws unconstitutional, despite dozens of challenges. (*"'unborn child' means a child in utero, and the term 'child in utero' or 'child, who is in utero' means a member of the species Homo Sapiens, at any stage of development, who is carried in the womb."*) To do so would require the Court to positively affirm that human life does not begin until much later, which no legal authority has done, and for which no evidence exists.

The 14th Amendment is *Roe's* foundation for legalizing abortion. (*"...the word 'person,' as used in the Fourteenth Amendment, does not include the unborn."*) That right, defended as "privacy", may seem logical to those unable to tell if it exists at the expense of the lives of other human beings. (*"...when life begins[?]...the judiciary, at this point in the development of man's knowledge, is unable to speculate...."*) But *Roe* rightly acknowledges that when we *can* tell, legal abortion must end.

Congress affirms, through 18 U.S.C. § 1841(d), that now we can tell.

Now, legal abortion must end.

Congress, not courts, has explicit 14th Amendment

authority to "enforce, by appropriate legislation, the provisions of" the Amendment. (Section 5) That necessarily encompasses the authority to establish the facts that are the basis for evaluating when "equal protection of the laws" needs to be "enforced". It gives Congress greater authority than courts to certify a discrete class of people whose enumerated rights are violated.

The right to life is an "*enumerated* right". The 5th Amendment says "No person shall be...deprived of life...without due process of law..." The right to "privacy" is a "*penumbral* right". ("...*personal, marital, familial, and sexual privacy said to be protected by the Bill of Rights or its penumbras.*" - *Roe*) An enumerated right must be protected even at the expense of an alleged penumbral right, not vice versa.

US. v. Caroline adds that the evidence in support of a law doesn't have to be overwhelming: "....the constitutionality of a statute predicated upon the existence of a particular state of facts may be challenged by showing to the court that those facts have ceased to exist. ...But by their very nature such inquiries, where the legislative judgment is drawn in question, must be restricted to the issue whether any state of facts either known or which could reasonably be assumed affords support for it."

Heartbeats & Brain waves are evidence of Life

Finding #4: Detectable heartbeats and brain waves are evidence that a person has not yet died, throughout state and federal law. Reason demands they be accepted as evidence that a person has begun to live, although of course that isn't when lives begin.

> **Finding #5:** "Are babies people or tumors?" is a question that can only be answered to the satisfaction of society by factual evidence, not rulings. If "fetuses" are *in fact* no more human than tumors, then "of course" killing nonpersons isn't murder, and taking care of your health is a fundamental right. But if unborn babies are *in fact* as fully human as any judge, then "of course", as *Roe* concedes, abortion must be outlawed. Reality is the standard by which rulings are judged. *Stare Decisis* criteria acknowledge that an erroneous factual premise is a ground for overturning precedent.

Justice Brett Kavanaugh, during his confirmation hearing, described *Roe v. Wade* as "precedent upon precedent", and yet when asked by a Democrat about a precedent that *Democrats* don't like, he explained that discovery of a "mistake of facts" is one of the "Stare Decisis" grounds for overturning precedents. Here is an excerpt:

Whitehouse: "The hypothetical problem that I have has to do with an appellate court which makes a finding of fact. Asserts a proposition of fact to be true. And upon that proposition hangs the decision that it reaches. The question is, what happens when that proposition of fact...turns out not to be true?" ...

Kavanaugh: "[This is] wrapped up in a question of precedent and Stare Decisis. And one of the things you could look at, one of the factors you could look at, how wrong was the decision, and if it is based on an erroneous factual premise, that is clearly one of the factors... Mistakes of history. Sometimes there are mistakes of history in decisions and mistakes of fact." **Day 3 of the Brett Kavanaugh hearings.** Beginning at from 4:52:11 to 4:53:50 of the video posted at www.youtube.com/watch?v=mSyWoxGbpFg

Finding #6: Part of *Roe's* definition of "person" was "infused with a soul". *Roe* thus affirms the belief of most of society, a belief logically demanded by the common knowledge that humans are distinguished from animals by consciousness which features a capacity for (1) self awareness, (2) choice between good and evil – to behave either as an angel or as a demon, and (3) love: to choose to sacrifice one's interests for another. John 15:13.

These differences justify legal protection of humans beyond protections of animals. They are not explained by any known physical process.

Since "infused with a soul" not just *Roe's* definition but is commonly held, and a "soul" without consciousness has never been theorized and can't be imagined, the consensus of fact finders is, in effect, that abortion kills babies *with conscious souls*.

Souls have no known pre-conscious stage. The lack of any physical explanation for a conscious soul rules out any reason to infer immaturity of consciousness from physical immaturity, and is consistent with the report in Luke 1 that a baby at 6 months heard a righteous voice [and/or felt the righteous Presence of God] and responded with joy, a response not everybody chooses, indicating a preference for good over evil: a choice.

Even considering the body only, there is no objective line between birth and conception distinguishing "humans" from "nonpersons". Without such a line, there can be no stage of gestation at which killing a baby can be objectively distinguished from murder. No baby is safe while that line remains arbitrary.

The failure of some to grasp the humanity of babies at any given stage is a dangerous basis for permitting killing, since as many fail to grasp the full humanity of quite a number of distinct groups of *born* persons.

> **Finding #7:** Congress established in 2004 that: *"'unborn child' means a child in utero, and the term 'child in utero'...means a member of the species Homo Sapiens, at any stage of development, who is carried in the womb"*, 18 U.S.C. 1841(d). This *fact,* with the 14th Amendment, requires all states to outlaw abortion.
>
> This *fact* is *not* diminished by clause (c) which does not *"permit [authorize] the prosecution of any person for...an abortion for which the consent of the pregnant woman...has been obtained...."* A law out of step with facts does not block future lawmakers from correcting deficiencies, and states don't need Congress' "permission" to obey the 14th Amendment. *[Each state could add a similar point about its own "unborn victims of violence" law.]*

#7 responds to the official position of prolifers and Republican Congressmen that 1841(c) robs clause (d) of any power to undermine Roe. "By its express terms, the Unborn Victims of Violence Act does not apply to, nor in any way affect nor alter, the ability of *a* woman to have an abortion." *- House Judiciary Committee report, 2/11/2004* www.nrIc.org/uploads/unbornvictims/UVVAHJCreport2004.pcif

"The law explicitly provides that it *does not apply* to any abortion to which a woman has consented, to any act of the mother herself (legal or illegal) ...It is well established that unborn victims laws (also known as 'fetal homicide' laws) do *not* conflict with the Supreme Court's pro-abortion decrees *(Roe v. Wade,* etc.). The state laws mentioned above have had no effect on the practice of legal abortion." *- Key Facts on the Unborn Victims of Violence Act 4/1/2004* www.nrlc.org/federal/unbornvictims/keypointsuvva

They have had no effect on the practice of legal abortion, because no state has *cited* them to say what *Roe* said once said would end the practice of legal abortion.

Finding #8: *Roe v. Wade* equates the time an unborn child becomes "recognizably human" with the time the child becomes a "person": *"These disciplines variously approached the question in terms of the point at which the embryo or fetus became 'formed' or recognizably human, or in terms of when a 'person' came into being, that is, infused with a 'soul' or 'animated.'"* See also *Wong Wing v. United States,* 163 U.S.228, 242 (1896), *"The term 'person' is broad enough to include any and every human being within the jurisdiction of the republic...This has been decided so often that the point does not require argument." Steinberg v. Brown* 321 F. Supp. 741 (N.D. Ohio, 1970) *"[o]nce human life has commenced, the constitutional protections found in the Fifth and Fourteenth Amendments impose upon the state a duty of safeguarding it".*

The word "persons" in the 14th Amendment means *all* who are *in fact* humans. Had it been only for those who are *legally* recognized as human, every deprivation of fundamental rights would be "constitutional" so long as a law or ruling questions whether its victims are "persons in the whole sense"

Law doesn't have to call baby humans "persons" before killing them can be legally recognizable as "murder". "...laws treating feticide as murder do not need to define fetuses as persons. California's law is illustrative. It defines murder as the killing [not of a 'person' but] of a human being or a fetus. - *Professor Michael Dorf, Supreme Court clerk, cited by the National Right to Life Committee.* [www.nr1c.org/federal/unborn victims/roesupportersspeakuvva]

The myth that proof that babies are humans falls short of proving they are "persons" makes prolifers fail to appreciate how overwhelming the consensus is of court-recognized finders of facts, that all unborn babies "at all stages of gestation" have 14th Amendment protection.

The false impression that that isn't enough evidence yet to topple legal abortion keeps many prolifers from supporting legislation that will challenge legal abortion with the overwhelming evidence we already have, until we pass more "personhood laws" and add "babies are persons" to the U.S. Constitution.

The assumption that *Roe* ruled that not all humans are the "persons" protected by the 14th Amendment leads prolifers to think the consensus of fact finders that babies are humans doesn't count as evidence that will trigger *Roe's* "collapse" clause.

Had the 14th Amendment "equal protection of the laws" been only for those who are *legally recognized* as human, we could still have slavery simply by declining to legally recognize a minority as fully human.

All pro-slavery judges would need to do would be to rule that blacks are only 3/5 human according to the Constitution. Or that immigrants aren't treated by our laws as "persons in the whole sense" when they are prosecuted for what their parents did with them, bringing them here as babies, so we can enslave them.

It is the *fact* that unborn babies are living human children that makes killing them murder, not what any law says about it, or even what the Constitution says about it. That's what makes the consensus of court-recognized fact finders a stronger legal reason to end legal abortion than a Life Amendment.

Which makes it insane for prolifers to not even mention this legally recognizable evidence in each and every prolife case!

The quibble of Roe was not whether babies are "persons" or merely "humans", but whether very young babies depicted in *Dorland's Illustrated Medical Dictionary* as indistinguishable from pig fetuses are "recognizably human". (See p. 166.)

> **Finding #9:** *Planned Parenthood v. Casey*, 505 U.S. 833, 945, 954 (1992) did *not* replace *Roe's* constitutional basis for legal abortion — inability to tell "when life begins" — with *Casey's* new basis: how much women had come to "rely" on legal murder. *Casey* did not say "when life begins" no longer matters, or that relying on abortion can justify keeping abortion legal after it is known that it kills *people*.

#9 responds to a widespread view, articulated by Clark Forsythe of Americans United for Life, that "The 'collapse clause' fallacy also completely overlooks the fact that the rationale of Roe was substantially changed in *Planned Parenthood v. Casey* in 1992. The Court shifted from an historical rationale for Roe to a sociological rationale---the idea that women need abortion as a back-up to failed contraception. Blackmun's rationale for Roe became irrelevant with the Court's adoption of this 'reliance interest' rationale in Casey." (This statement was given by Forsythe to Chuck Hurley, legal counsel for The Family Leader, 10/27/2010. Hurley had asked Forsythe to comment on the opportunity I present. For his complete statement and my response see http://saltshaker.us/SLIC/AULmissingOpportunity.pdf)

Casey did not say it no longer matters whether the unborn are humans/persons.

Casey did not say *Roe's* rationale that "personhood is not established" has been replaced with "women rely on abortion now".

Neither the opinion nor the dissent even mentioned *Roe's* rationale. At least not explicitly. No evidence of human life was presented, discussed, or rejected.

However, an unidentified "outer shell of Roe" was discussed in a dissent:

> "The joint opinion...retains the outer shell of

> *Roe*...but beats a wholesale retreat from the substance of that case.... Roe continues to exist, but only in the way a storefront on a western movie set exists: a mere facade to give the illusion of reality." (p. 945, 954, Concurrence in part, dissent in part of Rehnquist, White, Scalia, Thomas)

What other "shell" is sturdy enough for legal abortion to "hang" on, than "personhood is not established"?

To say a thing "hangs" on another thing is to suggest that without the *other* thing, the thing would "collapse". So whatever still sustains abortion's legality must still be subject to *Roe's* "collapse" clause.

The majority opinion is silent on any "shell" or about any other principle upon which legal abortion might "hang". But the dissent's metaphor well describes what the majority did. It is obvious that "reliance interests" alone can't sustain doubt whether abortion murders conscious human beings, without which abortion is intolerable.

The same concurrence/dissent identifies "the whole argument" of prolifers as a finding of facts. "The unborn child *is* [in fact] a human life." There is no muddiness about "persons" versus "humans" or about "a matter of law" trumping facts. If prolifers are right that the unborn are "humans", then SCOTUS is wrong to protect their killers.

> The whole argument of abortion opponents is that what the Court calls the fetus and what others call the unborn child is a human life. Thus, whatever answer Roe came up with after conducting its "balancing" [between women's "privacy" and "potential life"] is bound to be wrong, unless it is correct that the human fetus is in some critical sense merely *potentially* human. *p. 982*

The SCOTUS majority has never said otherwise.

> "Indeed,...we would not have indulged in statutory interpretation favorable to abortion in specified circumstances if the necessary consequence was the termination of life entitled to Fourteenth Amendment protection." – *Roe v. Wade* at 159.

10. **SCOTUS** said that without penalties, a state personhood law can't *generate* a case, but as *evidence* in a case, it could be strong enough to end legal abortion. *Webster v. Reproductive Health Services*(492 U.S. 490) "It will be time enough for federal courts to address the meaning of the [Personhood law] should it be applied to restrict the activities of [the abortionists] *in some concrete way.*" Id at 506. In fact, *Webster* said clear state penalties for abortion might trigger SCOTUS review of Roe itself: "*there will be time enough to reexamine Roe, and to do so carefully... When the constitutional invalidity of a State's abortion statute actually turns upon the constitutional validity of Roe*", Concurrence by O'Conner, Id. at 526. If the finding of a single state *could be* strong enough to end legal abortion, the uncontradicted consensus of *38* states *is* strong enough.

Missouri's otherwise strong personhood law had no penalties restricting abortion. It even promised to obey SCOTUS. But SCOTUS reviewed the case only to tell the world that the case was not "ripe" for review! States can talk all they want; SCOTUS only cares what states *do*.

> "...until... courts have applied the [personhood] preamble to restrict appellees' [abortionists] activities in some concrete way, it is inappropriate for federal courts to address its meaning." - *Webster,* p. 491. (First paragraph)

Nor has any other SCOTUS ruling made any attempt to decide unborn personhood, or consider what triers of facts say about it, or even treat it as a a topic of interest.

Webster left the impression that when SCOTUS finally decides if *one* state's affirmation is enough, it could go either way. Now 38 states concur with Missouri.

Finding #11: Evidence of Life is not disproved by an *"exception...for the purpose of saving the life of the mother"* and/or by not charging the mother with being a *"principal or an accomplice"* to murder, as *Roe's* footnote 54 is interpreted. N. 54 was part of a 65 page search for some explicit statement by fact finders; had *Roe* found them, that would have satisfied SCOTUS, so far as *Roe* indicates.

Although the ideal of law is equal protection of all humans, "innocent until proved guilty" illustrates the inability of courts to equally protect everyone, without that inability proving that not all crime victims are human!

A legal reason for stiffer penalties for abortionists than for moms is (1) to get moms to testify against abortionists, and (2) the greater ease for juries of imputing culpability to adult doctors than to mothers suffering varying degrees of youth, deception (by culture, schools, pastors, and judges) and pressure (by family and fathers). (See this principle in Luke 12:47-48.) A legal reason for a "life of the mother" exception is that while we are *inspired* by people who give their lives for others, we can't *require* them to by law. (Deuteronomy 20:8 illustrates how God calls us all to be heroes, but does not force anyone by law; cowards may retreat from risk without penalty.) Even our Good Samaritan laws, requiring people at accident scenes to help, are sparse and inconsistent.

It would be hypocritical to charge aborting moms with being accessories to murder, without first charging judges. The degree to which laws fail to give "equal protection" to all humans is no evidence of the degree to which people are not humans. Such a legal theory is absurd, unknown outside Footnote 54, and cannot be taken seriously.

> **Finding #12:** Court-recognized finders of facts have never treated abortion as legal in the whole sense. Their consensus that unborn babies are fully human makes abortion legally recognizable as killing human beings, which is murder, which is neither constitutionally protected nor legal, but rather is what *Roe* said would require abortion's legality to end. No judge can squarely address this evidence and keep abortion legal, much less classify abortion as a "fundamental right", because to the extent judges protect what everyone knows are the worst of crimes, they eliminate the reason for judges.

The goal of this defense is a challenge to legal abortion that is irresistible to judges. How could anyone, confronted with this evidence, still demand legal abortion?

The standard defense of legal abortion is "But abortion is legal". This argument is trusted to trump the opinions of legislatures, doctors, biologists, and the Bible. This defense will evaporate as this evidence survives the scrutiny it will receive as it progresses through any legislature, and as courts are forced by the evidence to agree that babies are living, fully human beings whose lives must be protected by law.

Even before courts agree, public confidence that "abortion is legal" will further erode as the public realizes that even before prolifers get this evidence before courts, abortion is already legally recognizable as murder, with which courts will most certainly agree if they squarely address the evidence.

Most Americans, Democrats or Republicans, would never deliberately support murder. Not even *Roe v. Wade:*

> "...we would not have indulged in statutory interpretation favorable to abortion...if the necessary consequence was the termination of life entitled to Fourteenth Amendment protection."

Finding #13: There now remains no court-recognizable basis for doubt that abortion kills innocent, human beings, which is not a fundamental right. Therefore states no longer need to enact "the least restrictive means possible" of achieving some OTHER "compelling government interest" than saving lives whose humanity used to be beyond the grasp of the Supreme Court. States are no longer barred from "substantial" criminalization of abortion for the *express purpose* of restricting abortion in order to save lives. States have no further legal obligation to refrain from criminalizing abortion, or to support or protect abortion in any way. No "burden" on murder can be "undue". In view of the uncontradicted consensus of court-recognized fact finders, this State's legal liability from noncompliance with the 14th Amendment, by failing to outlaw abortion, is greater than any legal liability from taking corrective constitutional action in advance of indecisive courts.

> **Finding #14:** Criminal laws against abortion by this state are not bold, legally dubious attempts by one state to rewrite the legal landscape for the entire nation, but will merely bring state law into conformity with federal law and precedent, including the requirements of *Roe v. Wade* itself. (However, the evidence of unborn reality which requires an abortion ban in this state will also require an abortion ban in every state.)

Tragic Assumption: *outlawing abortion in every state is impossible – our greatest hope is to overturn Roe so states can again individually decide whether to protect infanticide.*

This view dominates prolife legal thinking, for good reason: it has been the view of conservative Supreme Court justices Scalia, White, and Thomas. In *Casey*, they wrote, "There is, of course, **no way to determine [whether the unborn are human] as a legal matter;** it is, in fact, **a value judgment."**

That was 27 years ago, that they hadn't noticed the growing evidence of court-recognized fact finders. By that time, there had been thousands of expert witnesses in genetics and medicine and dozens of juries, in those embarrassing abortion prevention trials, but the unborn victims of violence legislation that is now law in 38 states and Congress hadn't begun. If they have noticed since, however, they haven't said so.

Are unborn babies people, or tumors? This is a question with which society will not be made at peace by opinions, laws, or "value judgments", but only by evidence. *This is a question about reality, not rulings.*

If unborn babies are *in fact* as fully human as any judge, with the discernment a judge has between good and evil, which a famous unborn baby once demonstrated by leaping for joy at the sound of a good voice as Luke 1:39-44 reports — the mark of a conscious "soul" which *Roe* correctly observes is part of the meaning of "person" and of "recognizably human", then "of course", as *Roe* concedes, abortion needs to be outlawed.

In every state, *Roe* meant.

Conversely, if unborn babies are *in fact* only humans "potentially" in the uncertain future, but meanwhile are tumors threatening their human hosts, then "of course" abortion must remain legal *in every state.*

Killing nonpersons really isn't murder, and taking care of one's own health really is one's fundamental right. For as long as SCOTUS can dodge evidence that challenges its premise that judges are "in no position to speculate" whether abortion is murder, the 14th Amendment really does empower courts to stop states from trampling fundamental rights. (Its original mission was to stop states from legalizing slavery.)

The question must be answered with evidence. If there is evidence that unborn babies are *not* as fully human as any judge, why has no court-recognized fact finder in 46 years been able to find any?

Reality is the standard by which the law is judged; law is not the standard by which facts are determined. Law needs to get in step with reality, because reality is not disposed to get in step with law.

In ruling that unborn babies are not "persons" "as a matter of law", lower courts have not only violated Supreme Court precedent, but plain reason. The only legitimate reason for the Supreme Court to stop protecting a woman's fundamental right to take care of her own health is *evidence* that her unborn baby is a distinct human soul whose health must be equally protected; and when that kind of evidence is finally presented to the Supreme Court *in a way the Court cannot dodge,* how will it be possible for the Court to allow *any* state to continue the carnage?

The spread to every state of the outlawing of abortion

would occur as judges face the overwhelming consensus of court-recognized fact finders that babies are, in fact, humans/persons. This would void the rationale for legal abortion, that "the judiciary...is in no position to speculate" about whether babies are humans. After it is established/acknowledged by judges that babies are fully human, with rights to life protected by the 14th Amendment, how could they then allow *any* state to continue the slaughter?

The Fallout of the Assumption. Because of the myth that the end of *Roe* will return to *each* state the choice between life and death, prolife legislatures and lawyers have not presented the evidence of unborn personhood from *other* states.

If there are 39 witnesses to a murder, should a prosecutor bring forward only two? But legislatures have supported abortion bans with only their own say-so, and maybe with a few medical authorities from within their own state's borders. No 37 other states. No Congress. No thousands of uncontradicted expert witnesses. No dozens of juries. Only a trace of the overwhelming evidence for the claim that "life begins" at fertilization.

Only two legislatures have completely outlawed abortion with serious penalties. When Rhode Island's did it, it didn't cite any other court-recognized fact finders than itself, because there wasn't that much to cite in 1973.

But when the Alabama legislature did it May 15, 2019, the only rationale for omitting evidence outside Alabama's borders was articulated in an Amicus brief by an Alabama legal team in an Alabama case whose stated goal is to let Alabama decide what is allowed within its own borders. [http://48w41x2exf1mzi1dezjx6mll5.wpengine.netdna-cdn.com/wp-content/uploads/2018/01/Alabama-Pro-Life-Organizations-Amicus-Brief-West-Alabama-Womens-Center-v.-Miller-1.pdf]

If each state can decide for itself "when life begins", (as opposed to this being a fact-driven question which, once established, must bind every state), then the consensus of fact finders outside Alabama's borders really is irrelevant.

Roe clearly accepted as possible that fact finders

might eventually "establish" what Wade presumed, but *Roe* declined to be moved by the evidence from only one state, when Mr. Wade, Texas' Attorney General, claimed that it was Texas' position that unborn babies are fully human. Unfortunately the Supreme Court has never said *how much more evidence* would be necessary to "establish" that.

However, it is clear that the Court didn't think just one single state's assertion was enough. So can prolifers today logically expect the assertion of one single state to be enough, with no need of more, when prolifers *could* be citing Congress, the 38 states, thousands of uncontradicted expert witnesses, dozens of juries, and several individual judges who have taken a position?

For as long as prolifers, their lawmakers, and lawyers, concede the goal of outlawing abortion in every state, it would seem unlikely, indeed not fully rational, for them to cite the full range of court-recognizable uncontested evidence from *all* court-recognized finders of facts in *every* court-recognized category of finders of facts.

And for as long as prolifers do not justify their restrictions of abortion with the full range of evidence available from all states, it seems unlikely, indeed not fully rational, that the Supreme Court will allow the fundamental right of women to take care of their own health to be compromised for the sake of embryonic pigs and rabbits – which is how human embryos were depicted in the illustration cited by *Roe*, published in *Dorland's Illustrated Medical Dictionary*. (See p. 166.)

Finding #15: Any judge or court which attempts to block this state's effort to bring its laws into conformity with the Constitution violates *Roe v. Wade,* interferes with this state's compliance with federal law, and is an accessory to genocide according to federal law. Any *state* judge interfering with this state's obligation to obey the 14t[h] Amendment is guilty of exercising the legislative function, in order to perpetuate genocide through an unconstitutional ruling, which exceeds the judicial powers given by the Iowa Constitution, which is Malfeasance in Office, a ground of impeachment. Should any *federal* judge so interfere, Iowa appeals to its congressional delegation to examine similar grounds for disciplinary action. (For example, see *Bringing the Courts Back Under the Constitution.* http://osaka.law.miami.edu/~schnably/GringrichContractWithAmerica.pdf)

Legislatures have considerable untapped potential for restraining their activist courts when they become confused about which branch of government they are.

Page XXXIII offers suggestions. Briefly, any legislature is well within its constitutional authority to prohibit any district court from invalidating a law – only a supermajority of the Supreme Court should be allowed to do it, and within 90 days. After they do, the legislature should be able, within the next year, to compel the attendance of judges under their jurisdiction to discuss and debate, with specified legislators in a public hearing, the constitutional justification for [or necessity of] that judicial exercise of the legislative function. A supermajority of the legislature might then overturn the ruling, and the final verdict will be made by very well informed voters at the next election.

NO American legal authority has ruled that legally protected "life begins" any later than fertilization

New York's 1/22/2019 law is no exception

This needs to be clarified because conservative news has reported as if New York became the first exception.

The law says ""Person," when referring to the victim of a homicide, means a human being who has been born and is alive." [https://nyassembly.gov/leg/?
default_fld=&leg_video=&bn=S00240&term=2019&Summary=Y&Actions=Y&Committee%26nbspVotes=Y&Floor%26nbspVotes=Y&Memo=Y&Text=Y]

As grim as this sounds, this is not a statement that babies are not in fact humans until they are born, as conservative news like Breitbart, Townhall, and Tony Perkins indicated. This isn't even a statement added in 2019. It has been there for years. It simply means, in context, that when the coroner investigates dead bodies found in his county, or in a jail, he will not investigate unborn babies. It also means a judge, when excluding the public from divorce or rape trials, will not exclude unborn babies.

The 2019 law repeals New York's "unborn victims of violence" law, but not through that definition. The law had previously read " Homicide means conduct which causes the death of a person [or an unborn child....]" The 2019 law deleted the part in brackets.

The definition previously had two more paragraphs which the 2019 law deleted. They defined the terms "abortional act" and "justifiable abortional act" which had been used in the now deleted law against late term abortion. You can read the deleted paragraphs at   [https://law.justia.com/codes/new-york/2016/pen/part-3/title-h/article-125/125.05/]

This point is worth clearing up because it is a very strong, important argument for the legal recognizability of all unborn babies as humans/persons, and of all abortions as murder, that no American legal authority has ruled that constitutionally protected "life begins" any later than conception. Not one.

Stare Decisis' Limit: Facts

In the words of Supreme Court Justice Brett Kavanaugh

Even though Supreme Court nominee Brett Kavanaugh said *Roe v Wade* is "precedent upon precedent", during his confirmation hearings the second week of September, 2018, he later explained the basis upon which "precedent upon precedent" must be overturned, at the insistence of Democrat Senator Whitehouse who was concerned about a precedent that *Democrats* don't like.

More analysis of *stare decisis* and how it applies to abortion begins in Part 2, page 52. But for now, here is a glimpse of our hope, in the words of Justice Kavanaugh.

Kavanaugh says, in this excerpt, that "clearly one of the factors" in overturning "precedent upon precedent", is whether it was based on "an erroneous factual premise".

Day 3 of the Brett Kavanaugh hearings. Beginning at 4:52:11 (4 hours, 52 minutes, 11 seconds) of the video posted at www.youtube.com/watch?v=mSyWoxGbpFg Senator Whitehouse, Democrat, grilling Bret Kavanaugh, Supreme Court nominee

Whitehouse: The hypothetical problem that I have has to do with an appellate court which makes a finding of fact. Asserts a proposition of fact to be true. And upon that proposition hangs the decision that it reaches. The question is, what happens when that proposition of fact actually in reality, reference to real world so often, actually reality, turns out not to be true?

What is the obligation of an appellate court, if it has hung its decision on a proposition of fact, and then the proposition of fact turns out not to be true, does it have any obligation to go back and try to clean up that discrepancy? To clean up that mess?

Kavanaugh: I think, Senator, that's probably hard to answer that question in the abstract...

White: But if I give you specifics you will say you can't answer that because that will be talking about a case. So I'm in kind of a quandry here with you.

Kavanaugh: Let me give a couple of thoughts which are — I think that would be wrapped up in a question of precedent and Stare Decisis. And one of the things you could look at, one of the factors you could look at, how wrong was the decision, and if it is based on an erroneous factual premise, that is clearly one of the factors...

Whitehouse: (finishing Kavanaugh's sentence for him) ...you would look at and whether the would ree...

Kavanaugh: (interrupting) Mistakes of history. Sometimes there are mistakes of history in decisions and mistakes of fact.

4:53:50   (End of excerpt)

The premise of *Roe* is its statement of a *fact* that might arguably in the past have been reasonable, but it certainly is not now: that "the judiciary, at this point in the development of man's knowledge, is not in a position to speculate as to the answer...[to] the difficult question of when [constitutionally protectable human] life begins." So therefore "We need not resolve" the question!

> [Prolifers] argue that the fetus is a "person" within the language and meaning of the Fourteenth Amendment. In support of this, they outline at length and in detail the well-known facts of fetal development. If this suggestion of personhood is established, the appellant's case, of course, collapses, for the fetus' right to life would then be guaranteed specifically by the Amendment. The appellant conceded as much on reargument. - *Roe*

As if to say "We *know* having a baby may change a mother's professional and financial future, but we *cannot tell* if *killing* her baby is murder. So we will stand on what we know and *hope* it isn't murder. Now 'of course' the 'case' for legal abortion must 'collapse', if 'the well known facts of fetal development' 'establish' that our guess is wrong, and that *a person is a person no matter how small* after all."

SCOTUS was shown "the well known facts of fetal development" and didn't consider that sufficient evidence that very young babies are "recognizably human", but it is past time for an update from the fraudulent illustrations that made human and pig fetuses look the same, in *Dorland's Illustrated Medical Dictionary,* p. 166.

Here is an excerpt from the oral arguments of Roe v. Wade acknowledging how much hinges on alleged ignorance of facts:

> Justice Stewart: Well, if – if it were established that an unborn fetus is a person, with the protection of the Fourteenth Amendment, you would have an almost impossible case here, would you not?
>
> Mrs Weddington, the attorney for baby killers: (Laughing) I would have a *very* difficult case.

The legitimate purpose of *Stare Decisis* is to stabilize law so Americans don't feel like they are on a roller coaster trying to guess how courts will apply laws THIS year.

How Legislatures Can Keep Judges from Legislating

This way to tame judges uses verbiage from Iowa law.

<u>Preamble/Explanation</u>: the intent of this section is a mechanism for resolving disputes about the Constitutionality of laws between the Courts and the Legislature, both of whom contain constitutional scholars.

The Iowa Constitution, Article 5 Section 4, makes the Iowa Supreme Court "a court for the correction of errors at law, under such restrictions as the general assembly may, by law, prescribe". Article 3 Section 20, gives the legislature the power to impeach judges for "malfeasance in office", which is generally defined to include "acting without authority" and "abusing power."

The Iowa Constitution does not give Courts the power to invalidate laws enacted by the Legislature, require the Legislature to enact different laws, or publish rulings which have the same effect as new legislation. This violates Article 3 Section 1 "Departments of government. The powers of the government of Iowa shall be divided into three separate departments — the legislative, the executive, and the judicial: and no person charged with the exercise of powers properly belonging to one of these departments shall exercise any function appertaining to either of the others...."

Although Iowa's courts have usurped those powers without Constitutional authority, it has been done for reasons which the Iowa Legislature respects: the Legislature welcomes the expertise and guidance of the courts in evaluating the constitutionality of its laws.

But when the reasoning of rulings which function as legislation appears to be not only unsound but unconstitutional, the Legislature has the constitutional duty and authority to determine that judges have abused power and exceeded their authority, which are grounds for impeachment under the "malfeasance in office" clause.

A remedy should advance wisdom, build consensus, and educate voters so that informed voters may hold both judges and legislators accountable. "All political power is inherent in the people. Government is instituted for the protection, security, and benefit of the people, and they have the right, at all times, to alter or reform the same, whenever the public good may require it." (Article 1 Sec. 2)

Iowa 602.2201 New Section: POWER TO COMPEL HEARINGS

DELAYED EFFECT, SUPERMAJORITY. Any ruling of the Supreme Court which invalidates existing law or has the effect of creating a new law shall not have any effect for one year, and not unless six of the seven justices (IA 602.4101) agree. The Court shall have the power to suspend implementation of a *new* law provided it produces an expedited ruling within three months.

JURISDICTION. No district court shall have power to invalidate a law: the Supreme Court shall have discretionary [the Court doesn't have to hear the challenge] original jurisdiction over any challenge to any law.

PUBLIC HEARING. Within one year, the legislature may, by a resolution, compel the attendance of specified Iowa judges to discuss and debate, with specified legislators in a public hearing, the constitutional justification for [or necessity of] that judicial exercise of the legislative function. A public record will be made, and on the basis of the hearing, any judge may alter his contribution to the ruling, and the legislature may determine if grounds for impeachment exist for acting without authority, which is malfeasance in office.

LEGISLATURE SUPERMAJORITY. After one year the ruling will take effect, unless before that time 2/3 of the

House and of the Senate overturn the Court's finding with a resolution giving clear reasons, documented by expert testimony and constitutional authority but not limited by precedent, that are responsive to the Court's findings.

LEGISLATURE REPORT. The legislature within one year may add its own statement to the published ruling.

Impeaching judges: Views, and History

The norm is that "judicial acts – their rulings from the bench – would not be a basis for removal from office by impeachment and conviction." So said Chief Justice William Rehnquist, in his history of judicial impeachment. (https://tinyurl.com/y9xjlw5t) That preserves "judicial independence...so that judges are deciding cases based on their understanding of what the law requires, and not worrying that they could be removed from office if powerful political actors disagree with their rulings." "The Constitution does not provide for resignation or impeachment whenever a judge makes a decision with which elected officials disagree."

The example offered to justify this policy was President Jefferson's attempt to get Justice Chase impeached for criticizing him. *Not* addressed was an example of where a ruling violates the Constitution. Shouldn't judges be made to worry about losing their jobs for violating the Constitution? "Judicial Independence" should not require "judicial unaccountability".

When a unanimous Iowa Supreme Court ordered county clerks to start issuing marriage licenses to same sex couples, the Iowa legislature began considering impeachment, but Republican Governor Branstad said "There's a difference between malfeasance and over-reaching." Other lawmakers had less difficulty concluding that the imposition of what the Bible identifies as abomination on three million souls, with only the most imaginary support of any Constitution, easily "over-reached" all the way to malfeasance. Voters agreed, turning out three of the seven justices in the next election.

But had the measure proposed here been in place, there would have been a third choice between impeachment and doing nothing. The error could have been corrected without terminating otherwise good judges.

Of 19 people impeached by Congress over 230 years, (https://history.house.gov/Institution/Impeachment/Impeachment-List) 15 were judges. "Abuse of power" and "misuse of office" were among the charges. Impeachment started against 37 state judges; https://tinyurl.com/y3l7cpr6 11 were impeached. https://tinyurl.com/kj2td2a]

The Resolution Option

As state customs permit, a simple resolution stating the Findings proposed in this book may help launch public education in advance of a bill. Resolutions face no deadlines, less scrutiny over precise wording, and less concern with length. Resolutions usually receive little attention because they have no legal consequences, but a resolution making these claims won't be ignored.

Where state customs discourage Findings of Facts lengthy enough for our needs, a resolution may be a vital supplement to a bill. A formal response to objections through either will (1) free individual lawmakers from having to always be ready to address objections and (2) from the time it takes to explain misunderstandings to hundreds of constituents one at a time, (3) make it easier for constituents to digest the explanations, and (4) establish agreement and accuracy among lawmakers.

A Resolution is no substitute for a "Finding of Facts" in the bill. If no trace of the bill's legal defense is in the bill, there is no assurance that the defense of the law in court will include points from a separate Resolution. And if the defense attorneys don't raise it, judges won't address it.

Examples: Expedited Review Grounds (from p. VII)

(Speedy review can be required in a prolife law.)

DC Circuit Federal Court: A party seeking expedited consideration generally "must demonstrate the delay will cause irreparable injury and that the decision under review is subject to substantial challenge"; but "[t]he Court may also expedite cases . . . in which the public generally [has] an unusual interest in prompt disposition" and the reasons are "strongly compelling." - *U.S. Court of Appeals for the DC Circuit, Handbook of Practice and Internal Procedures 40 (1987).*

9th Circuit: The requesting party must make a showing of "good cause," where irreparable harm might occur or an appeal might become moot. Rutter 6:149.

10th Circuit: Appeals can be expedited under 28 U.S.C. 1657 for "good cause."

Iowa: Iowa Rule of Appellate Procedure 6.902 has special rules for children's issues (since children might not remain children through a years-long case) and lawyer disciplinary proceedings. (Babies are children.)

3rd Circuit: Rule 4.1 says a motion for expedited appeal must set forth the exceptional reason that warrants expedition and include a proposed briefing schedule.

4th Circuit: Rule 12(c) says "A motion to expedite should state clearly the reasons supporting expedition...."

7th Circuit: Appeals can be expedited under 28 U.S.C. § 1657 for "good cause." (Reasons must be given.)

Expedited Appeal Law and Legal Definition (An explanation at uslegal..com): "The court will speed up cases involving issues of child custody, support, visitation, adoption, paternity, determination that a child is in need of services, termination of parental rights, and all other appeals entitled to priority by the appellate rules **or statute.**" Other grounds: "**the constitutionality of any law**, the public revenue, and public health, or otherwise of general public concern or for other good cause,"

(Source: https://www.rcfp.org/privilege-sections/2-expedited-appeals/)

Facts that are against the law

Comedy

"Can a law change a fact?" I asked a Congressman.

"Can a law, that is out of touch with reality, *change* reality?"

He said he wasn't sure, but he didn't think so. He said that for example if Congress passed a law requiring bicycles to fly, he wasn't sure the law would make bicycles able to fly.

It was quite another matter, though, when I asked a *judge* if he thought a *court ruling* could change facts.

He was irritated that I doubted his power over the universe.

"Court rulings change facts all the time," he told me. "The proper question is not whether a court ruling can be out of touch with reality, but whether reality can be out of touch with a court ruling.

"Take, for example, people.

"The Supreme Court can rule that certain kinds of people aren't people, and whammo, after 6,000 years of them being people, they are people no longer. Not only that, but they *never were* people! History itself is altered! Why, the Supreme Court even has jurisdiction over time.!

"So since they aren't people any longer, if it is convenient for you to kill them, go ahead – it's not murder! God bless America!"

Those weren't his exact words. He used a lot of technical jargon which I have broken down so you can understand him.

And I didn't ask the judge over coffee, or in an email. We common people don't get to talk to judges like that. I talked to him in a court case.

Court! What an experience! No matter how sweetly, how politely, or how respectfully you talk to a judge in court, they call it "arguing". So I "argued" with the judge in court, and in 50-page essays that are called "briefs". When the judge finally answers you, it is not an answer. It often doesn't address the question, It doesn't feel like an answer, and it isn't called an answer. it is called an "order".

Actually I've argued like that several times, in several courts, helping several people, and what I told you the judge told us is pretty much what all those judges told us. They said they have to say that, because that is what the Supreme Court Of the United States (SCOTUS) said.

I've even asked SCOTUS. But they didn't answer me. I wish they had, because what SCOTUS has said, to other people (whom the courts have not yet ruled are *not* people), is very different than what all those other judges *said* SCOTUS said.

Those lower appeals courts said SCOTUS said it is "irrelevant" whether all those unborn people are *in fact* innocent people, which would make their unprovoked killing *murder*. Those lower courts said the reason the *fact* that those babies are people is irrelevant is that SCOTUS ruled that they are *not* people *"as a matter of law"*. Which a legislature can't change – hold on –merely by passing a law.

Let me see if I have this straight.

A *law* can't change reality. The same facts remain the facts, before and after any law passes. Lawmakers can only change laws; not facts.

But a *judge* can "order" reality to change, if he rules that a fact is not a fact *as a matter of law*. And once a fact is "a matter of law", then *evidence* that a fact is still a fact is *irrelevant.*

I kid you not. I told my wife all this and she thought I was joking. I am not!

XL

And it wasn't just one judge, or a dozen, who said these things. *In tens of thousands of abortion prevention trials,* you know, where the defendant is on trial for trying to prevent abortions, you know, by blocking a door, or burning it down, or shooting it, or just by standing outside on the sidewalk and telling what the Bible says about murdering your own baby, all those tens of thousands of judges said just about what I have reported.

In fact, maybe I have sugar coated their orders too much. What they actually said, to a man, was that because SCOTUS ruled "as a matter of law" that murdering your own baby isn't murder because your baby isn't really a baby, therefore what your jury, the "finders of facts", says about whether your baby is *in fact* a baby is irrelevant, so they needn't be asked. Juries oughtn't judge "a matter of law", so they needn't be asked.

In fact, not only needn't they be asked, but they are not allowed to know that is the defendant's defense. Even when that fact is the defendant's ONLY defense – that babies are real babies so saving them saves real human lives – the defendant is not allowed to even HINT to the jury, in a jury trial, that that fact is his defense; if he does, he is held in contempt of court and jailed! (See www.saltshaker.us/Scott-Roeder-Resources.htm for entertaining videos about this.)

(Excuse me for just a moment while I take a sedative. Ah, that feels better.)

Now where was I? Ah, what I thought was a problem only a moment ago, suddenly seems pregnant with opportunity. Why, if a court ruling can change the fact that people are people, so *killing* them isn't murder, then *enslaving* them would be even *easier* to justify since enslaving somebody – er, some*thing* – is a lot kinder to him – er, *it* – than murdering him! - er, oh well.

So why couldn't a court declare "as a matter of law" (SCOTUS thinks it is Congress anyway) that, for example,

Democrats are not "people" so we can enslave them? No, wait, there are two many Democrats with guns. Their leaders even have hired guns. That would never work.

How about "illegals"? Yes, that is the future of American law. We don't have to go to the expense of a Wall. We don't have to keep out "illegals", or *deport* them. We now understand how, legally, to simply *enslave* them.

But wait – isn't there a constitutional amendment against slavery? Like, *two* constitutional amendments – the 13th and 14th? That were enacted to stop courts from ruling that black people are "property"?

The 14th Amendment stops any law that doesn't protect all people equally. Laws treating some people as the "property" of others aren't treating all people equally! But now we can get around that by ruling that large populations are not *in fact* "people", "as a matter of law", which of course would make the *fact* that they *are* still people, *in fact,* irrelevant.

I *used* to think it was whether babies are people "as a matter of law" that is irrelevant.

I can remember back before 1973 when babies of humans always used to be humans. So much progress I have seen over the years! I remember before there were washing machines or air conditioners or TV, when all cars did was go, when all phones did was talk, and when babies of humans were humans.

And when killing innocent humans was murder.

And when everyone who were humans were just automatically "people".

Ah, progress!

In 1973 the U.S. Supreme Court ruled, as everybody knows, that babies of humans are not persons. Even if they are humans, they aren't persons.

Oh no, I think it's wearing off. I feel my mind returning.

Another thing I've noticed over the years is that sometimes "what everybody knows" *ain't so.*

For example, SCOTUS did *not* say there are any humans who aren't "persons". SCOTUS said the opposite: that anyone we can recognize as a human is a "person" with a "soul".

You didn't know SCOTUS believes in souls, did you?

> "These disciplines variously approached the question [of when life begins] in terms of the point at which the embryo or fetus became 'formed' or recognizably human, or in terms of when a 'person' came into being, that is, infused with a 'soul'..." *Roe v. Wade* 410 U.S. 113, 133 (1973)

What SCOTUS *did* say, was that how could mere lowly Supreme Court judges TELL if babies of humans are humans, when doctors and preachers can't agree?

> "When those trained in the respective disciplines of medicine, philosophy, and theology are unable to arrive at any consensus, the judiciary, at this point in the development of man's knowledge, is not in a position to speculate as to the answer." *Roe v. Wade,* p. 159

Think about that for a minute. Actually I'm not going to let you think about that for a *whole* minute, because I can't stop talking that long.

It is everyone else, not SCOTUS, who said SCOTUS said what SCOTUS never said: that babies of humans are *not "persons".* SCOTUS said they COULDN'T say that, because no judge is smart enough to tell.

But if you think that is amazing, that's nothing. Not only does everyone else say SCOTUS said babies of humans are NOT humans: everyone else says SCOTUS said babies of humans are NOT humans, AS A MATTER OF LAW!

Like, it's a LAW that babies of humans are not, IN

FACT, humans.

Like, SCOTUS figures it is unnecessary for SCOTUS to conform its rulings to reality, because reality will always conform itself to court rulings.

Like, if you thought SCOTUS passing laws, thinking it was Congress, was something, that's nothing! SCOTUS *passes facts*, thinking it is God! The Ruler of *natural* law! Gravity, the speed of light, the distance between atoms, all are but things of wax in the expert hands of SCOTUS!

That is, according to everybody but SCOTUS.

Fortunately for America, and for sanity in general, SCOTUS, at least, doesn't think or say any of that.

(Except for thinking it is Congress.)

Roe even has a "collapse" clause which says states will have to outlaw abortion again "if" unborn "personhood" is "established". Take a look:

> "If this suggestion of personhood [of the unborn] is established, the...case [for legalizing aborticide], of course, collapses, for the fetus' right to life is then guaranteed specifically by the [14th] Amendment." *Roe v. Wade*, p. 156

Well, does that pop a question into your mind?

It does mine. And not just one.

"IF...personhood is established"?

You mean, *Roe* justices, that you *didn't* rule that unborn personhood could never be established? Why, who are you to disagree with every other appellate court in the nation, which said you ruled "as a matter of law" that unborn personhood could *never* be established? You mean *you didn't know* if personhood might in the future be established, and yet *they* all know you know it can never be? You mean you expected that *it could* be – you *didn't know* you ruled that it could never be? How did they all get to be so much smarter than you?

"the...case, of course, collapses"?

You mean, you thought it possible that some other authority than yourselves could "establish" what you could not? That could "collapse" your case for legal abortion?

What sort of authority has more authority than the world's experts in American law? Presumably not some other *legal* authority. What does that leave? Some *fact-finding* authority? Like juries, expert witnesses, or legislatures, whose fact-finding you generally defer to?

But "everyone knows" you made facts irrelevant.

"for the fetus' right to life is then guaranteed specifically by the [14th] Amendment"?

Listen, *Roe* justices, you need to be more careful how you talk. People are liable to misunderstand you.

Why, everyone knows the 14th Amendment is what gives mothers the constitutional right to "choose" to murder their babies. How can the very same Amendment require states to *outlaw* that "choice"? Isn't that a little inconsistent? I mean, just from a silly little circumstance like finding out that "choice" makes you a murderer?

Who even wants states to all have to outlaw abortion, anyhow? Even Justices Scalia and Thomas don't call for that. They only want states to have the same "right to choose" that mothers have.

"Of course"?

You mean it is *obvious* that abortion's legality cannot survive knowing it is murder? Meaning your alleged ignorance cannot rationally or legally be made an obstacle to letting fact finders "establish" this fact?

The only thing that is obvious to everyone is that you didn't mean that at all. So you should stop saying you said it. You need to go back through your ruling and correct it so it says what everyone knows you really said.

The way *Roe v. Wade* copies erroneously read now, it looks as if you said abortion's legality and aura of "constitutional protection" can continue only in the *absence* of this "establishment" of the fact that abortion is genocide — only as long as uncertainty is alleged whether the unborn babies of human mothers are humans.

What is obvious to everybody else but you, is that you said abortion's "constitutional protection" *can and will* continue no matter who establishes, or how well they establish, the *fact* that abortion is genocide. Because it is *irrelevant* whether abortion is, in reality, *in fact,* murder, when, *as a matter of law,* the Constitution protects it. If the Constitution wants to deliberately, knowingly, protect murder, who are mere citizens to question why?

Those old inaccurate records of what you really said make it sound as if you said "of course" abortion must be outlawed as soon as you know it's murder, because you can't knowingly have the blood of innocents on your hands.

> "...we would not have indulged in statutory interpretation favorable to abortion...if the necessary consequence was the termination of life entitled to Fourteenth Amendment protection." – *Roe v. Wade*

You need to set the record straight so people know you don't care about that at all.

You didn't want the blood of innocents on your hands, indeed. Why, some of the most important figures of human history were mass murderers.

The Political Strategy

for getting this bill and/or resolution passed,
and for then forcing courts to squarely address the
"when life begins" "elephant in the room"

Developing an irrefutable legal defense which no judge can squarely address and keep abortion legal is only half the challenge. That was done decades ago, although this book updates the defense raised then. The defense was solid enough, in thousands of prolife cases, that to keep abortion "legal", judges below SCOTUS had to mischaracterize the defense, mischaracterize Roe, and not let juries decide the only contested issue in jury trials.

The failure was of the political strategy. Prolifers were divided, leaving the predominant popular pressure on judges to rule against Life. So the other half of our challenge is to create the political conditions that will force judges to squarely address our legal argument. That requires public discussion and education so that many voters will be able to recognize if a judge sidesteps the issue, and will be motivated to support measures like the proposal on page XXXII; also see http://osaka.law.miami.edu/ ~schnably/GringrichContractWithAmerica.pdf (sic)

Abortion law won't fall alone. When the "abortion is legal" mask is ripped off, many who never meant to support the ethics of Hell will leave the party and the anti-religions that feed them. These truths will begin national repentance.

Perhaps the easiest and most effective way for a prolife lawmaker to start this snowball down Heaven's Hills towards Fort Abortion may be to ask a prolife lawyer to review at least the first 30 pages of this book and tell you if he thinks a judge could keep abortion legal, if there were enough political pressure to make the judge squarely address this manner of arguments and evidence.

Let the lawyer know it looks to you like it could work but you would value his opinion.

If his analysis proves positive, that is a green light for introducing the bill proposed here. His analysis can be shown to other lawmakers to encourage them to cosponsor.

If it is negative, but specific, it can help us understand and fix vulnerabilities. If it is completely general, such as simply "this can't work", not only does it not help us understand why not, but it raises the question whether he actually read it.

When the bill is introduced, that will launch the public education needed later.

As a baby step towards outlawing abortion, the "Findings" section of our bill can be introduced as a Simple Resolution, in states where Simple Resolutions are used to educate and lay groundwork for a bill.

> Simple Resolutions...do not become laws, but rather function as statements of intent...[that] "express fact, principles, opinions, or purposes....Most...deal with mundane...affairs, but occasionally they can cause a real stir [when they] force members to go on the record with opinions....Sometimes this is just a tactic to get members to take a position on a potentially controversial topic....Other times it's a real opportunity to get the ball rolling on substantive legislation. [www.nolabels.org/blog/just-the-facts-congressional-resolutions]

Threats command attention, and this bill is a threat. It isn't a threat to *violate* law, but to *restore* law. It threatens evil. Those who love evil won't ignore it. They will lie about it – mischaracterize it as some absurdity that is much easier to refute. That will discourage vote counters, but prolifers who are paying attention will be encouraged that the devil's most affluent apologists appear unable to refute an honest presentation of our bill. Prolifers will hopefully respond by educating each other about the legal arguments.

XLVIII

Abortion is no longer a "fundamental right", so states no longer need to enact "the least restrictive means possible" of achieving some OTHER "compelling government interest" than saving lives whose humanity *used* to be beyond the grasp of the Supreme Court. Now that no possible doubt remains that unborn babies are humans, this state must act without restraint to outlaw their murders.

That excerpt from the "findings" of our bill threatens evil more than evil has been threatened for awhile.

A **dare** also commands attention. Whether as a "finding" of a law or a separate Resolution, this is a challenge to one of the American judiciary's most sacred cows. This dares any judge to refute its evidence. This claims that will be impossible for any judge who honestly addresses the defense.

"Abortion is legal" is no longer quite true. Legal abortion will soon *officially* end when judges squarely address the unanimous findings of court-recognized fact finders that abortion kills innocent human beings, which is legally recognizable as murder, which is neither constitutionally protected nor legal, but is what Roe said would end abortion's legality. It is impossible for any judge to squarely address this evidence and keep abortion legal. Judges only need a case that turns on this evidence. We are preparing that case.

When David challenged Goliath, when Elijah challenged the priests of Baal, when Moses challenged Pharaoh, when Jesus challenged the Pharisees, that drew attention. Crowds of thousands gathered. Millions paid attention. And when evil fell, God was glorified.

The role of **public education** is to equip voters to recognize when judges mischaracterize the defense, and/or mischaracterize *Roe v. Wade,* as judges have in so many thousands of prolife cases already, and to be emotionally ready to support action when judges do that again.

The political strategy will go into overdrive with a bill completely outlawing surgical and/or chemical abortions, that includes a "finding of facts" that previews the legal argument.

> *("Findings of Facts" are sometimes added to laws as introductions to explain the principles underlying laws, for the guidance of courts. For example, 38 states including Iowa, along with Congress, have "unborn victims of violence" laws which create a separate charge of murder when injury to a woman causes the death of her unborn child. 28 have "findings of facts" which say babies are humans/persons from conception. Page 13 cites a precedent that lists them.)*

Such a finding of fact, including enough of the legal argument to give a hint of its irrefutability in court, must be embedded in any fundamental attack on abortion's legality in order to (1) encourage other prolife lawmakers to see that it really is a practical goal,

> *(If a criminalization of abortion embeds no credible legal argument in its defense, the bill will not be taken seriously even by other prolife lawmakers. It will be universally dismissed as just another pie-in-the-sky pipe-dream of some newbie lawmaker who wants to be "pure" but who has no grasp of what it takes to get legislation passed, much less of what it takes to get prolife legislation through courts.)*

(2) force the attorney general to present those arguments when it is tested in court, and

(3) prod liberal news reporters into starting the public education by getting comments from law school professors who will prove unable to refute them without mischaracterizing them, if they even read them.

Of course the longer they do ignore it, the easier it will be for informed prolife lawmakers to advance their cause in peace. The more they try to trash it, the sooner it will become obvious that the argument is irrefutable when squarely addressed – it can only be attacked by lying about what it is. Which will encourage informed prolifers, seeing that their bill is beyond honest criticism.

The Court of Public Opinion

You may ask, how can juries settle "when a 'person' came into being, that is, infused with a 'soul'"?

That is how *Roe* defines "person". *Roe v. Wade* 410 U.S. 113, 133 (1973). Indeed, if a human baby lacks a "soul", the baby lacks what distinguishes a human from an animal. But how can the time a soul is infused into a human body be determined by a jury, or by expert witnesses, or by state legislatures, or by Congress, or by individual judges?

The consensus of court-recognized fact finders is overwhelming evidence *in courts of law*. It is hard to imagine how any judge could squarely address the unopposed consensus of court-recognized fact finders that abortion kills fully human beings, and keep abortion legal.

But what about "we the people" - the "judges" in the Court of Public Opinion? How can court-recognized fact finders be as persuasive in the Court of Public Opinion as in Courts of Law? Who are juries, experts, legislatures, or judges, to really know such a thing?

Victory in courts of law, without victory in the Court of Public Opinion, could spark violence, or at least a displacement of legal abortion with "back alley" abortions.

What do medical doctors, geneticists, or psychiatrists know about souls? If they lack expertise about souls, can they acquire expertise about "persons" by becoming certified as "expert witnesses" in court? If *they* can't know, can juries and legislatures supply that information?

Yes, fortunately. The vision of this book is total victory over abortion in courts of law that will simultaneously ignite victory in "the Court of Public Opinion". The goal is evidence so simple, persuasive, and self evident that the public will not merely *tolerate* the outlawing of abortion, but will shudder at its very memory, as our ancestors finally came to regard slavery – though without war, violence, or the mere displacement of legal abortion with "back alley" abortions. The goal is a challenge to legal abortion irresistible to the public and to judges.

Even though juries, judges, expert witnesses, and legislatures are all human with imperfect knowledge and imperfect commitment to truth which creates gaps between "legally recognizable" and "true".

Juries. The reason court-recognized juries, expert witnesses, and legislatures can "establish" these truths with the kind of authority acceptable to whole societies is that unlike public opinion surveys or petitions, which are normally *not* admissible evidence of facts in court, we test jurors for impartiality and educate them with the most qualified expert witnesses we can find. Juries contribute impartiality to the search for Truth.

Unfortunately states have not, so far, cited the consensus of juries in abortion prevention trials, in which judges let juries know about the Necessity Defense, and juries acquitted because the defendants were saving lives. This is a powerful resource which prolifers need to use.

Expert witnesses. The reason expert witnesses testifying in court records are more persuasive to whole societies than experts outside court is that in court, (1) the very top experts that the litigants can afford are called, and (2) those experts are scrutinized by the top experts called to refute the opposing side.

That is a standard that news reporters make a show of meeting, but reporters will (1) talk to a source for an hour and select maybe two sentences for a quote, (2) take the quote as far out of context as necessary to suit the prejudices of the reporter, (3) get the quote wrong, (4) make no public record available of all that was said so readers can double check the accuracy of the report, and (5) cram all that into 300-1,000 words.

Judges at least write a summary of the proceedings, reporting the positions of both sides, in more detail than news reports. *Roe* was 65 pages. And anyone can get a transcript of the proceedings, and copies of the legal briefs filed, if they are rich enough. At least records exist.

The value of expert witnesses in abortion prevention trials who testified that fully human life begins from the first minute is that they were never, or at least virtually never refuted. Which is breathtaking considering that Planned Barrenhood invests billions in legally attacking prolifers, demonstrating their extremely high motivation to refute prolifers in court, and yet the closest they came to refuting the expert witnesses was to say that Life is "irrelevant". In *normal* trials, if a litigant argues that the opposing evidence is *irrelevant*, he will also bring in contrary evidence to show the opposing evidence is also *wrong*, in case the judge doesn't agree that it it is irrelevant. But in abortion trials, that apparently never happened. No witness, in thousands of trials, was ever brought forward to testify that protectable "life begins" any later than fertilization. The fact was dismissed as irrelevant, but *the accuracy of the fact was for all practical purposes conceded,* being left unchallenged.

Unfortunately prolife litigants have not cited this overwhelming evidence in court. Some litigants cite the expertise of new authorities that have not yet been tested in court, but not the tested evidence. This is a powerful resource that prolifers should use.

Legislatures. Societies respect the findings of their legislatures as much as any other authority because all the lawmakers are there with the support of a majority of voters, and to remain there, they suffer the bombardment of opinions and information that would make the average citizen cry. And even once there, they are scrutinized by other lawmakers who continually look for ways to be contrary.

They are elected from jury "pools", and expert witnesses are routinely clamoring to give them information for free. They pay the salaries of judges, and have the power – seldom exercised, but they have it – to impeach judges who stray too far from their duties. When they impeach judges, they then hold trials just like courts do; except that the judges are senators and *the defendants are judges*.

So when legislatures agree on facts, their verdict is as persuasive and acceptable to society as any authority.

It is therefore for good reason that these fact-finding authorities are recognized by courts and are persuasive in the Court of Public Opinion, even though not many think about these details. Still, these points should be made.

The influence of the Bible. Even *Roe v. Wade* acknowledged the authority of religion in determining "when [protectable] life begins". ("When those trained in...theology are unable to arrive at any consensus....(how are judges supposed to figure it out?)")] *Roe* even quoted a Bible verse: Exodus 21:22, which, properly interpreted, affirms that fully human life begins at fertilization, but which has also been improperly interpreted.

SCOTUS' claim that legal abortion has the support of many theologians, and of the Bible, though without citing a single modern Christian theologian, or more than one verse of the Bible and that without discussion, certainly "opens the door", as lawyers say, to making Bible discussion a part of the defense. The example legal brief in this book offers such a discussion, although it is tucked away in "Appendix E: Scriptures SCOTUS must address before saying Christianity supports abortion."

The Bible tells us what science cannot, about human souls. It is the only reason there are prolifers, even though prolifers rarely state, publicly, the real reason they are prolife: the Scriptures they learned from rare sermons or from their own reading.

But many in this generation hate God and His Word. For them, courts, and the fact-finders recognized by courts, will be the highest authority they are likely to accept. For them, it will make an impression that all American legal authorities who have taken a position have ruled that fully human life begins at minute one, and no court-recognized authority has said it begins any later.

The Bible has contributed indirectly to this result. Although our society prides itself in being called "secular", the correlation of our freedoms with Biblical principles, compared with the correlation of tyranny abroad with religions and atheism abroad, make it pretty clear that our nation is a lot more "Christian" than it is Communist, Hindu, or Moslem, for example.

Besides that, the fact finders who have ruled for Life are often Christians, personally, which shapes their respect for infant life when they function as fact finders.

Society accepts the fact that a variety of world views contribute to society's findings. And on one side of the balance is the certainty of Christians; on the other, the strongest opposition is "we don't know."

A full presentation of all the evidence can only bring glory to God, Who said as much centuries ago.

The power of God is not limited to reporting facts correctly and persuasively even to unbelievers. Nor is He glorified only by being proved correct by all the evidence that man can assemble.

The love required to want to rescue others, and the faith to believe we can, only God can supply in the measure we need. No other religion makes promises about what He will help us accomplish, like God does.

Jesus told us that God has made a way to topple the tallest mountain of evil. Jesus said even mountains will fall if we have enough faith to not give up, so undoubtedly God has made a way for legal abortion to fall, too.

The only thing you may legitimately question is whether I have found it. You many *not* legitimately assume that I have not, as proved by the "impossibility" of that goal, without doubting God.

Nor may you legitimately presume that I have not, as indicated by how unlikely a messenger of God's answer to your prayers I am, because if you read the Bible you know God typically gives His blessings through the unlikeliest of messengers, in order to teach us to value even His "least".

Nor may you expect to hear God's answer to your prayers if you limit your attention to only a handful of top experts, because God says it is through a *"multitude* of counsellors" that we reach our goals – that our "purposes are established", Proverbs 15:22.

"But abortion is *legal!*" The standard defense of legal abortion given in response to pictures of what abortion does or evidence of who abortion kills is "But abortion is legal". This argument is trusted to trump the opinions of legislatures, doctors, biologists, and the Bible.

This apology will evaporate as courts agree with legislatures that babies are living, fully human beings whose lives must be protected by outlawing their murders.

Even before courts agree, this apology will be weakened as this evidence survives the public scrutiny it will receive as it progresses through a legislature. As the public realizes, even before prolifers get this evidence before courts, that abortion is already legally recognizable as murder, with which courts will most certainly agree if they squarely address the evidence, public confidence that "abortion is legal" will further erode.

Most Americans, Democrats as well as Republicans, would never deliberately support murder. Even Roe v. Wade confessed: "...we would not have indulged in statutory interpretation favorable to abortion...if the necessary consequence was the termination of life entitled to Fourteenth Amendment protection.”

Just as the major argument for legal abortion in courts of law is “we don’t know if it is a human”, the major argument in the Court of Public Opinion is “every child a wanted child”, splattered all over billboards in the past by Planned Barrenhood.

“How cruel it would be to make parents raise a child they don’t love, and will abuse. They could adopt, but most won’t. It is compassionate to spare a child from that.”

If women are spared the burden of “unwanted” children, the argument goes, they will be free to pursue education and economic opportunities and welcome “wanted” children only when they are stable enough to support them. “Unwanted” children grow up in loveless, broken homes and become a menace to society. “Wanted” children enjoy life and contribute to society.

Love is a choice, too. The choice not to love is the root cause of all evils. We enable that choice at our peril.

If a mother can’t love her very own baby, how can she ever hope to love her husband, or any man, who is far less innocent, less cute, and much harder to shut up by plopping milk in his mouth?

Without love, how can families survive? The obvious answer: they don’t. They are crumbling all around us.

Without love, even sex is cruel. To get it, couples lie to each other to overstate how “true” their love is, and to understate their STD’s.

“Oh, don’t worry about killing those babies. God has plans for all of them. Wonderful plans. They will be OK. They will go right to Heaven.” An abortionist once offered up that rationale on the Jerry Springer show.

That’s like the B’hagavad Gita, the latest Hindu holy book, written about 500 AD. General Arjuna dreads the civil war battle of the next day; many of his own relatives are on the other side. Lord Krishna tells him, "Oh, don't worry about killing them. You'll only be killing bodies, and freeing their souls to progress forward. Besides, you were born to kill – born a warrior. It is your dharma, your duty. So go out there and see how much blood you can spill!"

Yes, God still has plans for babies. And judgments against all who love evil. Yes, I *care* for the souls of unborn babies. I am *concerned* for the souls of American voters.

It will be hard for these legal arguments to be ignored once they are taken seriously enough to be introduced in bills. Before that point, news reporters who know about the opportunity can ignore it and avoid drawing attention to it.

There are several deadlines bills must meet to become law, in many states. The survival of "our" bill by each deadline, called a "funnel" date, is potentially the occasion of another news story, more public discussion, and more education. Historically reporters let even the least promising prolife bill "have it with both barrels" (of ink). Good! IF the defense is solid, and prolifers know it.

A "Straw Man" that the public must watch for.

A lot of public education is necessary because when "our" law is "tested" in court, judges *will* try the "straw man" approach of misprepresenting our law as something much easier to ridicule. Judges will try very hard to get away with something like:

> To allow the personal, ethical, moral, or religious beliefs of a [state], no matter how sincere or well-intended, as a justification for...preventing a law-abiding citizen from exercising her legal and constitutional rights would not only lead to chaos but would be tantamount to sanctioning anarchy. *City of Wichita vs. Tilson*, 855 P.2d 911 (Kan. 1993)

Do you see the misrepresentation? "Our" legal argument has nothing to do with religion, although *Roe* did base its alleged inability to "speculate" about "when life begins" on the alleged inability of preachers to agree, which theoretically "opens the interesting door" explored in Appendix E, beginning on page 80.

Other than that footnote-level point, "our" argument is based on American law, on court-recognized finders of facts, on legally recognized facts, and on *Roe v. Wade* itself.

So was Elizabeth Tilson's defense in 1993. She even flew in the world's top geneticist from France to testify about "when life begins". District Judge Paul Clark, summarizing the defense and *ruling in her favor*, did not indicate religion was *any* part of the defense. (See excerpts in Appendix H, p. 145.) Yet the Kansas Court dismissed all that world-class scientific evidence as a "personal religious belief" of some dowdy no-account religious kook housewife who expects law to bow to her superstitions.

This is not an isolated "straw man" misconstruction of a defense. Appellate courts did it routinely. Appendix F in Part 2 gives examples. We can expect it will be done again. The public needs to be prepared to recognize such evasions for what they are, and to be ready to hold judges accountable who rule lawlessly, in violation of the Constitution, and even in violation of *Roe v. Wade*.

To the extent the public is prepared to recognize a lawless ruling, and to be ready to support measures to hold judges accountable, it is unlikely that any judge will rule lawlessly! That very public *readiness* to act, without the necessity of public action, will surely be enough political pressure on judges to make them squarely address "our" legal argument, and formally acknowledge the evidence which ends abortion's legality.

Therefore, an irrefutable legal argument, *and* enough public education to recognize when it is not squarely addressed, should be enough to court-proof "our" law against abortion.

Why these bills will be hard for liberal media to ignore

Bills containing *these* findings of facts challenge assumptions no one has questioned for years. *Roe* is "precedent upon precedent", even Justice Kavanaugh said. Even prolifers who see it is *bad* law, think it is *law*.

So "Abortion is *legal*", its supporters say with confidence, their premise not having been seriously challenged for decades.

Even if the unborn are humans, they are not "persons", *Roe* ruled, according to dozens of lower appellate courts. *Roe* ruled that babies are not "persons" as a "matter of law", courts said, and even prolifers agree: nothing will change until we have a Constitutional Amendment that states "as a matter of law" that unborn babies are "persons".

But now, all categories of court-recognized finders of facts have unanimously established that constitutionally protected "life begins" at fertilization – no American legal authority says it begins later. (See p. XXXIX.) It is impossible for any fact to be any more legally "established". If judges *still* "are not in a position to speculate" about "when life begins", [phrases from *Roe* reminescent of the Pharisees' answer in Matthew 21:27], no judge can know *anything*.

And we don't even have to overturn *Roe! Stare Decisis* is not in our way! In fact, we *rely* on *Roe!* We present what court-recognized authorities said about what *Roe* said must be said for legal abortion to end and for states to become obligated by the 14th Amendment to protect babies from baby killers.

So these arguments contradict what almost everyone has assumed for decades, about the most divisive issue in American politics for decades, and these arguments are irrefutable. (If you find a flaw, please tell me where it is.)

A very difficult combination to ignore.

Emperor Abortion parades down Main Street showing off his glorious legal clothes. Half the crowd marvels how glorious they are! The other half thinks they are the worst clothes since Adam took up leaf stitching, but at least they agree Emperor Abortion has clothes.

It may not *look* like Emperor Abortion is wearing a legal stitch, but the consensus of dozens of appellate judges convinces us our eyes are liars. The Emperor's legally recognizable vesture is magnificent. Who are we non-lawyers to question them, with no better reason for doubt than our own senses?

These arguments make clear enough for even a lawyer to understand, why Emperor Legal Abortion is, after all, just as our senses report: as naked as a shaved pig.

This is not just about a legalistic defeat of abortion. The consensus of court-recognized finders of facts do not have mere legal authority. They also have genuine fact-finding expertise. Their consensus establishes reality.

This is the kind of realization that makes people switch political parties (away from the one which still imagines legal clothes). It makes people realize their family, their neighbors, their coworkers, their pastors, their fellow church members, if not themselves, have tolerated murder, committed it, and voted for it, making them guiltier before God than they had assumed.

This is the kind of realization that turns hearts to God in repentance. The kind that sparks national revival.

Legal, Political, and Biblical Reasons to Not *Initially* Address Exceptions or Contraceptives in an abortion bill

Many prolifers will support a bill banning abortion only if it bans it all – even contraceptives. They have both a legal and a spiritual reason. (Such bans may be explicit only in the interpretations of their sponsors.)

Their **legal reason** is that when the penalty for killing younger babies is less than for killing older babies, younger babies are not treated as "'persons' in the whole sense" according to *Roe v. Wade.* So we need the penalty for killing in the first hours to be the same as for killing in the last months or we deny that "life begins" at fertilization.

Their *spiritual* **reason** is that a law against murdering only some but not all babies would not be "pure". It would be "compromise". I don't know if that reasoning is *Biblical*; Christians rarely cite any verses that drive them.

But there are legal, political, and Biblical reasons to *not* address more than people will tolerate – in the *first* bill.

Biblical considerations: Exodus 1:15-21, God rewarded women who saved lives by making impure statements. 1 Samuel 8 shows how God *warns* a majority who "have rejected me" through political stupidity, but will not *force* them to be smart. God mitigates the harm as much as we allow: He selected their king, ch. 9, and subjected him to a constitution, 10:25.

God works with less than pure humans whether the problem is ignorance, Acts 17:30, Luke 12:48, or hardness of heart, Mark 10:5. Hardness of heart stores up "wrath", Romans 2:5, but 1 Corinthians 3:1-4 shows how God works with what He has: when we act like little babies, He warms up some milk. "Incremental" describes the progressive revelation of God's whole plan of salvation, from Abel thru Noah, Abraham, Moses, the prophets, Jesus, the Apostles. 1

Corinthians 14:40 tells us, act "decently and in order."

The **political reason** is that outlawing surgical abortions may interest half the population, but outlawing contraception doesn't interest even half of prolifers. Thus, putting that in a bill will kill babies by default, by killing the bill. Shall we save lives, or make a "pure statement"?

The first **legal reason** is that courts will evade "when life begins" if they can. If there is another issue before them, such as "exceptions" or contraceptives, they will use that to dodge "life". They will say that because the law fails over some such detail, the Court needn't "reach" the issue of "when [protected] life begins". Forcing courts to squarely address that issue is the goal of this book.

The second legal reason is that evidence of contraceptives which are mailed from other countries is harder to get than evidence of surgical abortions in known locations. Even RU486 is already mailed from abroad. [www.operationrescue.org/archives/the-abortion-cartels-back-up-plan-should-roe-v-wade-be-overturned] It will take creativity and study for lawmakers to develop a solution, for which they will not take time before they know if they can even get it through courts.

Once courts step out of the way, which could be within a year of when prolifers support all three measures in this book, most of the public will step out of the way with them, including many Democrats, assuring lawmakers that time given to refining abortion law will not be wasted.

Before courts got in the way in 1965 and 1972, (*Griswold* and *Eisenstadt*) there were enough Christians who regarded contraceptives as a violation of Genesis 1:28, "Be fruitful and multiply", to support *laws* against them!

The public education generated by court rulings that "life begins at fertilization" will heal public understanding, making the impossible possible, and facilitating revival.

Part Two

A model legal brief from which any state Attorney General may borrow, to defend any state law criminalizing abortion. Legal terms are explained in brackets, to enable anyone to understand.

The next 8 pages are required introductory pages for Supreme Court briefs. The "argument" itself follows, where page numbering starts over with page 1.

A central argument that this book urges legislatures to make is that court-recognized fact finders in *every* category of court-recognized fact finders (juries, experts, states, Congress) has unanimously ruled that "life begins" from hour one. But what about juries? How is it even possible to prove or disprove that claim from court records, since juries rarely give reasons for their rulings?

A law review article (p. 15) says juries in abortion prevention cases, informed about the Necessity Defense, (blocking doors was "necessary" and "justified" to save real people) acquitted often enough that judges looked for a way to keep juries from learning about the defense.

I was a defendant in what may have been the last trial where a jury was allowed to hear the defense. The case was *State v. Brouillette*, et al, Johnson County, Iowa, 1989. 155 of us were arrested January 26, 1989 for blocking the doors of the Emma Goldman clinic in Iowa City, Iowa. Rather than pack all 155 in the court room, 16 of us were tried in the first batch. It was assumed that what happened to them would drive what happened later to the rest; especially since J. Patrick White, the prosecuting county attorney, had told newspapers that if the first 16 were acquitted there is no way he would prosecute the others.

But after the jury acquitted the first 16, White refused to dismiss, and that is the only reason we have an official court record documenting that the Defense of Justification was the only issue before the jury. The jury didn't say so, but the judge did, in his ruling dismissing the remaining charges.

He wrote that both sides stipulated to (officially agreed about) the facts. "Each Defendant stipulated to his or her identity; to entering and remaining upon public property; and to failing to leave said public property after being notified and requested to vacate by persons whose duty it was to supervise the use and maintenance of this property. By this stipulation, the sole element of the offense of Criminal Trespass which remained to be proven was **whether each defendant acted without justification**. The verdict of the jury indicates the State failed to prove, beyond a reasonable doubt, **the one essential element of the charge which remained in issue.** In a trial of the remaining 138 Defendants, [one of the 155 arrested was juvenile and was not charged], a jury would be presented with this identical issue. (So the remaining charges should be dropped by the theory of Issue Preclusion - if Joe is found innocent after doing something, Jack should be after doing the same thing.)"

Northern Virginia Women's Medical Center v. Balch, 617 F.2d 1045, 1048-49 (4th Cir. 1980) refers to two unreported cases where "necessity" led to acquittals, where it is not clear whether it was a jury or "bench" trial.

No. _________________

IN THE
SUPREME COURT OF THE UNITED STATES
State of Iowa, Petitioner

vs.

Planned Parenthood of Greater Iowa, Respondent
ON PETITION FOR A WRIT OF CERTIORARI TO
THE 8th CIRCUIT COURT OF APPEALS
PETITION FOR WRIT OF CERTIORARI
Attorney General of Iowa
Des Moines, Iowa

Question for the Court: "Has the fact that all unborn babies are humans/persons been sufficiently established by juries, expert witnesses, state legislatures, individual judges, Congress, and the absence of any contrary affirmation, to invoke Roe's ruling that state legislatures and courts should now protect their 14th Amendment rights?"

[This is not an actual legal brief that has been or will be filed in any court case, although it builds on legal arguments I have made in briefs submitted by "pro se" defendants in their court cases. This brief is an example of legal arguments available to defend, in court, a state or federal law that completely outlaws abortion. In order to make this readable for all readers, legal terms and idioms will be explained in this font, in brackets like these.]

Attorneys
For the State: Honest Joe, Attorney General
For Banned Parenthood: Bloody Harry, Esq.

TABLE OF CONTENTS

(How to read case citations in the following section: first are the names of the two sides opposing each other in court. Next is the volume number of the book in which the court's ruling may be read; for example, "580" means it is in the 580th book in that series – enough books to cover the wall of an average size living room, as an alternative to painting it. Then is the abbreviation of the name of the series. Then come two numbers: the page number on which the case begins, and then the page number where the quote is found. Finally in parenthesis is the year the case was decided. So if you want to read any of these cases, search online for everything except the second page number.)

TABLE OF AUTHORITIES CITED

Statutes

U. S. Constitution

Other legal authorities

Bible   *Roe's* claim of Christian support for abortion
"opened the door" rather wide *["When those trained*
in...theology are unable to arrive at any consensus....]

Definition: *"Opening the door"* is a Common Law legal
doctrine that allows for the admission of previously
inadmissible evidence after the other side has "opened the
door" to it by first bringing up the forbidden subject at trial.
"Evidence is admitted under the doctrine when deemed
necessary to counter the evidence that opened the door." -
USlegal.com

[The following "Opinions Below" and "Statement of the Case" are fiction, but they present an idea of how a case may proceed. One appeal for which I wrote briefs actually did have the deadline for Planned Barrenhood to respond fall on Christmas Eve. They forgot to respond, as it turned out, but the judge forgave them. These two sections, in this fictional case, will use Iowa law and rules for an example; after that, the actual legal arguments offered by this book, "Reasons to Grant the Writ", will no longer mention Iowa but will be applicable in any state.]

IN THE SUPREME COURT OF THE UNITED STATES
PETITION FOR WRIT OF CERTIORARI

[A "writ of certiorari" orders a lower court to deliver its record of a case to the higher court so the higher court can review it. This is a "petition", or request, for the Supreme Court to take a case. The first round of briefs before SCOTUS – Supreme Court Of The United States – are just to persuade SCOTUS to take the case.]

Petitioner respectfully prays [*asks*] that a writ of certiorari issue [*be issued*] to review the judgment below.

OPINIONS BELOW [*How the lower courts ruled*]

The opinion of the 8th Circuit Court of Appeals appears at Appendix A to the petition and is reported at Planned Parenthood v. Iowa, #123456. The date the highest federal court decided the case was October 24, 2019. The jurisdiction of this Court is invoked under 28 U. S. C. § 1257(b). The trial court entry of judgment is in Appendix B. [*The case number, name, and date are fictitious. The U.S. Code number and Appendix section are set by court rule.*]

CONSTITUTIONAL AND STATUTORY PROVISIONS INVOLVED

Iowa's arguments are based on and involve the Preamble to the U.S. Constitution, 14th Amendment "equal protection", and 5th Amendment "Due Process". The text of these is in Appendix C. The text of the Iowa law challenged here is as follows: [*This is what I propose saying in a law so that judges will not be able to overturn it.*]

Iowa Code 707.7 Feticide.

New Section: **Findings of Fact:** The Iowa Legislature finds itself obligated to protect the Right to Life of all unborn babies by Roe v. Wade's order that when the fact is "established" that "when life begins" is at fertilization, then "of course" the 14th Amendment requires states to outlaw abortion. Iowa finds that no fact could be more legally established than this fact, which is the consensus of all American legal authorities who have taken a position, in all categories of court-recognized finders of facts [*Courts recognize courts as the best qualified of all legal authorities to understand law, but defers to the following legal authorities as having a better grasp of facts*] – juries, expert witnesses, state legislatures, individual judges, and Congress with 18 U.S.C. § 1841(d). [*Chapter 18 of the U.S. Code, section 1841, paragraph d.*] Iowa finds that no American legal authority has affirmed that any unborn baby of a human is not a human/person, or that protectable "life begins" any later than fertilization. [*Fertilization – when a sperm joins to an egg – is earlier than conception – when the fertilized egg implants itself in the wall of the uterus.*] In view of this uncontradicted consensus, Iowa finds that its legal liability from noncompliance with the 14th Amendment, by failing to criminalize abortion, is greater than any legal liability from taking corrective action in advance of indecisive courts. [*In the next two paragraphs, what is underlined is what should be added to the law. What is struck through is what should be deleted from the law. The rest is what the law already says that should be left alone.*]

1. Any person who intentionally terminates a human pregnancy <u>at any stage of gestation</u>, with the knowledge and voluntary consent of the pregnant person, ~~after the end of the second trimester of the pregnancy~~ where death of the fetus results commits feticide. Feticide is a class "C" felony.

2. Any person who attempts to intentionally terminate a human pregnancy <u>at any stage of gestation</u>, with the knowledge and voluntary consent of the pregnant person, ~~after the end of the second trimester of the pregnancy~~ where death of the fetus does not result commits attempted

feticide. Attempted feticide is a class "D" felony.[1]

3. Any person who terminates a human pregnancy <u>at any stage of gestation</u>, with the knowledge and voluntary consent of the pregnant person, who is not a person licensed to practice medicine and surgery or osteopathic medicine and surgery under the provisions of chapter 148, commits a class "C" felony.

4. This section shall not apply to the termination of a human pregnancy performed by a physician licensed in this state to practice medicine or surgery or osteopathic medicine or surgery when in the best clinical judgment of the physician the termination is performed to preserve the life ~~or health~~ of the pregnant person or of the fetus and every reasonable medical effort not inconsistent with preserving the life of the pregnant person is made to preserve the life of a viable fetus. [R60, §4221; C73,...]

A companion resolution, laying out additional legal arguments in support of this law, was enacted the same day. It is copied in Appendix I. (The letter "i".) [*Legislatures can pass both laws and resolutions. The difference is that laws have penalties which can fine people and put people in jail. They can include short statements of facts that justify the law or explain how to apply the law. Both are numbered to show where they are added to the state's law books. A resolution is just a statement of facts with no penalties, that can be longer. Resolutions are not added to the state's law books.*]

STATEMENT OF THE CASE [2]

[*What got us in Court*]

---

1   This section would criminalize distribution of RU486. Because even if the existence of a baby can't be proved absolutely, the law criminalizes mere intent.

2   Since this is a model defense for a case which has not yet occurred, this section, stating what has happened in the case so far, is of course fiction. However, it contains elements from past cases, and may be prophetic.

The Iowa Legislature outlawed abortion in January of its 2019 session. Iowa's governor signed the bill on Sunday, January 22, the 46th anniversary of *Roe v. Wade.* Iowa's law was immediately enjoined from taking effect by a single federal judge. In his expedited ruling, the judge did not address the defense for Iowa's law embedded in section (a). He instead refuted arguments Iowa had not made, that were unrelated to Iowa's actual defense, about what he called "religious" statements made by some lawmakers during the legislature's deliberations.[3]

In expedited action, the 8th Circuit Court of Appeals ruled on October 24, 2020, leaving the deadline for Iowa's petition before SCOTUS to fall on the 48th Anniversary of Roe v. Wade.

It was never challenged in court that Iowa's law would save unborn human beings. Nor was it ever denied that unborn babies of human mothers are humans, but neither was it ever acknowledged. That was the "element in the room".

Neither the district judge nor the appellate Opinion Below rules on whether 18 U.S.C. § 1841(d)[4] legally establishes Iowa's view – that unborn babies of humans are humans/persons – as correct and controlling. [*"Controlling" means having the authority to determine how a court must rule*] Or on Congress's authority to determine this fact. Or on Iowa's reliance on the statute. The record outside Iowa's own

---

3   Again, this is fiction. But it is realistic. It was the Iowa Supreme Court's approach in *Planned Parenthood of Mid-Iowa v. Maki* 478 N.W.2d 637 (1991), which is summarized later, and in cases reviewed in Appendix F. As for court deadlines falling on significant dates, that has happened several times in cases I have been involved in; sometimes in ways that no man could have planned, and sometimes deliberately such as when Judge Huppert overturned Iowa's Heartbeat Law on the 46th Deathday of Roe v. Wade.

4   18 USC §1841(d) ...the term "preborn child" means a child in utero, and the term "child in utero" or "child, who is in utero" means a member of the species homo sapiens, at any stage of development, who is carried in the womb.

briefs [*the rulings of the lower courts, the briefs of the abortionists, and the transcript of oral debate*] omits any mention of 18 U.S.C. § 1841(d).[5]

No federal judge ever acknowledged Iowa's key defense, its fact issue, [*its claim that the unborn are legally established as being, in fact, persons/humans, which ends legal abortion*] its reliance [*its defense, based*] upon federal law, or on Iowa's reliance on Roe v. Wade's "collapse" clause. [*The clause in Roe v. Wade which explains what will cause legal abortion to "collapse".*] Iowa is still waiting for a court to rule on the facts and arguments that Iowa has *actually* presented, instead of the *straw man* [*the debating trick of characterizing an idea you don't like but which you can't refute as something different than it is which is much easier to ridicule*] which the Court substituted:

> The legislature has no legitimate interest in "simply interfer[ing] with a...person's right to lawful activity". That "is generally not available to excuse" an undue burden on the fundamental right "under the Constitutions of the United States and of the State of [Iowa] to terminate a pregnancy...."[6]

The alleged "evidence" that Iowa claimed a "legitimate state interest" in interfering with lawful activity was not submitted *by Iowa* at trial, but by Planned Parenthood and the National Abortion Federation in its amicus, presumably to divert the court's attention from the federal law upon which Iowa's defense relies.

---

5   Again, this is fiction, but it is realistic. The 18 USC §1841(d) argument was raised in two cases for which I wrote briefs, but was never acknowledged by the judges. These scenarios are included to prepare readers for the breathtaking ability of judges to imagine a "Straw Man" much easier to knock down as an alternative to addressing the actual defense.
    It is a mistake to expect courts to squarely address the defense presented here. Only a very aware, informed public can *make* them. Otherwise they definitely will dodge the evidence; because if they squarely address *this* evidence, it will be impossible for them to leave abortion legal.

6   Again, this is fiction, but there is precedent for expecting a similar "straw man" dismissal of a state's defense. These phrases are taken from actual abortion cases: *State v. Sahr*, 470 N.W.2d at 191-192; *U.S. v. Kabat*, 797 F.2d 580, 591 (8th Cir.1986); and *People v. Garziano* 230 Cal. App. 3d 242, 244 (1991).

One doesn't have to be religious to realize that the babies of humans are humans. One only needs respect for U.S. law. Every U.S. legal authority which has taken a position on the subject has unanimously agreed they are.

REASONS TO GRANT THE WRIT

Judges are forcing this state to violate the Constitution. The most urgent reason SCOTUS must grant Iowa's writ is that the injunctions of federal judges are forcing Iowa to violate the 14th Amendment of the Constitution, according to *Roe v. Wade.*

> "If this suggestion of personhood [of unborn babies] is established, the...case [for legalizing aborticide], of course, collapses, for the fetus' right to life is then guaranteed specifically by the [14th] Amendment." *Roe v. Wade,* 410 US 113, 156

This "suggestion of personhood" is now "established."

But every court but SCOTUS says *Roe v. Wade* made that irrelevant.

Since the 14th Amendment directly obligates states to protect fundamental rights, preventing a state from protecting these rights is an unacceptable situation in which to place any state. Iowa has been out of compliance with the Constitution since at least 2004 when Congress joined every other court-recognized category of fact finders in establishing what *Roe* said must end legal abortion. For a state to finally realize its noncompliant condition, and promptly make itself compliant, only to be prevented by federal courts from obeying the Constitution and avoiding any further liability for noncompliance, is error which must be corrected immediately. How can there be a more "important question of federal law that has not been, but should be, settled by this Court"?[7]

---

7 This is one of two reasons SCOTUS will hear a case that are given in Supreme Court rule 10c.

Lower courts violate Roe by misapplying Roe. A second reason to grant the writ is to correct a long line of appeals courts precedents whose conflict with *Roe v. Wade* was widened by the 2004 federal law, and which continue to prevent states' compliance with the Constitution.

The contrast between *Roe* and the long line of lower appellate court decisions could not be greater.

Roe professed inability of "the judiciary" to determine "when life begins", a "question" upon which doctors and preachers have more expertise than themselves.[8] Since SCOTUS could not expect superior expertise on a question of *law* from doctors and preachers, SCOTUS had to have meant to treat the question as one of fact. Because of SCOTUS' inability to answer the question, the *Roe* justices invited unspecified but impliedly greater authorities than themselves to do so, and said abortion's continued legality would hinge on what they "establish"[9]. *Roe* said if abortion is proved to *in fact* kill people, then *Roe's holding* must "of course" become irrelevant.

Lower courts said the opposite. They said *Roe* made abortion so absolutely constitutionally protected that it is whether abortion *in fact* kills people that is irrelevant.

That error [*"error", in legal briefs, means not just a small mistake, but a mistake critical enough to reverse the entire ruling*] was pioneered in the first abortion case, a 1973 review of [*court challenge to*] Rhode Island's law which had a strong statement that unborn babies are persons, and strong criminal penalties for aborting them. *Doe v. Israel,* 358 F.

---

8   "We need not resolve the difficult question of when life begins. When those trained in the respective disciplines of medicine, philosophy, and theology are unable to arrive at any consensus, the judiciary, at this point in the development of man's knowledge, is not in a position to speculate as to the answer." *Roe v. Wade* 410 US 113, 159

9   "If this suggestion of personhood [of unborn babies] is established, the...case [for legalizing aborticide], of course, collapses, for the fetus' right to life is then guaranteed specifically by the [14th] Amendment." *Roe v. Wade,* 410 US 113, 156

Supp. 1193 (1973)

That reasoning was replicated in a long line of criminal abortion prevention cases (where the charge was usually trespassing or door blocking) but never again until now in a review of a state law.

Not that there were no further reviews of state laws. But none of those reviews of state restrictions of abortion (ie. informed consent, 20 week bans, medical standards), after Rhode Island, required courts to revisit "when life begins", so it was not revisited, leaving *Roe's* declared indecision about Life untouched.

"When [constitutionally protected] life begins" was usually the *only* contested issue in the thousands of criminal abortion prevention cases. That issue was the focus of the key element of the defense raised in virtually all those cases, which was most commonly called "The Necessity Defense". The defense was that trespassing was necessary to save lives. The contested issue was whether there were any lives to save; there are none, if unborn babies of humans are not humans. It was in those criminal cases that the judicial doctrine became entrenched that whether human lives were *in fact* saved was irrelevant because SCOTUS made a mother's right to kill whatever they are a "fundamental right" *"as a matter of law"*.

Possibly the most remarkable thing about all those cases was that even after dozens of appellate courts had ruled that SCOTUS made the unborn nonpersons "as a matter of law" so whether they were humans *in fact* was made irrelevant, defendants by the thousands *continued* raising the Necessity Defense as if they were simply unable to let go of the idea that whether abortion kills human beings *is* relevant.

Courts won't allow States to assert their "Legitimate State Interest." States were more submissive, after every court but SCOTUS told states that their "legitimate state interest" of saving unborn human beings from abortion was made unavailable "as a matter of law" by SCOTUS. In the line of reviews of *state* restrictions, no state between Rhode Island's and today's case challenged the status of abortion as a "fundamental right".

Courts overturn laws that restrict fundamental rights unless they serve a "legitimate state interest" or a "compelling government interest" by "the least restrictive means possible". Since abortion is officially a "fundamental right", laws must restrict it as little as possible.

But abortion must be restricted as *much* as possible, to serve the only genuine "legitimate state interest" compelling enough to cause such struggle between legislatures and courts: "saving unborn human lives". *That* legitimate state interest demands that *every* human life be saved from abortion (except in those rare cases where saving one life kills another) – in other words that virtually every abortion be *outlawed*.

Obviously the "legitimate state interest" of saving as many unborn babies from abortion as possible, and the "fundamental right" of mothers to kill what SCOTUS was not sure were unborn human lives with as *few* restrictions as possible, cannot coexist.

So those state restrictions became a search for some *other* "legitimate state interest" that courts *would* allow – that is, some *other* "legitimate state interest" than saving what SCOTUS was not sure were unborn human lives – that is able to indirectly mitigate some of the harm and still survive the court's "strict scrutiny". [*"Strict scrutiny" is the name for the process of "reviewing" whether a law achieves a "legitimate state interest" by "the least restrictive means possible".*] ("Strict Scrutiny" changed its name to "Undue Burden" in *Casey* and *Hellerstedt*.[10])

---

10 *Planned Parenthood v. CASEY,* 505 U.S. 833 (1992), *Whole Woman's Health v. Hellerstedt,* 579 U.S. ___ (2016) *Hellerstedt* said it was not enough for a statute to be "reasonably related to (or designed to further) a legitimate state interest." That standard was dismissed as "the less

But states could not even openly admit that any part of their purpose was to mitigate, as much as possible, the harm of killing unborn human lives, because of lower courts saying it is irrelevant whether those killed are humans combined with *Casey* which bars any restriction that *"has the purpose* or effect of placing a substantial obstacle in the path of a woman seeking an abortion of a nonviable fetus." *Planned Parenthood v. CASEY,* 505 U.S. 833, 877 (1992)

That made it a liability for a state's legislative "finding of facts" to say the reason for a regulation is to save as many unborn people as the courts will allow. That would be a confession that the real purpose of its regulation is to place *as great an obstacle as possible* in the path of abortion, which isn't allowed. So the only acceptable goal of a "finding of facts" would be to prove that the state has a legitimate interest that would not be an "undue burden" on abortion.

That approach concedes that abortion will always remain a "fundamental right", no matter how clearly the legally recognizable facts are that unborn babies' right to life is protected by the 14th amendment.

Although this fatalistic view is demanded by every lower court which has considered the issue, it is fortunately the opposite of the position taken by the Supreme Court. SCOTUS said that when it is established what now has been unanimously established by every category of court-recognized fact finders, then the 14th Amendment, instead of protecting a mother's right to murder, must require states to outlaw abortion.

This constraint on reason has stifled the ability of states to even state what their real legitimate state interest is. Not only because *Casey* threatens states that their regulation will not be allowed if part of their motive is to save unborn people, but also because it is legally awkward

---

strict review applicable where, for example, economic legislation is at issue." Courts must go beyond that to "consider whether any burden imposed on abortion access is 'undue.'"

for an "informed consent" defense, for example, to cite the evidence that abortion is legally recognizable as killing people, and then to ask only for "informed consent". So states are pressured to limit any "finding of facts" to some other goal that restricts abortion as little as possible.

Courts below [*below the U.S. Supreme Court*] **conduct counterfeit Trials by Jury.**

Since juries do not decide constitutional challenges to state laws, this point does not affect Iowa's case directly. But it does, indirectly. Because if this error of courts below, the judicial doctrine has become entrenched that is against Iowa, that it is irrelevant whether those killed by abortion are *in fact* human beings with 14th Amendment protection.

The line of abortion cases which produced this state-stifling contradiction of *Roe* was not, except for one case, the line of cases about state restrictions like "informed consent", medical standards, "heartbeat bans", etc. It was, rather, criminal cases where *individuals* prevented abortions, mostly by blocking abortionists' doors, and argued in their defense that unborn babies are in fact humans/persons, so that their actions *saved lives.*

In those cases, courts said *Roe* made abortion so irreversibly "constitutionally protected" "as a matter of law" as to make irrelevant factual evidence of its harm to infant humans/persons, so juries should not be encouraged to think it matters — *or even be allowed to hear the evidence.*

Judges in thousands of trials have so ruled. They were called "jury trials", but when the jury is not allowed to even know the only contested issue of a case, and especially when that issue is a fact question, but the fact question in those jury trials is decided by the judge, that is a trial by a judge, not a trial by jury. The right to trial by jury is denied.

Both categories of cases share in common the error by which lower courts have ruled *irrelevant* the fact inquiry which *Roe* said was not only relevant, but *dispositive.*

ARGUMENT IN SUPPORT
OF THESE REASONS

Iowa has no more authority to legalize abortion than slavery. The 14th Amendment restrains states from depriving any discrete [*distinct, identifiable*] class of humans/persons of "equal protection" of their rights, and especially of their *fundamental* rights, beginning with the *most* fundamental right: life. Unborn babies are such a class, according to every American legal authority who has ruled on the fact question.

The 14th Amendment protects all who are *in fact* humans. All case law including *Roe* treats all humans as "persons",[11] and what is irrelevant is whether they are "persons" *"as a matter of law"*. In fact, the Amendment was passed *specifically* to protect those who "as a matter of law" were never treated as "persons in the whole sense".

Roe almost says the opposite.

Roe said "the unborn have never been recognized in the law as persons in the whole sense." *Roe v. Wade*, 410 U.S. 113, 162 (1973). This was Roe's rationale for presuming that legislatures did not regard the unborn as in fact "recognizably human", *Roe*, p. 133. And because legislatures, in *Roe's* view, did not treat the unborn as fully human, SCOTUS was "in no position to speculate" whether they are.

Roe did not say lack of protection by law was, and it obviously is not, evidence that one is not in fact human or that one has no constitutionally protected "right to life".

It was a finding of Congress which was the final piece of evidence that turned *Roe's* alleged doubt about "when life begins" into a demand that Iowa obey the 14th Amendment by outlawing abortion. Congress said in 2004 what Roe said

---

11 "These disciplines variously approached the question in terms of the point at which the embryo or fetus became 'formed' or recognizably human, or in terms of when a 'person' came into being, that is, infused with a 'soul' or 'animated.'" *Roe v. Wade*, 410 US 113, 133.

must be said to end abortion. Congress "established" the unborn as being legally recognizable as humans/persons:

> 18 USC §1841(d) ...the term "unborn child" means a child in utero, and the term "child in utero" or "child, who is in utero" means a member of the species homo sapiens, at any stage of development, who is carried in the womb.

Here is where *Roe* said what must be said for legal abortion to end:

> "If this suggestion of personhood [of unborn babies] is established, the...case [for legalizing abortion], of course, collapses, for the fetus' right to life is then guaranteed specifically by the [14th] Amendment." *Roe*, p. 156.

According to *Roe*, now that federal law has "established" that all unborn babies, "at all stages of gestation", are humans/persons, "the fetus' right to life is [now] guaranteed specifically by the [14th] Amendment." That is, it is the constitutional responsibility of states to "guarantee" "the fetus' right to life"; and any state which fails to do so violates the Constitution.

Congress' authority to find facts is especially deferred to by SCOTUS.[12]

All fact finders agree. 2004 is not when the conflict between lower courts and SCOTUS started; it is when the final category of court-recognized Finders of Facts – Congress, whose fact finding is especially deferred to by

---

12 ...the existence of facts supporting the legislative judgment is to be presumed...not to be pronounced unconstitutional unless in the light of the facts made known or generally assumed it is of such a character as to preclude the assumption that it rests upon some rational basis within the knowledge and experience of the legislators....the constitutionality of a statute predicated upon the existence of a particular state of facts may be challenged by showing to the court that those facts have ceased to exist. ...But by their very nature such inquiries, where the legislative judgment is drawn in question, must be restricted to the issue whether any state of facts either known or which could reasonably be assumed affords support for it. *U.S. v. Carolene Products*, 304 U.S. 144, 152 (1938)

SCOTUS – added its voice to the growing consensus of all court-recognized finders of facts that all unborn babies are humans/persons from conception/fertilization. No legal authority in America affirms that they are not.

Juries. When juries in criminal abortion prevention trials [for trespassing] were allowed to rule on whether human "life begins" at conception (or at least before abortions are possible) – the key element of the Necessity Defense, they agreed it does, and acquitted.

That defense was claimed in tens of thousands of abortion prevention trials.[13] That defense, often called the Necessity Defense, (In Iowa it is "Compulsion", Iowa 704.10), says that what is normally against a relatively minor law is not against the law when it saves lives. The contested fact issue, therefore, was only rarely *what the defendant did* at the abortion doors; those defendants proudly admitted what *they did*. The only *contested* fact issue, which belonged before "the triers of facts" (juries), was, rather, whether unborn babies count as being *in fact* humans whose lives merit being saved.

That was almost always the *only* contested issue of the trial, and it was a fact issue, and its submission to fact finders was invited by *Roe,* and yet after several jury acquittals, judges stopped allowing defendants to tell juries about their only defense. But before judges started doing that, those early jury acquittals established the consensus of juries that all unborn babies are humans/persons.

The consensus of Triers of Fact "establishes" the fact.

> After the court ruled that it would allow the [Necessity] Defense to go to the jury, the Women for Women Clinic dropped the prosecution. If the defense is permitted, evidence is introduced that life begins at conception. This

---

13 60,000 was the number of arrests reported in Operation Rescue literature in about 1990, after which there were thousands more arrests.Online, the figure is confirmed at http://letstalkbooksandpolitics.blogspot.com/2018/06/ and www.pnj.com/story/news/2017/10/31/pensacola-plays-pivotal-role-abortion-struggle/819921001/.

evidence is rarely contradicted by the prosecution, which is merely proving the elements of criminal trespass. Rather than risk such a precedent, many clinics prefer to dismiss. In fact, defense counsel have admitted that their intent is to bring the abortion issue back before the United States Supreme Court to consider the very question of when life begins, an issue on which the Court refused to rule in Roe... (The *Cincinnati Law Review* footnote analyzes the case *of Ohio v. Rinear,* No. 78999CRB-3706 (Mun. Ct. Hamilton County, Ohio, dismissed May 2, 1978)

By calling the goal of triggering Roe's "collapse" clause through jury verdicts and appeals an "admission", this law review author treats the resort to our court system as some sort of nefarious scheme which the clever author has finally exposed. The readiness of juries to acknowledge harm to unborn humans is seen as a threat grave enough to justify *keeping the "triers of facts" from weighing the only contested issue in jury trials, which was a fact question.*

This law review article documents the readiness of juries, invited to do so, to "establish" that unborn babies are humans/persons – a pattern otherwise difficult to survey because juries seldom explain their verdicts, and because few juries were ever informed of the contested issue.

This suppression of the evidence which juries would have supplied abundantly, had they been allowed, is like the suppression of evidence in the John Peter Zenger trial of 1735,[14] in which Zenger wasn't allowed to submit evidence that his "zingers" aimed at the royal New York governor were the truth. "Truth is not a defense against libel", the judge told him. In fact, proving those zingers were true would only make them sting worse, the judge explained, making them doubly "libelous".

Zenger's lawyer told the jury there should be no rule against telling the truth. (Had the jury also been censored from hearing the legal argument, we might not have

---

14 Apparently the only record of the trial was the one published by Zenger himself.

Freedom of the Press today.) But how could Zenger persuade the jury that his zingers were the truth, with his evidence ruled irrelevant? "The suppressing of evidence ought always to be taken for the strongest evidence", his lawyer told them. The jury agreed, and acquitted, giving us Freedom of the Press.

Today we may similarly reasonably infer, from the routine judicial suppression of evidence from juries about the nature of the unborn, in abortion prevention trials, that judges generally agree that juries, if allowed and informed, would virtually always find that unborn babies of humans are humans/persons from conception/fertilization.

The Cincinnati article only makes that inference official. We may take this inferred expectation for evidence in addition to the handful of jury acquittals where juries *were* allowed to rule on the fact question, that the consensus of Triers of Fact is that the unborn are humans/persons. Certainly among those juries who were allowed to take a position, there is consensus.

You may ask, how can juries settle "when a 'person' came into being, that is, infused with a 'soul'"?[15]

Human courts suffer gaps between "legally recognizable" and "true". But "legally recognizable" jury findings are about as close as courts can get to "true".

Unlike public opinion surveys or petitions, which are normally *not* admissible evidence of facts, we test jurors for impartiality and educate them with the most qualified expert witnesses we can find.

Expert witnesses. Another category of court-recognized fact finders is expert witnesses. As the preceding Cincinnati Law Review article reported, it was typical of thousands of abortion prevention trials to bring in a doctor to testify that fully distinct human life begins from conception. It was "rarely contradicted", implying sometimes it *was* contradicted; but in the absence of any

---

15 This is how Roe defines "person". *Roe v. Wade* 410 U.S. 113, 133 (1973)

physical medical evidence in support of any later time "when life begins" than conception/fertilization, we may presume that any such contradiction was not on the merits.

Appendix H contains excerpts from District Court Judge Clark's ruling in favor of a defendant who flew in probably the world's leading geneticist, from France. Judge Clark addressed the evidence and was persuaded by it. The Kansas Supreme Court overruled, but not on the merits of the defense. The Court did not even acknowledge that the defense or its evidence existed, choosing instead to shoot down a defense of the Court's own invention which the defendant had not raised. See Appendix F.

Of tens of thousands of abortion prevention trials, thousands featured expert witnesses documenting the reality that unborn babies of humans are humans, long after judges stopped allowing juries to hear them. These offers of proof, of thousands of expert witnesses, in abortion prevention trials, were uncontested. They were almost never heard by juries, and never acknowledged by appellate courts.

Their unanimous testimony legally establishes that unborn babies are humans/persons, requiring states, according to *Roe,* to protect their fundamental rights.

Genetic evidence is routinely not merely tolerated but sought by courts to prove both that a human was there, and which individual human it was. In these cases, the existence of human genetic material is taken as proof that a human was there. So far, every unborn baby of a human mother has been discovered to contain genetic material which is certifiably human.

This mountain of unrefuted evidence in abortion prevention trials fulfills the test of the Supreme Court[16] for

---

16 "We start from the premise that illegitimate children are not 'nonpersons.' They are humans, live, and have their being... They are clearly 'persons' within the meaning of the Equal Protection Clause of the Fourteenth Amendment." *Levi v. Louisiana,* 391 U.S. 68, 70 (1968) (discussing illegitimate children).

personhood and fulfills the requirement of *Roe*, p. 156, that if the preborn are humans/persons, abortion is "of course" unlawful.

State legislatures. "At least 38 states", a Constitutional Majority,[17] "have enacted fetal-homicide statutes, and 28 of those statutes protect life from conception."[18] *Hamilton v. Scott*, 97 So. 3d 728 (Ala. 2012)

Most of them incorporated findings of facts about the humanity of the unborn, and most of them have had their constitutionality challenged. All survived. In addition, a few states have enacted stand-alone personhood laws outside the context of Unborn Victims of Violence laws.

No state has affirmed that "when life begins" is later than conception.[19]

There is a statement in *Roe v. Wade* which, read carelessly, could be taken to minimize the evidentiary value of Unborn Victims of Violence laws. But *Roe's* respect for their value is actually underlined by analysis of their value in the footnote *Roe* gives in this paragraph, and double underlined by the curious fact that *Roe* does not mention it.

> In areas other than criminal abortion, the law has been reluctant to endorse any theory that life, as we recognize it, begins before live birth or to accord legal rights to the unborn except in

---

17 Am I making up a term? Anyway, 38 is the 3/4 of the states needed to ratify a Constitutional Amendment.

18   *Hamilton v. Scott's* basis: "See *State v. Courchesne*, 296 Conn. 622, 689 n. 46, 998 A.2d 1, 50 n.46 (2010) ("'[As of March 2010], at least [thirty-eight] states have fetal homicide laws.'" (quoting the National Conference of State Legislatures, Fetal Homicide Laws (March 2010) (alterations in *Courchesne*))

19 A careless reading of New York's repeal of its partial birth ban on January 22, 2019, led to reporting in conservative media that the new law for the first time positively declares that unborn babies are not "persons". They report that the new law says " "Person," when referring to the victim of a homicide, means a human being who has been born and is alive." But that is the old law that has been there for years, and in context simply means that when the coroner investigates dead bodies found in his county, or in a jail, he will not investigate the bodies of unborn babies.

narrowly defined situations and except when the rights are contingent upon live birth. ...some States permit the parents of a stillborn child to maintain an action for wrongful death because of prenatal injuries.[65] Such an action, however, would appear to be one to vindicate the parents' interest and is thus consistent with the view that the fetus, at most, represents only the potentiality of life. ...In short, the unborn have never been recognized in the law as persons in the whole sense. *Roe v. Wade*, 410 U.S. 113, 162 (1973)

A careless reading of that paragraph could lead to the conclusion that Unborn Victims of Violence laws do not necessarily prove that legislatures think babies are people. Because maybe those laws only "vindicate the parents' interest [which] is thus consistent with the view that the fetus, at most, represents only the *potentiality* of life."

But *Roe* was talking about parents bringing civil lawsuits against people whose negligence had caused the deaths of their unborn children, ["some States permit the parents of a stillborn child to maintain an action for wrongful death because of prenatal injuries"] in which case obviously it *is* the parents' interests who are being vindicated. (Except that the legislative regard for the unborn is shown by the phrase "wrongful death" - phrases not applied in law to tumors, dogs, or refrigerators.)

Unborn victims of violence laws are different: they are *criminal* charges, brought by county or state prosecutors, to vindicate the *states'* interest in protecting life, without asking the parents for permission first. And the fact that the penalties for killing an unborn baby are the same in 38 states as the penalties for killing the mother disposes of the argument, even in the 10 states which currently do *not* explicitly "find" that all babies are people from hour one, that unborn babies are regarded as any less human.

In addition, Unborn Victims of Violence penalties take effect well *before* birth, ruling out the theory that rights which are only "contingent upon live birth" treat preborn babies as merely *potential* life.

It is interesting that Roe backs up its mention of lawsuits to vindicate parents' interests with footnote #65, which is to an <u>article</u>[20] whose section B is "The Law of Torts and the Unborn Child". But Roe avoids mentioning that Section D is "The Criminal Law and the Unborn Child", which lists 10 states which already had criminal penalties for causing the deaths of unborn babies apart from abortions consented to by mothers.

The analysis in Section D very persuasively disposes of *Roe's* conclusion that "the unborn have never been recognized in the law as persons in the whole sense." Section D's analysis is followed by a footnote listing the ten states with such laws. Here is a quote from the article:

> But some statutory protection for the unborn child after quickening has been provided by feticide statutes in several states. These statutes make it a separate offense (usually manslaughter) to kill an unborn quick child willfully and under such circumstances that, had the mother rather than the child been killed, the offense would have been murder. Even those writers who favor liberalized abortion have admitted that "conceptually **these [feticide] statutes clearly accord independent personality to the fetus, for the killing of the fetus under these circumstances is called manslaughter,** and the sections themselves are usually found with the other homicide sections. Statutes of this type, it will be noted, do not require the child to be born alive before he is entitled to the protection of the law. Under the feticide statutes, **both the quick child and the mother are human beings and**

---

20 <u>https://scholarship.law.nd.edu/cgi/viewcontent.cgi?article=2972&context=ndlr</u>

to unlawfully kill either constitutes homicide. Footnote 118:   Arkansas: ARx. STAT. ANN. §§ 41-2223, 41-2224 (1964); Florida: FLA. STAT. ANN. §§ 782.09, 782.10 (1965); Georgia: GA. CODE AN'N. §§ 26-1101 to 1104, 26-9921a (1969 Revision); Michigan: MICH. STAT. ANN. §§ 28.554, 28.555 (1954); Mississippi: Miss. CODE ANN. § 2222 (1956); Missouri: Mo. ANN. STAT. §§ 559.090, 559.100 (Vernon 1953); Nevada: NEv. REV. STAT. §§ 200.210, 200.220 (1967); New York: N.Y. PENAL CODE § 125.00 (McKinney 1967); North Dakota: N.D. CENT. CODE ANN. §§ 12-2502, 12-2503 (1960); Oklahoma: OKLA. STAT. ANN. tit. 21, §§ 713,714 (1958).

As this analysis points out, these laws of 10 states treat the death of the baby as equal to the death of the mother, which persuasively refutes *Roe's* conclusion that "the unborn have never been recognized in the law as persons in the whole sense."

Why then did *Roe* not address it, or even mention it? Could *Roe* have thought it so utterly unpersuasive, or legally sophomoric, as to be not worth their consideration? But *Roe* treated the article's legal qualifications as worthy of one of their footnotes, and the analysis *is* persuasive.

The only alternative is that *Roe* did not want to draw attention to it precisely because it refutes the conclusion which the justices wanted to draw. If that is the explanation, then its omission in *Roe* further underlines SCOTUS' respect for the evidentiary power of Unborn Victims of Violence Laws to establish that fully human, constitutionally protectable life begins at fertilization.

Individual judges. Although SCOTUS ruled itself incompetent to determine "when life begins"[21], and it is

---

21 "We need not resolve the difficult question of when life begins. When those trained in the respective disciplines of medicine, philosophy,

hard to imagine any other court more competent than SCOTUS to judge the matter, and in fact no appellate court majority has taken a position on the matter either way except to say *Roe* made the matter irrelevant which *Roe* did not, a handful of individual judges have ruled that "life", meaning human life, which merits protection of its fundamental rights beginning with the Right to Life, begins at conception/fertilization.

No American judge has ever ruled, on his own authority, that unborn babies are *not* human persons, which makes the finding unanimous among all judges who have taken a position.

For example, Wichita District Judge Paul Clark ruled for Elizabeth Tilson in 1992:[22]

> I will find Mrs. Tilson's evidence proffered through witnesses Lejeune, Hilgers, McMillan and Rue relevant to the issue here. ... life in homo sapiens begins at conception; and harm is the result of termination of life under most circumstances. That opinion...has always been foundation for the public policy in Kansas.

Judge Clark conceded that SCOTUS let

> "a pregnant woman...make a decision whether to terminate her pregnancy without governmental interference...." [and]
>
> "Any corporation authorized to do business and its clientele still have a right to do lawful business without interference...."

BUT "*Roe* and its progeny" did not reverse

> "the public policy of the state of Kansas that the voluntary act of prematurely terminating a pregnancy...is a wrongful act." [Thus it is illogical to say abortion "cannot be a harm because it is legal."]

---

and theology are unable to arrive at any consensus, the judiciary, at this point in the development of man's knowledge, is not in a position to speculate as to the answer." Roe v. Wade 410 US 113, 159

22 July 21, 1992, Case No. 91 MC 108, "Memorandum of Opinion Following Bench Trial". Appendix H contains extensive excerpts. The complete ruling is posted at www.Saltshaker.US/SLIC/PaulClark.

That is, the Supreme Court stopped *states* from outlawing abortion. But the Court could not make abortion *harmless* (in fact *Roe* explicitly declined to rule on whether abortion is a "harm") – and thus *Roe* has no effect on the right of *individuals,* through the Necessity Defense, to prevent abortions. The "harm" of abortion is legally recognizable as serious enough to justify stopping it. In fact, Judge Clark said the Bill of Rights, in whose "penumbra" the *Roe* court saw a right to kill babies,

> ...is law that protects the people from their government. [It] was [not] meant to protect people from fellow citizens.

Justice Dimond, on the Alaskan Supreme Court, has emphatically denounced the indecision of *Roe* and declared the unborn to be both human and persons. In *Cleveland v. Municipality of Anchorage,* Alaska, 631 P.2d 1073, 1084, he wrote:

> (Concurring:) I empathize with the defendants' sorrow over the *loss of human lives* caused by abortions. I believe the United States Supreme Court *burdened this court with a tragic decision* when it held in Roe...that the word "person, as used in the fourteenth amendment, does not include the unborn...", and that states cannot "override the rights of the pregnant woman" by "adopting one theory of life."
>
> I do not agree with the Court's conclusion that a state's interest in potential life does not become "compelling" until the fetus has attained viability. It stated its explanation for this conclusion as follows:
>
> "With respect to the State's important and legitimate interest in potential life, the 'compelling' point is at viability. This is so because the fetus then presumably has the capability of meaningful life outside the womb. State regulation protective of fetal life after viability thus has both logical and biological justifications." ~ "(410 U.S. at 163, 93 S.Ct. 731-32, 35 L.Ed.2d at 183) As Professor Tribe indicates, "One reads the court's explanation [of the magic line called "viability"] several times before becoming convinced that nothing has inadvertently been omitted." (Tribe, Forward to *The Supreme Court 1972 Term,* 87 Harv.L.Rev. 1. 4 (1973] (footnote omitted]). I agree with Professor Tribe when he

states, "Clearly, this [analysis] mistakes a definition for a syllogism", and offers no reason at all for what the Court has held. (Id., quoting Ely, *The Wages of Crying Wolf: A Comment on Roe v. Wade*, 82 Yale L.J. 920, 924 (1973] (footnotes omitted]).

In effect, the Supreme Court held that because there is no consensus as to when human life begins it can act as if it were proven that human life does not begin until birth so as to preserve to women the right to make their own decision whether an abortion takes a human life or not. It would make more sense to me if, in the face of uncertainty, any error made were side in favor of the fetus, which many believe to be human life.

The development of a zygote into a human child is a continual, progressive development. No one suggests that the born child is not a human being. It seems undeniable, however, that human life begins before birth. As Professor Curran states:

"[T]he fetus one day before birth and the child one day after birth are not that significantly or qualitatively different – in any respect; Even outside the womb the newborn child is not independent but remains greatly dependent on the mother and others. Birth in fact does not really tell much about the individual as such but only where the individual is--either outside the womb or still Inside the womb.' (C. Curran, *Transition and Tradition in Moral Theology*, p. 209 (1919]). Similarly, viability does not mark the beginning of the truly human being.

[V]iability again indicates more about where the fetus can live than what it is. The fetus immediately before viability is not that qualitatively different from the viable fetus. In addition viability is a very inexact criterion because it is intimately connected with medical and scientific advances. In the future it might very well be possible for the fetus to live in an artificial womb or even with an artificial placenta from a very early stage in fetal development.

I join with those persons who believe that truly human life begins sometime between the second and third week after conception....[23]

---

23 Oops, there goes our claim that no American legal authority has established that "life begins" any later than fertilization. And yet we will not count this as a clear exception because (1) it sounds more

A dissent by Justice Mahoney said

> "Until the Court decides when a fetus is a person, I see no
> reason to deny the defense of necessity to those who believe
> that the fetus is viable and is a person...At least it would get
> the issue squarely before the U.S. Supreme Court...."
> *Detwiler v. Akron,* C.A. No. 14385 at 22 (9th App. Dist. 1990)

Congress, Guardian of the 14th Amendment

> 18 USC §1841(d) ...the term "unborn child" means a child in
> utero, and the term "child in utero" or "child, who is in utero"
> means a member of the species homo sapiens, at any stage of
> development, who is carried in the womb.

Roe said the "penumbra" of the 14th Amendment[24] is
what gives women the right to kill whatever that is in their
wombs, although if it is ever "established" that what that is,
is "recognizably human, or...a 'person'...that is, infused with
a 'soul'...",[25] then "of course" that same 14th Amendment
must require states to protect those humans/persons by
outlawing abortion.[26]

Congress was given the constitutional authority

---

like speculating out loud than a positive finding backed by evidence.
And it is not an official ruling, but a dissent; (2) the distinction
between "fertilization" and "2 or 3 weeks" has no impact on surgical
or chemical abortions, although it could affect future restrictions on
contraception; and (3) Dimond's reasoning that there is no particular
difference between pre or post viability applies equally to the lack of
any qualitative difference between 3 weeks and fertilization.

24 "The principal thrust of appellant's [abortionist's] attack on the
Texas statutes [which had outlawed abortion] is that they
improperly invade a right, said to be possessed by the pregnant
woman, to choose to terminate her pregnancy. Appellant would
discover this right in the concept of personal 'liberty' embodied in the
Fourteenth Amendment's Due Process Clause; or in personal,
marital, familial, and sexual privacy said to be protected by the Bill
of Rights or its **penumbras**,..." *Roe, p.* 129 (1973)

25 *Roe v. Wade* 410 U.S. 113, 133 (1973)

26 "If this suggestion of personhood [of unborn babies] is established,
the...case [for legalizing aborticide], of course, collapses, for the fetus'
right to life is then guaranteed specifically by the [14th]
Amendment." Roe v. Wade, 410 US 113, 156

under Section 5 of the Fourteenth Amendment to enforce by legislation the provisions of the 14th amendment. This is in addition to the SCOTUS-recognized authority of Congress to find facts. This authority certainly extends to defining whose rights the Amendment protects.

2004 was a banner year for personhood because not only was Congress the final category of court-recognized finders of facts to join the consensus, but Congress' authority to find facts is well regarded by SCOTUS,[27] and Congress is given authority by the 14th Amendment to clarify who merits its protection.

Congress' finding of this fact, that all unborn babies are humans "at all stages of gestation", is especially authoritative because *Roe's* trigger is "recognizably human", and Congress legally recognized unborn babies as human. No kind of recognition of a fact can satisfy a court's need better than formal, admissible, *legal* recognition of a fact.

American legal authorities are unanimous and undisputed. It is not possible for any fact to be any more legally recognized in America. If *any* "establishment" of this life-and-death fact can satisfy SCOTUS, *this* must, because no greater legal "establishment" of a fact is possible than the unanimous, undisputed concurrence of all court-recognized fact finders.

The fact that all unborn babies are humans/persons, triggering the legal obligation of states to protect their

---

27 ...the existence of facts supporting the legislative judgment is to be presumed...not to be pronounced unconstitutional unless in the light of the facts made known or generally assumed it is of such a character as to preclude the assumption that it rests upon some rational basis within the knowledge and experience of the legislators....the constitutionality of a statute predicated upon the existence of a particular state of facts may be challenged by showing to the court that those facts have ceased to exist. ...But by their very nature such inquiries, where the legislative judgment is drawn in question, must be restricted to the issue whether any state of facts either known or which could reasonably be assumed affords support for it. *U.S. v. Carolene Products,* 304 U.S. 144, 152 (1938)

fundamental right to life, was "established" well before 2004. But Congress' vote makes it complete.

If the unanimous consensus of all five categories of court-recognized fact finders were not enough to "establish" a fact, it would be impossible for courts to establish any fact.

Since courts obviously know many facts with far less consensus among fact finders, we must infer that courts *can* know "when life begins" now; and because Iowa's defense turns on that fact, this court's past "inability to speculate" is no longer an obstacle to resolving this issue.

It is impossible to legally recognize any fact with more certainty than the unanimous findings of all court-recognized categories of fact finders. Every court presented with these findings can now know that abortion is the legal equivalent of murder, and that our Constitution requires that Iowa criminalize it.

The dozens of appellate courts which have ruled, contrary to *Roe,* that *Roe* made all this overwhelming evidence irrelevant in abortion cases, are a long line of cases in which appeals courts have "decided an important federal question in a way that conflicts with relevant decisions of this Court".[28]

The 18 USC §1841(c) Delusion

("when [protectable] life begins" according to federal law)

18 U.S.C. § 1841

(c) Nothing in this section shall be construed to permit the prosecution...of any person for conduct relating to an abortion for which consent of the pregnant woman...has been obtained....

(d) As used in this section, the term "unborn child" means a child in utero, and the term "child in utero" or "child, who is in utero" means a member of the species homo sapiens, at any stage of development, who is carried in the

---

28 Supreme Court rule 10c.

womb.

§1841(c) doesn't make unwanted babies less human. Although §1841(d) defines all unborn babies as humans, §1841(c) exempts abortion from the penalties of §1841(a), which seems to some to mitigate paragraph (d). *Roe* similarly reasoned that lesser penalties for killing older unborn babies than for killing adults, and for killing younger unborn babies than for killing older unborn babies, showed that "the unborn have never been recognized in the law as persons in the whole sense". *Roe v. Wade* 410 U.S. 113, 161

But law contains many dissimilar penalties for dissimilar situations, for many reasons, without any implication that people in less protected situations have less value or right to live than better protected people. Nor do people ordinarily argue that less than perfect protection proves those people are not "persons in the whole sense".

For example, causing someone's death is not "first degree murder" if it is proved to be an accident. No one thinks this "exception" proves the legislature thinks people killed accidentally are not "persons in the whole sense".

§1841(d) is a categorical finding of fact. It establishes a fact. Laws, or their absence, do not change facts. §1841(c) says nothing about facts. It is only about penalties. Penalties do not alter facts, and facts are irregularly consulted when humans enact penalties.

The difference in treatment, then, requires some other explanation, than that loved babies are human while unwanted babies are tumors. There are many reasons penalties protect equally deserving citizens differently.

Sometimes the difference reflects the realities of the limitations of government in recognizing when citizens equally deserve rights. For example, a law student one week before taking his bar exam may be equally qualified with the lawyer who took it a week ago, but Courts are unable to recognize their equality until they actually take it and pass it.

Sometimes the difference is because of the difference in how criminal intent must be established. For example, no one says laws treat auto accident fatalities as less human than gunfight fatalities because drivers who kill with their cars are not penalized as greatly. The difference is one of intent, which is and should be an element of First Degree Murder.

Similarly, *Roe* may have misunderstood the point of Exodus 21:22 when *Roe* (in a footnote) gave the passage as a possible reason for treating unborn babies as not fully human. It says when a pregnant woman finds herself in the middle of a fight between two men, and gets hit, causing her child to go into labor, then if the child is unharmed, a jury shall set damages. This does not suggest the baby is less than human; but a jury can hear witnesses to establish how deliberate the punch to the womb appeared.

Sometimes the difference has nothing to do with merit, but with political reality. It would be absurd to conclude from repeal of prohibition, while marijuana criminalization increased, that drinking is "not legally recognizable as a harm". Or even that it is less harmful than marijuana. The disparity simply reflects political reality, and nothing else.

The newspaper headlines and Congressional debate about Laci's law (18 USC §1841(d)) proved beyond any reasonable doubt that the disparity of treatment of loved unborn babies, versus unwanted unborn babies, had nothing to do with a finding that a mother's choice can make you less than human, and everything to do with politics.

To imagine any deeper significance in Laci's Law's disparate treatment would quickly lead to absurdity. To imagine the disparity was Congress' choice, as opposed to the result of limitations beyond its control, would place Congress in a patently false, even absurd, and profoundly immoral theoretical position, where, to maintain any semblance of consistency when trying to explain the statute, it must concede that this statute implies that the right to life of an innocent human being depends purely on the choice of another. Congress would have to posit that the slaying of an unborn human child is a non-harm under United States law, provided solely that the child's mother wants the child dead.

18 USC § 1841(c) doesn't keep states from outlawing crime. The "abortion exception" clause states in relevant part

> "1. Nothing in this section shall be construed to permit the prosecution: a. of any person for conduct relating to an abortion for which consent of the pregnant woman...has been obtained."

Some think these words somehow hinder states from defending their own laws against abortion. But nothing in §1841(c) hinders any state, or Congress itself later, from criminalizing anything. These words only say *this* U.S. Code section does not create penalties for consensual abortion. Yet. They do not mitigate 1841(d).

Reality does not adjust itself to whatever section of law you are reading. No matter what section of the U.S. Code you are reading at any time, all unborn babies remain "members of the species homo sapiens".

Even if Congress *meant* to bar states from outlawing consensual abortion, Congress has no such authority. States do not need Congress' permission to penalize crimes.

Neither does 18 U.S.C. §248 make anyone less human. §248 [F.A.C.E., Freedom of Access to Clinic Entrances] restricts *individuals* from saving babies from abortionists. It does not restrict *states* from saving those same lives, any more than *Roe v. Wade,* which restricted *states* from saving those same lives, restricted *individuals* from saving those same lives. (Although most courts have erroneously assumed *Roe* did.)

The interaction of these laws and precedents may be illogical, but they are legal. Usually laws and precedents try to logically respond to relevant facts. So where they are premised on the facts being irrelevant, it should be no surprise when they are illogical.

A personhood challenge is ripe now that the facts are in

[A case is "ripe" when "nothing remains for the court but to render the appropriate judgment." - Black's Dictionary]

Iowa's "personhood" challenge is not that of a single state. It is the challenge of the unanimous rulings of expert witnesses, state legislatures, judges, juries, and Congress.

Iowa's constitutional obligation to criminalize abortion is demanded by unanimous American legal authority.

Rhode Island. Only one state previously challenged abortion's legality with a criminalization of abortion. *Doe v. Israel,* 358 F. Supp. 1193 (1973). *Doe v. Israel,* 1 Cir., 1973, 482 F.2d 156. This Court declined to hear the case. *Cert. denied,* 416 U.S. 993.

Just weeks after *Roe* alleged uncertainty about the unborn because "the unborn have never been recognized in the law as persons in the whole sense",[29] Rhode Island enacted that recognition.

> The Rhode Island legislature apparently read the opinion of the Supreme Court in *Roe v. Wade* to leave open the question of when life begins and the constitutional consequences [**12] thereof. *Doe v. Israel,* 358 F. Supp. 1193, 1199 (1973)

Rhode Island "established" the fact more than Texas had, in the sense that the Rhode Island legislature and governor made official, in law, what Texas Attorney

---

29 Roe v. Wade: 410 U.S. 113, 161

General Wade had only alleged in court as a fact understood by Texans without having to put it in a law.

District Judge Pettine didn't just respond "well, that's a little more of the 'establishment' courts will need before we outlaw abortion again, but that's still not enough." He went far beyond SCOTUS, saying *all the evidence in the world* was irrelevant.

> I neither summarize nor make any findings of fact as to their testimony [about whether unborn babies of human mothers are humans/persons]. To me the United States Supreme Court made it unmistakably clear that **the question of when life** [in fact] **begins needed no resolution by the judiciary as it was not a question of fact.** ... I find it all irrelevant.... *Doe v. Israel,* 358 F. Supp. 1193, 1197

If SCOTUS didn't treat Life as "a question of fact", but of law, how did doctors and preachers become more qualified to "answer" the "question" than SCOTUS?[30]

Roe said the court was "in no position to speculate as to the answer", not that the answer was irrelevant. *Roe* said the answer was not only relevant, it was dispositive: once "established", it must "of course" end legal abortion.

> (Continued:) It is true that the Court in Wade and Bolton did not attempt to decide the point "when human life begins." No reading of the opinions, however, can be thought to empower the Rhode Island legislature [alone] to "defin[e] some creature as an unborn child, to be a human being and a person from the moment of its conception." *Doe v. Israel*

Since when does a state legislature need SCOTUS to "empower" them to establish facts? Normally courts *respect* findings of facts by legislatures.

> (Continued:) Roe v. Wade and Doe v. Bolton can [not] be

----

30 When those trained in the respective disciplines of medicine, philosophy, and theology are unable to arrive at any consensus, the judiciary, at this point in the development of man's knowledge, is not in a position to speculate as to the answer. *Roe v. Wade,* 410 U.S. 113, 159

nullified by the simple device of a legislative declaration or presumptions contrary to the court's holding. *Doe v. Israel*

Except that *Roe's* holding was conditioned on no court-recognized legal authority establishing precisely the fact which Rhode Island established. And the Rhode Island legislature is a court-recognized finder of facts. The only thing Roe didn't clarify was how much establishment, by how many fact finders, was "enough" establishment to satisfy the court.

But now that issue is gone. There can be no more "establishment" than the uncontested consensus of every court-recognized fact finder in all five categories of court-recognized fact finders. If *Roe* was correct, that "establishment" was *possible*, then "establishment" has been *accomplished*.

SCOTUS never said "when life begins" was irrelevant, or that it was a question of law and not a question for fact finders, or that state legislatures are not court-recognized fact finders any longer. Therefore it was reasonable for Rhode Island to essentially ask SCOTUS, "is *this* enough more establishment for you to know those are babies?"

Roe had only said that the Texas Attorney General's assertion in court wasn't enough to establish that "life begins at conception", since his statement lacked the backing of even one state legislature in an explicit law. Which begs the question, what if *two* states affirm the claim? What if the second one, once informed that SCOTUS didn't already know it, affirms it with a crystal clear law enacted by its legislature and signed by its governor? Is *that* enough? It is enough. The issue is ripe.

The question remains unanswered. Cert denied.

Missouri. Before today, Rhode Island was the only state which placed that question squarely before the courts. Missouri almost did, 16 years later, but with no penalties for doing abortions. They even promised, in their otherwise strong personhood law, to obey SCOTUS, which let SCOTUS respond "we *still* don't need to decide."[31] SCOTUS heard Missouri's challenge only to point out that Missouri's challenge didn't actually prevent any abortions so it wasn't ripe for review.

Nor has any other SCOTUS ruling made any attempt to decide unborn personhood, or consider what triers of facts say about it, or even treat it as a a topic of interest.

At least the *Webster* ruling affirmed the definite *possibility* that a state's finding that "life begins at conception/fertilization" *might* be enough to satisfy SCOTUS that it is time for states to outlaw abortion.

Webster left the impression that when SCOTUS finally decides if *one* state's affirmation is enough, it could go either way.[32] Now *38* states concur with Missouri.

Was *Roe's* "collapse" clause nullified by Casey? What if *Roe v. Wade* is no longer what sustains abortion's legality? Did *Planned Parenthood v. CASEY*, 505 U.S. 833 (1992) say it no longer matters whether the unborn are humans/persons because *Roe's* rationale that "personhood is not established" has been replaced with "women rely on abortion now"?

Neither the opinion nor the dissent even mentioned *Roe's* "personhood is not established" rationale. No evidence of human life was presented, discussed, or rejected.

However, an unidentified "outer shell of Roe" was

---

31 *Webster v. Reproductive Health Services,* 492 US 490 (1989) said the impact of a state's "personhood" law on Roe's "collapse" clause was not properly before the Court. The issue was not ripe. "...until... courts have applied the [personhood] preamble to restrict appellees' [abortionists] activities in some concrete way, it is inappropriate for federal courts to address its meaning."

32 Sandra Day O'Conner concurred: "This Court refrains from deciding constitutional questions where there is no need to do so.... When the constitutional invalidity of a State's abortion statute actually turns upon the constitutional validity of Roe, there will be time enough to reexamine Roe, and to do so carefully." (Quoting from the syllabus.)

discussed.[33]

That "shell" upon which legal abortion continues to "hang" is "personhood is not established". Without that, *any* new rationale must "collapse".

To say a thing "hangs" on another thing is to suggest that without the *other* thing, the thing would "collapse". So whatever still sustains abortion's legality must still be subject to *Roe's* "collapse" clause.

A dissent in *Casey* identifies "the whole argument":

> The whole argument of abortion opponents is that what the Court calls the fetus and what others call the unborn child is a human life. Thus, whatever answer Roe came up with after conducting its "balancing" [between women's "privacy" and "potential life"] is bound to be wrong, unless it is correct that the human fetus is in some critical sense merely *potentially* human. *Planned Parenthood v. Casey*, 505 U.S. 833, 982 (1992) (Concurrence/dissent of Scalia, White, Thomas)

Whether I am human: a value judgment?

This dissent correctly dismisses any validity in deciding Life "as a matter of law", but neither does this dissent consider the possibility of establishing unborn personhood as fact. Which leaves a personal "value judgment" – a subjective judgment made independently of law or fact.

> There is, of course, no way to determine [whether the unborn are human] as a legal matter; it is, in fact, a value judgment. Some societies have considered newborn children not yet human, or the incompetent elderly no longer so. (Ibid, following paragraph)

Whether I am a human being is a "value judgment"? Not a question for fact finders but for policy makers?

---

33 "The joint opinion, following its newly minted variation on stare decisis, retains the outer shell of Roe v. Wade, <u>410 U.S. 113</u> (1973), but beats a wholesale retreat from the substance of that case.... Roe continues to exist, but only in the way a storefront on a western movie set exists: a mere facade to give the illusion of reality."
Planned Parenthood v. Casey, 505 U.S. 833, 945, 954 (1992) (Concurrence/dissent of Rehnquist, White, Scalia, Thomas)

Would we be any safer if our lives depended on whether decision makers "value" us, than if our humanity is "legally recognized"?

Only one thing holds up *Roe, Casey,* and all in between: alleged uncertainty whether unborn babies of human mothers *are* (in fact) humans. Smash that "shell" with legally recognized *certainty* that the unborn are human, and "reliance interests" must fall. Once abortion is "established" as killing innocent people, "women's schedules" are left a barbarically trivial excuse for it.

Even Justices Scalia and Thomas, noting the life-and-death importance of the question in their dissents, avoid affirming their own certainty that the unborn are humans/persons, or even that the question can be objectively resolved. Nor do they acknowledge the growing evidence that unborn babies of human mothers are humans.

Taking no position as SCOTUS justices is consistent with their theory that the right to kill babies is a "value judgment"[34] for states. The logical difficulty with that approach is that that "value judgment" won't be surrendered to states as long as SCOTUS' official inability to tell "when life begins" remains unchallenged, leaving the rights of the unborn less clear than the allegedly constitutional "woman's right to choose". (For more about "reliance interests", see Appendix G, #1.)

"There is, of course, no way to determine [whether the unborn are human] as a legal matter...." said the most conservative Supreme Court justice in 1992. Now that every American legal authority which has taken a position on "when [protectable] life begins" has ruled that it begins at fertilization/conception, the question is ripe to determine the fact as a legal matter.

Partial Birth. As late as *Stenberg v. Carhart* 530

---

34 *Planned Parenthood v. Casey*, 505 U.S. 833, 982 (1992)
  (Concurrence/dissent of Scalia, White, Thomas)

U.S. 914, 920-921 (2000) SCOTUS still did not address whether the unborn are in fact humans/persons. It dismissed the belief "that life begins at conception and consequently that an abortion [causes] the death of an innocent child" as a "point of view" which is "irreconcilable" with, and apparently canceled by, the "view" that murder is OK.

As for *Roe's* "speculation" whether abortion kills baby humans, or whether the babies that women are used to killing according to *Casey* are humans, "We shall not visit these *legal* principles."

This, despite the fact that even two of the liberal justices voting to perpetuate "partial birth" murders accepted Congress' description of them as "gruesome",[35] something one would not say of dismembering a tumor.

Even *Stenberg's* dissents avoid a position. Whether the unborn are "human life or [merely] potential human life" is "depending on one's view".[36] It "dehumanizes the fetus and trivializes human life", not because it *takes* human life, but because it *"approaches* infanticide".[37] Whether to save lives "is a value judgment, dependent upon how much one respects (or believes society ought to respect)...life...."[38]

Is it only sophistry to claim what Scalia and Thomas would not, that the consensus of all court-recognized fact finders represents something more objective than a "value judgment"?

It may be conceded that when many of those fact-

---

35 Justices Stevens and Ginsburg, concurring with the majority: "[I doubt if the abortion method used by George Tiller is] more brutal, more gruesome, or less respectful of "potential life" than the equally gruesome procedure [which the law still allows]." Justice Scalia, in his dissent, added, "The method of killing a human child -- one cannot even accurately say an entirely unborn human child -- proscribed by this statute is so horrible that the most clinical description of it evokes a shudder of revulsion."

36 *Stenberg v. Carhart,* 530 U.S. 914, 980 Dissent by Thomas, Rehnquist, Scalia.

37 *Stenberg v. Carhart,* 530 U.S. 914, 1006 Dissent by Thomas.

38 *Stenberg v. Carhart,* 530 U.S. 914, 954 Dissent by Scalia

finding authorities made their determination, they did not explain their reasons. However, thousands of expert witnesses, and a few judges, did. And many reasons are given in the record of legislative debates. Thousands more would be more readily available in court records had courts shown any interest in the evidence.

Reasons to outlaw abortion. The Legislative Findings include these reasons for joining the consensus of all other court-recognized fact finders that constitutionally protected "life begins" at fertilization:

> **Finding #6:** Part of *Roe's* definition of "person" was "infused with a soul". *Roe* thus affirms the belief of most of society, a belief logically demanded by the common knowledge that humans are distinguished from animals by consciousness which features a capacity for (1) self awareness, (2) choice between good and evil – to behave either as an angel or as a demon, and (3) love: to choose to sacrifice one's interests for another. John 15:13.
>
> These differences justify legal protection of humans beyond protections of animals. They are not explained by any known physical process.
>
> Since "infused with a soul" is a common definition of "person" besides being *Roe's definition*, and a "soul" without consciousness has never been theorized and can't be imagined, the consensus of fact finders is, in effect, that abortion kills babies *with conscious souls*.
>
> Souls have no known pre-conscious stage. The lack of any physical explanation for a conscious soul rules out any reason to infer immaturity of consciousness from physical immaturity, and is consistent with the report in Luke 1 that a baby at 6 months heard a righteous voice [and/or felt the righteous Presence of God] and responded with joy, a response not everybody chooses, indicating a preference for good over evil: a choice.
>
> Even considering the body only, there is no objective line between birth and conception distinguishing "humans" from "nonpersons". Without such a line, there can be no stage of gestation at which killing a baby can be objectively distinguished from murder. No baby

is safe while that line remains arbitrary.

The failure of some to grasp the humanity of babies at any given stage is a dangerous basis for permitting killing, since as many fail to grasp the full humanity of quite a number of distinct groups of *born* persons.

To whatever extent the objectivity of "life begins at conception" may be limited by the incompleteness of knowledge available to humans, the fact remains that all five categories of court-recognized finders of facts have "established" the fact, while no American legal authority has said it begins any later, including SCOTUS.

Therefore to whatever extent any heart fails to *emotionally* recognize the unborn as human, or any brain fails to *intellectually* recognize the unborn as human, there is no denying the *legal* recognizability of the unborn as humans/persons.

Roe's "Collapse".

"If this suggestion of personhood [of unborn babies] is established, the...case [for legalizing aborticide], of course, collapses, for the fetus' right to life is then guaranteed specifically by the [14th] Amendment." Roe v. Wade, 410 US 113, 156

This short "collapse" clause tells us five things:

(1) **"Collapse" is possible.** "Establishment" of the unborn as humans/persons, to an extent that SCOTUS will legally recognize it, is *possible*, and will transfer "constitutional protection" from *people who kill* babies to *babies*. *Roe* did *not* rule that unborn personhood could never be established by any other authority than itself. *Roe's* "if" explicitly acknowledges both the possibility, and *Roe's* own uncertainty whether it would happen.

(2) **Authority greater than SCOTUS?** The unspecified authority/agency of this "establishment" is not

SCOTUS. Some other authority is better able or more qualified, than SCOTUS, to "establish" personhood in a way that could "collapse" the case for legal abortion.

Since there can be no greater *legal* authority than SCOTUS, this can only mean an authority over facts, an area where SCOTUS does indeed routinely defer to fact-finders as having superior authority.

It may be supposed that an amendment to the Constitution is what the *Roe* justices were thinking of as an authority superior to that of SCOTUS.

Well, maybe. But there is something about an amendment to the Constitution establishing unborn personhood that argues against it being thought of by the *Roe* justices, because it argues against its appropriateness to address abortion: *no other Constitutional Amendment has attempted to establish a fact as true, as a matter of law.*

It is therefore hard to imagine that a Constitutional Amendment can have greater power to establish the fact that all unborn babies are humans/persons, than today's consensus of court-recognized fact finders that we already have.

(3) **Authority less in doubt than SCOTUS?** What must be "established" must be a fact question about which it is possible for the Roe court to be in doubt – not a question of American law, upon which SCOTUS is the world's expert and cannot possibly be in doubt.[39]

(4) **Evidence is welcome.** Fact finders (ie. juries, legislatures, or expert witnesses) are invited to "establish" this fact if they can – *SCOTUS' alleged ignorance cannot rationally or legally be made an obstacle to letting fact*

---

39 "We need not resolve the difficult question of when life begins. When those trained in the respective disciplines of medicine, philosophy, and theology are unable to arrive at any consensus, the judiciary, at this point in the development of man's knowledge, is not in a position to speculate as to the answer." *Roe v. Wade* 410 US 113, 159 Roe would not defer to doctors and preachers as their superiors on a question of law!

finders "establish" this fact - although we are not told which of them, or how many of them, must agree before SCOTUS will consider the fact established "enough".

(5) **As ignorance passes, so must abortion.** Abortion's legality and aura of "constitutional protection" can continue only in the absence of this "establishment" – *only as long as uncertainty is alleged whether the unborn babies of human mothers are humans.*

Roe's "of course" acknowledges that it is *obvious* that abortion's legality cannot survive knowing it is murder. That is, alleged ignorance cannot rationally or legally be made an obstacle to letting fact finders "establish" this fact. If there is evidence, it must be heard. Because it is unthinkable that we would knowingly want the blood of innocent human lives on our hands. So if the babies of human mothers turn out to be humans, we need to protect them.

Many abortion supporters hope, and prolifers fear[40], that even after our nation's laws and courts officially acknowledge that abortion is the legal equivalent of murder – that the babies abortion kills are humans/persons, it will be possible, even likely, for other rationales to replace *Roe's* rationale – *Roe's* official ignorance about "when life begins".

Appendix G deals with some of them inside and outside case law and shows this is simply impossible. It is just as obvious today as when Roe's "collapse" clause began with "of course", that SCOTUS can't decide who lives and dies as a question so exclusively of law as to render irrelevant whether SCOTUS' rulings protect murder.

The 14th Amendment "equal protection of the laws" is for all who are *in fact* humans/persons. *Had it been only for those who are legally recognized as human, we could still have slavery simply by declining to legally recognize a discrete class of people as fully human.*

---

40 A leader of this fear is Clark Forsythe:
   http://www.saltshaker.us/SLIC/AULmissingOpportunity.pdf

All that pro-slavery judges would need to do would be to rule that blacks are only 3/5 human according to the Constitution. Or that immigrants, already treated as less than "persons in the whole sense" by classifying people as "illegals" for a variety of circumstances beyond their control, for which they are therefore not culpable[41] yet may still be prosecuted. So because "they were never treated by our laws as persons in the whole sense", they may be enslaved, we might then reason.

All "humans" are "persons"

Abortion debate is clouded by the legalistic claim that 18 USC §1841(d) doesn't trigger Roe's "collapse" clause because it uses a different word for unborn baby: the former says "homo sapiens" and the latter says "persons". However, not only are the terms equated in the definitions of the U.S. Code and in all SCOTUS precedent, but *Roe v. Wade* itself acknowledges that babies who are "recognizably human" are "persons".

The confusion involves the statement in *Roe* that "the word 'person', as used in the Fourteenth Amendment, does not include the unborn." Roe, 410 U.S. at 156-157. Courts below interpret that as meaning that even if unborn babies are in fact human beings, they are not "persons" *as a matter of law,* so therefore, evidence that unborn babies of humans are *in fact* humans is irrelevant.

That interpretation of *Roe* ignores *Roe's* equation of "person" and "recognizably human".

> These disciplines variously approached the question [of when life begins] in terms of the point at which the embryo or fetus became 'formed' or *recognizably human, or in terms of when a 'person' came into being,* that is, infused with a 'soul'... Roe

---

41 For example, children brought here by parents are not culpable for being here. Immigrants are not culpable for visa overstays that exist only because the USCIS took years longer to process simple and legitimate application forms than anyone expected.

An interpretation of *Roe* consistent with both *Roe's* stated inability to "speculate" and *Roe's* equation of "person" with "recognizably human" is that *Roe* did not mean there is such a thing as a human being who is not a "'person', as used in the Fourteenth Amendment", but only that SCOTUS' inability to "speculate" was whether unborn babies are "recognizably human" when they are very tiny, at which point Dorland's medical charts (2nd paragraph in *Roe* after the "'person'...does not include the unborn" quote) portray human and pig embryos as identical, 35 years before the first human chromosome was decoded.[42]

Roe neither said the fact is irrelevant, nor that there is such a thing as a human being who is not a "'person', as used in the Fourteenth Amendment". *Roe* equates "person" and "recognizably human".

Therefore the expectation for this section is that it will not say what SCOTUS does not already affirm, but will be a double check against a legalistic distinction between "humans" and "persons" rising from courts below.

The U.S. Code equates "humans" and "persons" from birth. It avoids a position on the legal rights of preborn babies, but a distinction between "humans" and "persons" has no precedent in the U.S. Code.

> 1 U.S.C. 1 §8. **"Person", "human being", "child", and "individual" as including born-alive infant**
>
> (a) In determining the meaning of any Act of Congress, or of any ruling, regulation, or interpretation of the various administrative bureaus and agencies of the United States, the words "person", "human being", "child", and "individual" shall include every infant member of the species homo

---

42 P. 479 of Dorland's Illustrated Medical Dictionary - 24th edition, published 1965, has an illustration of embryos of a hog, calf, rabbit, and human side by side. It portrays the four as indistinguishable until about a human's third month. The illustration is attributed to Haeckel, who a century earlier confessed to his fraud in manipulating the images of the human by (1) adding gills, (2) redrawing the eye, (3) making the back twice as long proportionately, (4) shortening the head, (5) removed the arms and legs. See Appendix J.

sapiens who is born alive at any stage of development....

(c) Nothing in this section shall be construed to affirm, deny, expand, or contract any legal status or legal right applicable to any member of the species homo sapiens at any point prior to being "born alive" as defined in this section.

"Persons" in the Constitution and Declaration. The 5th and 14th Amendments say "[n]o person shall be deprived of life...without due process of law" and "[no] State shall. . . deprive any person of life, liberty, or property, without due process of law". The word "person" must be taken in these protections to include all human beings,[43] or no human being – no matter how educated or useful – can be safe from arbitrary exclusion from them by hearts hardened against recognizing in others the value they want recognized in themselves. When communism sweeps across nations the "useless eaters" targeted for eradication include the most useful – doctors, public servants, teachers.

This amendment secures protection for the basic, minimum human rights any state must respect. It is imperative that categories of human beings not be read out of the terms of this amendment without the clearest demonstration of justification for such exceptions.

Precedents equating "person" with "human". If there is any term whose broad scope demands unconditional respect, It is the term "person." For whoever is not a person lacks not only the privileges of citizenship, but even minimum human rights and is no better off than property, entirely subject to the whim of the owner and whatever regulations the state may impose.

It is as dangerous to drive any invidious [*unwanted, annoying, irritating*] class of human beings out from under the term "persons" in the 5th and 14th Amendments, as it is to read them out from under the term "men" in the legal

---

43 The following section on the unborn being humans borrows from a widely circulated brief by Cliff Zarzky, who <u>died</u> in 2011. The brief is posted at <u>https://personhoodeducation.files.wordpress.com/2009/06/cliff-zarsky-personhood-brief.pdf</u>

foundation of our Constitution: the Declaration of Independence, which says:

> "all men are created equal, and are endowed by their Creator with certain unalienable rights, among which are life..."

A legalistically narrow reading of "men" designed to exclude any human beings who are not "men" from this acknowledgment of God-given rights would not stop with babies, but would include children and women in its sweep. Obviously such a reading occurred to none of its authors. The absurdity of this result proves that "all human beings" are the meaning of the term "men" in this clause. It would be just as absurd to think not all human beings are meant by "persons" as used by a government founded on this declaration of rights. That our government was founded on this declaration is stated by this Court in *U.S. v. Cruikshank,* 92,U.S. 542, 553 (1875):

> The rights of life and personal liberty are natural rights of man. "To secure these rights," says the Declaration of Independence, "governments are instituted among men, deriving their just powers from the consent of the governed."

This opinion continues by noting the obligation of *states* to secure these rights:

> The very highest duty of the States, when they entered into the Union under the Constitution, was to protect all persons within their boundaries in the enjoyment of these "unalienable rights with which they were endowed by their Creator." Sovereignty, for this purpose, rests alone with the States.

The very idea of freedom presupposes some objective moral law which overarches rulers and ruled alike. Subjectivism about human value is eternally incompatible with democracy. We and our rulers are of one kind only so long as we are subject to one law. But if there is no "law of nature", the ethos of any society is the creation of its rulers, educators, and conditioners; and every creator stands above and outside his own creation, so unless we hold to the objective values stated in the Declaration, we will perish. "The laws of nature and of nature's God" contain no value distinctions between one invidious class of humans and another.

Abortion precedents. In *Steinberg v. Brown* 321 F. Supp. 741 (N.D. Ohio, 1970) the federal district court rejected a challenge to Ohio's laws against abortion. It treated an "embryo of a a fetus" as having a right to life which no abortionist or mother had any right to remove. It said the implied right to privacy

> ...must inevitably fall in conflict with the express provisions of the Fifth and Fourteenth Amendments that no person shall be deprived of life without due process of law. The difference between this case and Griswold [*the Supreme Court decision that legalized contraceptives*] is clearly apparent, for here [in this case] there is an embryo of a fetus incapable of protecting itself. There, [in Griswold] the only lives were those of two competent adults. Id. 745-46.

This case is acknowledged in *Roe*, at 155, where no error is identified in it. Seven more such cases are acknowledged in the same paragraph of *Roe*. It is unclear why *Roe,* after addressing this case and several others cited below, said "no case could be cited that holds that a fetus is a person within the meaning of the Fourteenth Amendment".

> Biologically, when the spermatozoon penetrates and fertilizes the ovum, the result is the creation of a new organism which conforms to the definition of life just given. ... Thus when a new life comes into being with the union of human egg and sperm cells, it may terminate, or be terminated, at any moment after it commences, and before, at, or after the particular developmental process called birth" takes place. Such terms as "quick" or "viable", which are frequently encountered in legal discussion, are scientifically

imprecise and without recognized medical meaning, and
hence irrelevant to the problem here presented. Id at 746,
and "[o]nce human life has commenced, the constitutional
protections found in the Fifth and Fourteenth Amendments
impose upon the state a duty of safeguarding it." *Steinberg v.
Brown,* Id 746-47.

This case says so precisely what *Roe* says that "no
case" says, that we would expect *Roe* to have to expose
something fundamentally erroneous about it to put it in the
category of not being a case. *Roe* identified no such error.

Gray v. State, 77 Tex Cr. R. 221 (1915), involves the
review of Gray's indictment for the abortion of Sadie
Moore's child. Though the indictment was tested to see if it
complied with state statutes, the court examined the
common law before doing so (and affirming the conviction)
and said *most states held abortion can be criminally
prosecuted any time after conception.* This case was also
mentioned in *Roe,* in footnote 27, with several other cases.
But it is listed as supporting a statement which seems quite
different than how we have just summarized it:

> ...most American courts ruled, in holding or dictum, that
> abortion of an unquickened fetus was *not* criminal under
> their received common law, <u>27</u>... (emphasis added)

**SCOTUS' "Personhood" Test: "humans, live,
and have their being".** There is no doubt that citizens of
hostile nations, children under eighteen, convicted,
comatose or mentally disabled individuals are each a class
of persons. This is so, not because members of each class
can prove their inclusion under the fourteenth amendment,
but because they are included by virtue of their humanity.
They are "humans, live, and have their being."

> We start from the premise that illegitimate children are not
> "nonpersons." They are humans, live, and have their being...
> They are clearly "persons" within the meaning of the Equal
> Protection Clause of the Fourteenth Amendment. <u>Levi v.
> Louisiana,</u> 391 U.S. 68, 70 (1968) (discussing illegitimate

children).

"Humans, live, and have their being" is a biological test, and a very simple, fundamental one for doctors today.

There are two simple ways to determine whether a creature is "human": one is to check its DNA – an option of course not available in 1973. An even simpler way is to see if the creature is living inside the womb of a human.

SCOTUS' test of personhood is a "biologic" test. *Glona v. American Guarantee and Liability Inc. Co.* 391 U.S. 73, 75 (1968). Any entity possessing those factors are clearly "persons" within the meaning of the Equal Protection Clause of the Fourteenth Amendment.

> To say that the test of equal protection should be the "legal" rather than the biological relationship is to avoid the issue. For the Equal Protection Clause necessarily limits the authority of a State to draw such "legal" lines as it chooses.

The Court held illegitimate children are clearly 'persons' because they are "human, live and have their being." These are all biological qualifications that the Court acknowledged and accepted that the illegitimate children possessed without any facts presented or questions asked by the Court. Why did the *Levi* Court hold the illegitimate children were clearly 'persons'? No proof of any kind was required. It was self evident truth to the *Levi* Court.

In what way are unborn children not "human, live and have their being"? There is no reference to the *Levi* case in *Roe*, but *Levi* has not been reversed, and therefore must be presumed to be the Supreme Court test for "personhood."

The *Levi* Court did not refer to any evidence presented for the children, so it is apparent they accepted as judicial knowledge that the children were "human beings, live, and had their being" and the same judicial knowledge should apply to all classes of human beings including the class of unborn humans. Especially since Congress' "establishment" of the fact that all unborn babies are humans, in 2004.

At present the only approved test for "personhood" by the Supreme Court is "human, live and have their being," Therefore, "[t]hey are clearly 'persons' within the meaning of the Equal Protection Clause of the Fourteenth Amendment." Id. Human offspring conceived but not yet born are likewise "humans, live and have their being."

Justice White joined by Rehnquist, CJ, in a dissent, explains more clearly the genetic and biologic test of the *Levi* Court:

> However one answers the metaphysical or theological question whether the fetus is a human "human being" or the legal question whether it is a "person" as is used in the Constitution, it must be at least recognized first, that the fetus is an entity that bears in its cell all the genetic information that characterizes a member of the species homo sapiens, and distinguishes an individual member of that species from all others, and second, that there is no nonarbitrary line separating a fetus from a child or indeed from an adult human being. *Thornburgh v. American College of Obstets., & Gyne.* 476 U.S. 774, 792 (1986)

They are "a form of human life," *Webster v. Reproductive Health Servs.* 492 U.S. 490, 520 (1989) (plurality opinion), as are infants, toddlers, teens, adults, and the elderly. They do not need to overcome any additional hurdle in order to establish their right to presumptive inclusion within the term "person" as used in the Constitution, and there is no justification for the arbitrary exclusion of such children from the protection of basic human rights under the Constitution.

Direct statements that all "humans" are "persons". In *United States v. Palme,* 14-17 U.S. 607, (1818), Chief Justice John Marshall stated, *"The words 'any person or persons,' are broad enough to comprehend every human being."*

Justice Stephen Field stated in *Wong Wing v. United States,* 163 U.S.228, 242 (1896), "The term *'person' is broad enough to include any and every human being* within the jurisdiction of the republic...This has been decided so often that the point does not require argument."

In 1971 an action was maintained on behalf of a stillborn child.

> The increasing weight of authority supports the proposition that *a viable unborn child,* which would have been born alive but for the negligence of defendant, *is a 'person'* within the meaning of the wrongful death statute. *Simmons v. Howard University* D.C. Cir. 323 F. Supp. 529 (1971)

This was the kind of case *Roe* dismissed with:

> In a recent development, generally opposed by the commentators, some States permit the parents of a stillborn child to maintain an action for wrongful death because of prenatal injuries. <u>65</u> Such an action, however, would appear to be one to vindicate the parents' interest and is thus consistent with the view that the fetus, at most, represents only the potentiality of life. Roe at 162.

But if that Court saw no human worth in the stillborn child apart from "the parents' interest", wouldn't that be the same "interest" the law would have, had another's negligence killed a fine horse or dog?

It is hardly necessary, to vindicate a plaintiff's "interest", to classify the thing or creature destroyed as a "person" if it is in fact not.

There was no reason for the Court to call the baby a "person" if the Court did not in fact believe the baby was.

Probate. [*when an inheritance is left to an unborn baby*] No one, not even *Roe,* denies that the unborn are "persons" in probate law.

> The preamble [of Missouri's personhood law] does not, by its terms, regulate abortions or any other aspect of appellees' medical practice, and § 1.205.2 can be interpreted to do no more than offer protections to unborn children in tort and probate law, which is permissible under *Roe v. Wade, supra,*

at 161-162. *Webster v. Reproductive Health Services* (492 U.S. 490, 491), 1989.

The Texas Supreme Court agreed with Lord Hardwicke,

> ...that a child in the mother's womb is a person in *rerum natura,* [*in the nature of things*] and that by rules of the civil and common law "she [the child] was to all intents and purposes a child. . . and is to be considered as living for all purposes. *Nelson v. Galveston,* 14 S.W. 1021 (1890)

The court ruled that a posthumous child may recover damages for the father's death. The case is not mentioned in *Roe*. "She was to all intents and purposes a child" certainly says, directly, that this finding of fact is not limited to probate, but would have been considered by SCOTUS as just as true in *any* 5th or 14th Amendment case.

It would appear to undermine *Roe's* statement that "...no case could be cited that holds that a fetus is a person within the meaning of the Fourteenth Amendment...."

Here is how *Roe* justified acknowledging "personhood" of the unborn only in probate but not in other law — as if broad assertions of unborn personhood throughout all case law did not exist:

> Such an action, however, would appear to be one to vindicate the parents' interest and is thus consistent with the view that the fetus, at most, represents only the potentiality of life. Similarly, unborn children have been recognized as acquiring rights or interests by way of inheritance or other devolution of property, and *have been represented by guardians ad litem.* <u>66</u> Perfection of the interests involved, again, has generally been contingent upon live birth. In short, the unborn have never been recognized in the law as persons in the whole sense. *Roe* at 162.

Guardian ad litems (*lawyers*) **for the unborn.** But is there not an internal inconsistency in the preceding logic? If the rights of the unborn are only at the mercy of the testator's (*the person who left the will*) interest, why isn't the lawyer *for the testator, hired by the executor appointed by the testator, to represent the interests of the testator,* the best representation for that interest? What legal purpose is served by a guardian ad litem for the baby, if the baby has no protectable interest of his own independent of the testator's?

There is no reason to appoint a guardian ad litem for the unborn, by a court which considers the beneficiary to have no greater legally protectable rights than those wished by the testator; such as in a will for the maintenance of a dog. No court has appointed a guardian ad litem to represent the interests of a dog. At least we hope not.[44]

We are unsure of what significance Blackmun found in saying "Perfection of the interests involved, again, has generally been contingent upon live birth", since the death of a plaintiff in any lawsuit ordinarily eliminates his claim. How do courts of equity treat adults differently than unborn babies, in that regard?

McArthur v. Scott, not mentioned in *Roe*, said preborn children in the womb should not have been cut out of a probated will without proper representation in court.

> "A decree annulling the probate of a will is not merely irregular and erroneous but absolutely void, as against [unborn] persons interested in [*who are beneficiaries of*] the will and not parties to the decree, [*who had no opportunity to defend their interests in the court hearing*] and as the parties these plaintiffs were neither actually nor constructively parties to the decree setting aside the will of their grandfather, it follows that that decree is no bar to the [*can't keep them from*] assertion of their rights under the will."

---

44 Apparently a judge's ruling April 21, 2015 is the closest any court has come to regarding animals as "persons". The judge allowed guardian ad litems to represent two chimpanzees in a habeas corpus proceeding, implying their status as "persons". www.theguardian.com/world/2015/apr/21/chimpanzees-granted-legal-persons-status-unlawful-imprisonment. Here is a 2002 article about the push for guardian ad litems to represent animals: www.proaviculture.com/guardian.htm. Here is a 2011 push: www.bradenton.com/2011/05/24/3218278/animals-to-get-guardians-in-court.html

This Court said a person must have the opportunity to present their side of the story in court. Id. 387, 391.

If it be argued that the plaintiffs are "persons" with representation rights only *since* their birth, this Court also held that preborn persons in the womb can hold vested [*not just potential or expected, but fully realized*] rights, not just rights "contingent upon live birth,"id. 384.

> ...it has long been a settled rule of construction in the courts of England and America that estates, legal or equitable, given by will, should always be regarded as vesting immediately, unless the testator has by very clear words manifested an intention that they should be contingent upon a future event.

Not only does *McArthur v. Scott* join those cases which would counter *Roe*'s claim that "no case could be cited that holds that a fetus is a person within the meaning of the Fourteenth Amendment", but its ruling would likely have significantly impacted *Roe* had not the lower courts in *Roe* denied a motion for a guardian ad litem to join in the arguments. *Roe, Doe v. Scott,* 321 F. Supp. 1385 (N.D. III. 1971), cert denied 409 U.S. 817 (1972).

The Fifth Amendment provides "no person shall be ... deprived of life...without due process of law." As a fetus is a person, neither a state nor the federal government may allow anyone to take innocent life without due process of law. Especially now that federal law defines every unborn baby "at all stages of gestation" as a human life, it has the right to representation to be heard on the question as to whether its life should be terminated. And every court ruling affecting their fundamental rights, in which they are not allowed representation, is null and void according to *McArthur. Roe* definitely affects the fundamental rights of unborn babies, some of whom are definitely impacted by a ruling protecting their killers, and those babies were definitely denied representation in that ruling.

The Judgments of the U.S. District Court and the Supreme Court in *Roe,* rendered without any representation of such victims by guardian or next friend (or by counsel for such guardian or next friend), constituted deprivation of life, liberty and property without due process of law, in violation of the 5th Amendment. Accordingly, such Judgments are unconstitutional and void with regard to them. *McArthur v. Scott,* 113 U.S, 340, 391-392, 404 (1885) (unborn children); *Pennoyer v. Neff,* 95 U.S.714,733-734 (1878) (U.S. citizens).

Neither the Supreme Court in *Roe* nor the U.S. District Court below had personal jurisdiction over any category of children affected vitally by those proceedings, who had a right to be represented before the Courts.

Unborn baby's interest *greater* than mother's interest. *Raleigh Fitkin-Paul Morgan Memorial Hospital v Anderson* 201 A.2d 537,538 (N.J. 1964) held that the interest of the unborn child was *greater* than the interest of the mother. This is contrary to *Roe's* contention that unborn babies have *no* protectable rights better established than whatever rights the mother *chooses* to grant.

The mother, a Jehovah's Witness, refused consent to any future blood transfusions which her hospital had advised will probably be necessary to save her and her baby. The hospital sued to require a transfusion if her doctor determines it is necessary, and a unanimous state Supreme Court agreed.

This doesn't technically contradict the verbiage of *Roe,* which supposedly allows states to restrict 3rd trimester abortions. But it certainly contradicts the jurisprudence since *Roe,* which throws impossible obstacles before states trying to restrain killing an unborn baby up to the moment of delivery and in some cases after, so long as the mother so chooses. Even the partial birth restriction, *Gonzales v. Carhart,* 550 U.S. 124 (2007), restricts only one method of abortion up to the moment of live delivery.

Corporations. The Supreme Court has applied the term "person" so broadly that it includes legal fictions. The fictitious entity of a corporation is a "person" meriting Fourteenth Amendment equal protection, *Santa Clara County v. Southern Pacific Railroad Company*, 118 U.S. 394 (1886) and for due process protection in *Minneapolis and St. Louis Railway Co. Beckwith*, 129 U.S. 26 (1889).

Can the 14th Amendment give "equal protection" to legal arrangements with real people, but not real babies from other real people? These cases stand for nothing if they do not stand for the principle that the word "person" in the fourteenth amendment is not to be construed in a strict or narrow sense.

Nothing in the constitution suggests fictional legal entities should be included as persons for constitutional protection. By contrast, unborn humans are specifically referred to in the Preamble of the Constitution as a purpose of the Constitution: ". . . (to) secure the blessings of liberty to ourselves and our posterity...." Presently living unborn humans are unquestionably posterity. There can be no pretense of consistency unless and until this Court holds either that a corporation is *not* a person or that an unborn human child *is*.

Executions of pregnant women. Women on death row can't be executed while they are pregnant, according to 400 years of U.S. law.

> The *writ de ventre inspiciendo* ["to inspect the body"], to ascertain whether a woman convicted of a capital crime was quick with child, was allowed by the common law, in order to guard against the taking of the life of an unborn child for the crime of the mother. *Union Pacific R. Co. v Botsford*, 141 U.S. 250, 253 (1891).

The prohibition was codified in the U.S. Code in 1994 (if not before) by HR3355. It now reads:

Blackmun might have seen, in the 1891 case just cited, confirmation of his theory that our ancestors didn't attach as much human worth to first trimester babies (which in his mind was the same as babies before quickening) since in the common law the protection didn't kick in before quickening. (When the baby's kicks can be felt by someone holding their hand on the mother's womb.) But the quickening trigger was obviously necessitated by prosecutorial necessity, regardless of what anyone thought about the value of preemies. Quickening was the only pregnancy test they had in those days, with which a warden could verify a prisoner's claim. Before delaying an execution they would of course want proof that the woman was pregnant rather than just take her word for it that she craves pickles and ice cream. Without a proof requirement, any woman would make the claim – even though no woman could really be sure either – to buy a few more months.

The codification of this prohibition changes "quick with child" to "pregnant". In other words, current law stops the execution as soon as the woman tests positive, which is as close as modern science can get to the time of conception.

Surely prosecutorial considerations explain other common law distinctions in penalties before and after quickening, too. Before quickening, prosecutors had no evidence that there was a live human being who was killed, not to mention the absence of a dead body to document death. The situation was the legal equivalent of attempted murder, where even if the attempt can be proved, the existence of a victim cannot be. Perhaps rather it was the legal equivalent of the kinds of contraception today which kill after fertilization; where not even the mother knows if there was ever a fertilization, or if fertilization was prevented or the embryo was killed after fertilization.

Slavery & abortion were outlawed together.

There was a concurrence of 14th Amendment ratification and stronger criminalization of abortion before quickening. Despite the prosecutorial hurdle, states passed stronger penalties against pre-quickening abortion, during the same time that they ratified the 14th Amendment.

As *Roe* reports, this tightening of penalties by almost all states was in response to lobbying of The American Medical Association, which had been assembling evidence of distinct, unique human life from the moment of conception.

The fact that almost all states tightened their penalties from conception in response to evidence of human individuality from that point, proves that states adopted the position, if they didn't already hold it but had withheld penalties because of courtroom reality, that all babies from conception are humans/persons. The fact that they simultaneously ratified the 14th Amendment with its "equal protection of the laws" clause protecting all humans/persons and invalidating any law that gives less protection to humans of any invidious class through some legal fiction, indicates that they believed the 14th Amendment obligated states to protect the unborn.

The purpose of the 14th amendment was to close a loophole in the 13th that had allowed slavery to continue. In other words the national consciousness that increasingly protected unborn babies at all stages of gestation was the same national consciousness that was nailing down slavery's coffin.

Stare Decisis, the principle, carried back centuries. By reasoning similar to that of *Stare Decisis, Roe* dismisses the reforms of post-slavery because they are so recent, having occurred a mere century before.[45] *Roe*

---

45 "It perhaps is not generally appreciated that the restrictive criminal abortion laws in effect in a majority of States today are of relatively recent vintage. Those laws, generally proscribing abortion or its attempt at any time during pregnancy except when necessary to preserve the pregnant woman's life, are not of ancient or even of common-law origin. Instead, they derive from statutory changes effected, for the most part, in the latter half of the 19th century." Roe v. Wade, 410 U.S. 113, 129 (1973)

argued that more ancient understanding of "when life begins" is a better guide for us today, than the popular understanding that grew in response to the newly discovered facts circulated by the American Medical Association.[46]

The past 50 years have seen a second explosion of knowledge of the nature of human life from fertilization to birth. Now that Americans know, we shouldn't be expected to tolerate abortion until that knowledge is lost again.

Unfortunately, knowledge is not directly proportional to behavior. The national acceptance of AMA's facts a century before *Roe* coincided with the maturing respect for all human life forced by the Civil War over slavery. National acceptance of facts about blacks presented before the War *could* have ended slavery without war. Today, political positions are formed not by disagreement over medical facts, but by personal responses to them.

Roe treats the maturing understanding of the AMA of preborn humans a century before, and the AMA's continued alarm a century later over weakening criminalization of abortion,[47] as mitigated by another somewhat medical association, the American Public Health Association, which urged legalizing abortion.[48]

---

46 ""the attitude of the [medical] profession may have played a significant role in the enactment of stringent criminal abortion legislatio...." Starting before the Civil War, the AMA resolved to address "wide-spread popular ignorance of the true character of" the babies killed by abortion. Roe v. Wade, 410 U.S. 113, 141 (1973)

47 "Except for periodic condemnation of the criminal abortionist, no further formal AMA action took place until 1967. In that year, the Committee on Human Reproduction urged the adoption of a stated policy of opposition to induced abortion, except when [familiar exceptions are listed]." *Roe,* p. 142. "In 1970, after the introduction of a variety of proposed resolutions, and of a report from its Board of Trustees, a reference committee noted 'polarization of the medical profession on this controversial issue'; division among those who had testified; a difference of opinion among AMA councils and committees; 'the remarkable shift in testimony' in six months, felt to be influenced 'by the rapid changes in state laws and by the judicial decisions which tend to make abortion more freely available;' and a feeling 'that this trend will continue.'" Roe, p. 143.

48 "American Public Health Association. In October 1970, the Executive Board of

But *Roe* cites no indication that the shifts in acceptance of abortion had anything to do with any shift in understanding of the facts of preborn human life.

Stare Decisis is properly set aside when the facts underpinning precedent are shown to be incorrect. The principle applies to our understanding of past culture. The more ancient laxity about killing the unborn was properly set aside in response to facts. Past ignorance belongs in the past. The challenge for humans of every age has been to live so as to avoid collisions with known facts.

Stare Decisis: we do not challenge *Roe*. We rely on it.

Roe v. Wade has been "the law of the land". We rely on it. We invoke *stare decisis* as a principle in our favor. As we argue under "Reasons to Grant the Writ", we challenge the violation of *Roe* by lower appellate courts which have ruled saying *Roe* said what *Roe* obviously did not say: that evidence was made irrelevant, "as a matter of law", that abortion *in fact* kills living human beings.

Of course, the holding of *Roe* that everybody knows is that abortion is legal. We concur that abortion *was* legal, but we rely on the "independent ground for the decision" which has equal authority with the holding,[49] which is that abortion must *stop* being legal after it is legally recognized as killing living persons. Now that every court-recognized American legal finder of fact that has taken a position agrees, *Roe* requires states to outlaw abortion. It is a basic principle of *stare decisis* that precedents must fall when the

---

the APHA adopted Standards for Abortion Services. 'Rapid and simple abortion referral must be readily available through state and local public health departments, medical societies, or other nonprofit organizations.'" *Roe,* p. 144

49 *Stare decisis* preserves the authority of reasons for rulings along with the rulings [holdings] themselves: "Although we gave other reasons for our holding in *Schleier* as well, we explicitly labeled this reason an 'independent' ground in support of our decision, id., at 334. We cannot accept petitioners' claim that it was simply a dictum." *O'Gilvie v. United States,* 519 U.S. 79 (1996)

facts upon which they are founded change.[50]

To the extent any ruling has precedential value, its value presumes it will be relied on in the context of its full reasoning rather than having parts selectively taken out of context.

> "Virtually every one of the Court's opinions announcing a new application of a constitutional principle contains some explanatory language that is intended to provide guidance to lawyers and judges in future cases. See, e.g., *Crawford v. Washington,* 541 U. S. 36 (2004); Strickland, 466 U. S. 668; *Miranda v. Arizona,* 384 U. S. 436 (1966); see also *Marbury v. Madison,* 1 Cranch 137 (1803). It is quite wrong to invite state court judges to discount the importance of such guidance on the ground that it may not have been strictly necessary as an explanation of the Court's specific holding in the case. Cf. *County of Allegheny v. American Civil Liberties Union, Greater Pittsburgh Chapter,* 492 U. S. 573, 668 (1989) (KENNEDY, J., concurring in judgment in part and dissenting in part); ('As a general rule, the principle of stare decisis directs us to adhere not only to the holdings of our prior cases, but also their explications of the governing rules of law'); Sheet Metal Workers v. EEOC, 478 U. S. 421, 490 (1986) (O'Connor, J., concurring in part and dissenting in part) ('Although technically dicta, . . . an important part of the Court's rationale for the result that it reache[s] is entitled to greater weight . . .'). *See *Yarborough v. Alvarado,* 541 U. S. 652, 660-661 (2004); *Lockyer v. Andrad* 538 U. S. 63, 71 (2003); *Tyler v. Cain,* 533 U. S. 656, 664 (2001)." Carey v. Musladin, 549 U. S. 70 (2006), Concurrence by Stevens

Had *Roe* been followed by the lower courts, they would have ruled abortion unconstitutional decades ago when they were first presented with overwhelming uncontested evidence that the factual underpinning of *Roe's* legalization of abortion – that judges are "not in a position to speculate" about "when life begins" – had "collapsed". Those courts should have ended abortion's legality both

---

50 Dictionary.com: "Stare Decisis: the doctrine that rules or principles of law on which a court rested a previous decision are authoritative in all future cases in which the facts are substantially the same."

because *stare decisis* does not preserve rulings whose factual underpinnings no longer exist, and because *Roe v. Wade* explicitly ordered that abortion's legality must "of course" "collapse" when it is "established" that its factual underpinnings no longer exist.

Stare decisis preserves constitutional rulings least, especially applications of constitutional principles. Although Iowa relies on *Roe's* "collapse" clause, we do so because it is compelling and persuasive, not because it ought to be preserved to keep law stable no matter how questionable it is.

Roe is in the category of cases whose authority is least preserved by *stare decisis:* it is a case "where correction depends upon amendment [of precedent by the Court], and not upon legislative action," and "particularly...when the decision believed erroneous is the application of a constitutional principle rather than an interpretation of the Constitution to extract the principle itself."

> In reaching this conclusion we are not unmindful of the desirability of continuity of decision in constitutional questions.[8] However, when convinced of former error, this Court has never felt constrained to follow precedent. In constitutional questions, where correction depends upon amendment [of precedent by the Court], and not upon legislative action, this Court throughout its history has freely exercised its power to reexamine the basis of its constitutional decisions. This has long been accepted practice,[9] and this practice has continued to this day.[10] This is particularly true when the decision believed erroneous is the application of a constitutional principle rather than an interpretation of the Constitution to extract the principle itself.[11] *Smith v. Allwright,* 321 U.S. 649, 665-666 (1944)

It is "strikingly true of cases under the due process clause", that "this Court has often overruled its earlier decisions". *Burnet v. Coronado Oil & Gas Co.,* 285 U.S. 393, 406–407, 410 (1932) (Brandeis, J., dissenting)

***Stare Decisis:* Past Crimes Don't Legalize future Crimes. Updated facts call for updated precedents.** Getting away with crime doesn't make crime legal.

This is another obvious limit to *stare decisis.* 46 years of killing the unborn doesn't make irrelevant the now unanimously "established" fact that the unborn are innocent living humans, and killing innocent humans is not protected by the Constitution. *Stare decisis* has no power to perpetuate deprivation of fundamental rights. The fact that the fundamental rights of sixty millions have been cut off for 46 years cannot turn the Constitution into the willing executioner of sixty million more.

As this Court emphasized in *Brown v. Board of Education,* 349 U.S. 294, 300 (1955) (Brown 11), "the vitality of these constitutional principles cannot be allowed to yield simply because of disagreement with them"; how much more *these constitutional principles must not be allowed to yield simply because of violation of them!*

If the state in fact is denying due process or equal protection to a class of humans, the remedy is to declare the discrimination unconstitutional, not to deny the personhood of the victimized class, nor to declare *evidence* of the personhood of the victimized class *irrelevant.*

Errors in abortion prevention cases

Iowa's defense relies on the evidence that every baby of a human is a human/person from conception/fertilization.

Courts below have erroneously said this court ruled that evidence irrelevant. Only one of those cases was a civil case like Iowa's: Rhode Island, in 1973. The rest were all criminal cases. All of them said this Court said it doesn't matter whether those killed by abortion are people. None of those cases were reviewed by this Court.

None of the abortion cases this Court *has* taken, which were all civil cases, addressed when protectable human life begins.

Since this is an Iowa case, the first precedent we should review should be Iowa's.

The principal error in *Planned Parenthood of Mid-Iowa v. Maki,* 478 N.W.2d 637 (1991), was that *the Court did not address her defense.* Judy Maki invoked the Necessity Defense *to justify actions necessary to save human lives.* The Court completely ignored that defense and substituted, for it, a defense which Maki did not raise, which Maki considered as ridiculous as everyone else thought it was: that Maki invoked the Necessity Defense *"to excuse criminal activity by those who disagree with the policies of government."*

> In October 1990, Planned Parenthood filed a petition seeking to permanently enjoin Maki from trespassing upon its property, disrupting its business, and interfering with its patients. Maki contends that her acts do not constitute a trespass but instead are justified based on the defense of necessity. We apply the necessity defense only in emergency situations where the threatened harm is immediate and the threatened disaster imminent; the individual must be stripped of all options available to avoid both evils. *State v. Walton,* 311 N.W.2d 113, 117 (Iowa 1981). The necessity defense is generally **not available to excuse criminal activity by those who disagree with the policies of the government.** *United States v. Kabat,* 797 F.2d 580, 591 (8th Cir.1986). Thus, we do not believe the necessity defense has been established here to excuse Maki's repeated trespasses. *NOW v. Operation Rescue,* 747 F. Supp. 760, 770 (D.D.C.1990).

Even if Maki had actually "disagreed with the government", as even courts do from time to time, and even if that were part of Maki's motivation, did the Court think that when there is an additional reason for doing something besides the reason that justifies it, that it isn't justified?

The ruling doesn't ignore the *name* of the defense or of its elements. But it did not acknowledge the *object* of the defense: the harm which the defendant's action had averted.

A third problem was giving Planned Parenthood standing to sue for the injunction against Maki. When a plaintiff in a lawsuit is at least partly responsible for the harm the suit seeks to correct, the plaintiff does not have the "clean hands" needed for standing to sue. Now that abortion is legally recognizable as the legal equivalent of murder, abortionists have no legal right to sue anybody for interfering with murder. The Court should have considered Maki's considerable evidence that human life/personhood begins at conception. It was not irrelevant.

A fourth problem with the ruling was that it so misapplied the *Kabat* case as to reach the opposite result that *Kabat* sought while citing *Kabat* as its authority for it.

Kabat said courts can't allow Necessity to establish, as a "harm", what *elected legislatures* have fixed as necessary and good – because (1) that would be tantamount to courts reversing legislatures, which courts must never do.[51] And because (2) they had an alternative way to reach their goal without breaking the law: the political process. (The case was about protesters at a nuclear facility.) But Judy Maki (1) supported what legislatures were trying to do and only wanted the lower appellate court to do what SCOTUS directed them to do, and (2) when laws are vacated by courts, the political process is a fragile remedy.

Maki ruled that courts can't allow Necessity to establish, as a "harm", what nearly every legislature in America had established as a *crime* until SCOTUS overturned them all on the ground that SCOTUS wouldn't

---

51 Kabat said "the necessity defense was never intended to excuse criminal activity by those who disagree with the decisions and policies *of the lawmaking branches* of government: in such cases the 'greater harm' sought to be prevented would be the course of action chosen by elected representatives, and a court in allowing the defense would be making a negative political or policy judgment about that course of action. Judgments of that type, however, are not the province of judge (or jury) under the separation of powers established by our Constitution." [797 F.2d 592]

be "in a position to speculate" whether it was a harm, before being informed by fact finders such as those which *Maki* silenced.

See Appendix F for analysis of errors in several other criminal abortion prevention cases.

God's Relevance. *Roe v. Wade* treated

the findings of theologians, along with those of doctors and philosophers, as not only relevant, but as controlling. [*"Controlling" means having the authority to determine how a court must rule*]

> "When those trained in the respective disciplines of medicine, philosophy, *and theology* are unable to arrive at any consensus, the judiciary, at this point in the development of man's knowledge, is not in a position to speculate as to the answer." *Roe v. Wade*, 410 U.S. 113, 159 (1973)

This followed *Roe's* section VI, whose first three subsections touched on treatment of abortion among three ancient pagan empires, three Greek philosophers, and two Christian theologians 800 years ago trying to speculate when souls enter preborn bodies. *Roe*, pp. 129-136.

Roe gave surprising weight to those authorities, according to the final statement in section VI: "It is with these interests, and the weight to be attached to them, that this case is concerned." *Roe*, p. 152.

Roe did not identify disagreement between the two Christians, leaving us to wonder *whose* "inability to arrive at any consensus" left *Roe* "unable to speculate" whether unborn babies of humans are humans. Was it the contradiction between Christians and pagan philosophers? Was it between 800-year-old speculations and the findings of modern medical science?

Roe was correct to recognize a spiritual dimension to the abortion issue beyond medical facts such as those pointed out by Justices White and Rehnquist:

> However one answers the metaphysical or theological question whether the fetus is a human "human being" or the legal question whether it is a "person" as is used in the Constitution, it must be at least recognized first, that the fetus is an entity that bears in its cell all the genetic information that characterizes a member of the species homo sapiens, and distinguishes an individual member of that species from all others, and second, that there is no nonarbitrary line separating a fetus from a child or indeed from an adult human being. *Thornburgh v. American College of Obstets., & Gyne.* 476 U.S. 774, 792 (1986)

But how does one grasp that a dozen cells merit the same protection as an important adult with a Ph.D.?

It is also a fact that without a nonarbitrary line, there can be no stage of gestation at which the deliberate killing of a baby can be objectively distinguished from murder.

But still, a dozen cells? One cell?

It is also a fact that the failure of some adults to grasp the humanity of babies at any given stage is a dangerous basis for permitting their killing, since as many adults fail to grasp the full humanity of quite a number of discrete *[distinct]* groups of born persons.

And yet even at two months, can a baby only an inch long have a soul? And suffer like any adult when it is torn apart? Very hard to grasp.

It is also a fact that the capacity to choose between good and evil – to choose to behave either as an angel or as a demon – is a capacity that distinguishes humans from animals. It is not related to brain size, since animals with much larger brains lack this capacity, while toddlers with much smaller than adult brains demonstrate this capacity. No known physical process accounts for this ability, supporting the belief acknowledged in *Roe*[52] that a soul

---

52 These disciplines variously approached the question in terms of the point at
   which the embryo or fetus became "formed" or recognizably human, or in

attaches to the body whose capacity for discerning good from evil, and choosing between them, and being harmed by evil and blessed by good, is not limited to physical body size.

It is hard enough for humans to believe that someone who *disagrees* with him is fully human. It takes something beyond logic – faith – to reverence the right to life of someone too little to even find without a microscope.

Much the same may be said of the 14th Amendment.

The idea that everyone should be treated equally by law might be a popular idea among a few people who realize they would probably be slaves without it, but *logic* does not require it. Greek philosophy does not imagine it. Atheistic Communism does not tolerate it. Hinduism has no caste for it. Islam outlaws it. All Europe said equal rights could never work, when America began.

The same things may be said of the Declaration of Independence, "We hold these truths to be self-evident, that all men are created equal...." They didn't mean "self evident to everybody". It wasn't self evident to the British king or parliament. They took it as a declaration of war.

And the rest of the world? Seeing a few born to privilege, while masses fight over crumbs of opportunity, such a declaration was incomprehensible and counter intuitive to most.

So who *was* the "we" who "hold these truths to be self-evident, that all men are created equal...."?

The only people to whom equality seemed self evidently innate in us were those who accepted a principle found in only one place. The principle: *Imago Deo* – we are created in the Image of God. The foundation of freedom.

Without that vision, there could never have been a 14th Amendment, an "all men are created equal", or Fundamental Rights. There could never have been Freedom. *Imago Deo* is larger than all those. It gave birth to all those. It calls us still higher than all those.

To the extent we sideline the One who gave us all

---

terms of when a "person" came into being, that is, infused with a "soul" or "animated." *Roe*, p. 133

those as irrelevant, we abandon all those. We revert to frail logic. We revert to the little that imperfect humans are able to grasp. Without a standard higher than ourselves, it is very difficult for our logic to grasp very much more than ourselves.

It is interesting to ponder, in a nation where even most Christians agree the Bible has no place in courtroom or political discussion because "America is not a theocracy", why *Roe v. Wade* declared that the views of theologians were part of the basis for its holding. But *Imago Deo* is the elephant in freedom's room.

Imago Deo inspires Americans to press for ever more equal rights and opportunities for all. Americans separated church and state, freed slaves, let women vote, and moved children from factories into schools. We are still struggling with the unborn, homosexuals, and immigrants. But it is only because of *Imago Deo* that anyone struggles.

But what about a mother's rights to control her own body? What about the slave master's right to control his own property? What about the husband's right to control his own household?

Whatever right any husband ever had to control his wife lost the support of voting laws and equal pay laws as evidence failed to materialize that women are less competent, level headed, or hard working than men. Masters lost their property rights in their slaves as masters were unable to produce evidence for their "inferior race" myths in response to Bible preaching – although not without tremendous struggle. Nor can the right of a mother to kill a dependent survive forever in a society with any equal rights at all, as the public processes the evidence that an unborn dependent, like any other dependent, is a human being equal in value to that of his or her mother, and that there is no such thing as a partial human.

The Book in which *Imago Deo* is found contains many more helpful details which our Founders consulted as they fashioned our freedoms. Details which help us correctly identify a "suspect class" [*a class of people who have historically been subject to discrimination*], and whether there is anyone who is not a "person in the whole sense". Appendix E lists a few of the verses which have led many Americans to see *Imago Deo* even in a tiny unborn baby.

However, SCOTUS need not openly perform the task of consulting the Bible in order to correctly understand what abortion kills. Every category of court-recognized finders of facts, and every American legal authority that has taken a position on "when [protectable] life begins", has already done that work, it would appear.

They seldom say the Bible influenced their finding as openly as *Roe* said theologians were part of the basis of their ruling, but logic alone can't explain their unanimity.

Nor can the remarkable absence of any official legal affirmation that unborn babies are *not* humans/persons, not even by this Court, nor by any other court which instead of taking responsibility for the claim has laid the responsibility on this Court, and even then has avoided declaring it a fact but kept it a "matter of law", be accounted for by anything other than fear of pushing too far people who reverence *Imago Deo*.

All this Court needs to consult is the unanimous establishment of this fact by every American legal authority which has taken a position.

Possibly what motivated the *Roe* justices to say they found it relevant to consult theologians, is that a relevant, practical problem is created for courts by the conflict between *Imago Deo* and logic alone.

Faith looks at this virtually unrestrained killing of lives whose humanity logic struggles to grasp, and sees genocide. It sees the blood of 60 million slain running down the steps of the U.S. Supreme Court. This dangerously erodes public confidence in American justice. The only reason "we the people" created courts was to prosecute crime. Murder is the ultimate crime, and genocide is the ultimate murder. To the extent judges promote genocide, and especially after it becomes clear that is what is done, judges undermine the reason for their existence.

Fortunately the American legal system is able to balance doubt and faith and allow America to move forward, although no one is happy that it takes so long.

People debate facts and faith. Their debate spills into courts. America's court-recognized fact finders rule. As the facts become clearer to everybody, there is a point of decision whether to ignore reality or accept and accommodate it. The process of legal recognition through fact finders is for a nation like the conscience is for an individual, from which courts stray at peril to their own credibility.

"We hold these truths to be self evident, that all men are created with unalienable rights...life...."

The "self evident" status of our fundamental "rights" establishes the role of popular understanding in legal reasoning. Rights are the Gift of God, our Declaration says. But in few nations during few centuries have they had the support of popular understanding. Popular understanding of our rights, which can exist only to the extent of reverence for *Imago Deo,* acts as a nation's acceptance of God's Gift. Popular understanding is not to be ignored. Not to be dismissed as irrelevant. Without it, no rights are safe.

No *Roe* backup is possible. Several wannabe replacement rationales wait in the wings to take *Roe's* place when it "collapses". 12 of them are addressed in Appendix G. None of them can survive "establishment" that all unborn babies of humans are humans/persons.

> "Indeed, our decision in *United States v. Vuitch,* 402 U.S. 62 (1971), inferentially is to the same effect, for we would not have indulged in statutory interpretation favorable to abortion in specified circumstances if the necessary consequence was the termination of life entitled to Fourteenth Amendment protection." – *Roe v. Wade* at 159.

In oral arguments in *Roe v. Wade*, Justice Potter Stewart asked Sarah Weddington "If it were established that an unborn fetus is a person, you would have an almost impossible case here, would you not?" Weddington audibly laughed and acknowledged "I would have a very difficult case." Stewart pursued, "This would be the equivalent to after the child was born...if the mother thought it bothered her health having the child around, she could have it killed. Isn't that correct?" Weddington answered, "That's correct."

This exchange is what presumably provoked Justice Blackmun to write "[If the] suggestion of personhood is established, the case, of course, collapses, for the fetus' right to life is then guaranteed specifically by the [14th] Amendment."

Is it true that abortion's fragile "legality" must "collapse" along with *Roe*? Can it be sustained, after *Roe's* burial, by SCOTUS rationales added after *Roe*, to *Roe's* "outer shell"?

> The joint opinion, following its newly minted variation on stare decisis, retains the **outer shell** of Roe v. Wade, 410 U.S. 113 (1973), but beats a wholesale retreat from the substance of that case. (Rehnquist, joined by White, Scalia, and Thomas, in Planned Parenthood v. Casey, 505 U.S. 833 (1992)

What is *Roe's* "outer shell"? Can any rationale hanging on it stand alone, without it?

Since it does not appear to be identified anywhere, it must be taken as a metaphor of whatever it is about *Roe* that keeps abortion legal despite the shifting sands of legal rationales for it.

There is only one skeletal sustaining principle Iowa can think of in *Roe*, to which a succession of rationales may attach in turn: *alleged uncertainty whether the unborn babies of humans are human.*

This alleged uncertainty is articulated in *Roe's* "collapse" clause where it is explicitly identified as *Roe's* sustaining principle, in the sense that without it, *Roe's* holding cannot stand.

This uncertainty as a matter of law cannot still seriously be alleged. Granting that the unborn babies of humans are humans, making their killing the legal equivalent of murder, will this Court still insist their murder is some kind of "private and personal right", a "sacred choice" with which courts and lawmakers ought not interfere? Once this "outer shell" of alleged uncertainty who is human "collapses", no rationale can stand.

Let us be clear that *Roe* does not merely "collapse" and leave states free to outlaw abortion or keep it legal. The terms of *Roe*'s "collapse" clause make it clear that the "establishment" that will overturn *Roe*'s holding that abortion is a constitutional right will also overturn every law and court ruling which obstructs protection of the 14th Amendment right to life of every unborn baby.

Summary: Abortion on trial. It is not possible to invalidate Iowa's law without squarely addressing whether abortion is murder. The defense for abortion must prove that Iowa's law will *not* save human lives.

Every court-recognized legal authority in America, and every court-recognized fact finding authority in America, which has taken a position on it, has unanimously found that unborn babies are humans/persons from conception. No legal authority or court-recognized fact finding authority has said the unborn are *not* humans/persons.

Abortion, and its sustaining rationale that we can't tell if babies of humans are humans, threatens more than unborn babies. By successfully dehumanizing millions of persons over a term like "fetus", *Roe* demonstrates the device of denying defensible rights to any group the state considers "unwanted" (ie. PVS [*Persistent Vegetative State*], seniors, mentally ill, or prisoners) by simply alleging inability to define certain elements of humanity or personhood.

It is impossible for a "right to privacy", which gives

mothers jurisdiction over the lives of unborn babies, to exist in the "penumbra" of the 14th Amendment, once legal recognition is "established" that these babies are "persons", which *Roe* equates to "recognizably human", requiring 14th Amendment protection of their Right to Life.

This impossibility is declared in *Roe*'s "collapse" clause. The trigger of *Roe*'s "collapse" clause was pulled by 18 U.S.C. 1841(d) if not long before.

Roe's holding that abortion is legal has "collapsed" by *Roe*'s own order. No legal rationale, whether attached by SCOTUS to its "outer shell", or waiting in the philosophical wings, can stand in its place.

To the extent our Constitution stands, *Roe*'s holding cannot.

CONCLUSION. Iowa wants to stop the murder of thousands of Iowa humans every year. Iowa wants to comply with the 14th Amendment which requires Iowa to protect them. Iowa asks this Court to save all still in danger, by granting Iowa's petition for a writ of certiorari to affirm that the babies Iowa would save are humans and persons, and abortion's legality has "collapsed".

Respectfully submitted, ______________________

Appendix A   (The Ruling of the 8th Circuit Court of Appeals, or of the Iowa Supreme Court)

Appendix B (The federal trial court or Supreme Court entry of judgment)

Appendix C

Constitutional and Statutory Provisions: text

Preamble to the U.S. Constitution: *We the People* of the United States, in Order to form a more perfect Union, establish Justice, insure domestic Tranquility, provide for the common defence, promote the general Welfare, and secure the Blessings of Liberty to ourselves **and our Posterity,** do ordain and establish this Constitution for the United States of America.

14th Amendment, § 1, sentence 2: No State shall make or enforce any law which shall abridge the privileges or immunities of citizens of the United States; nor shall any State deprive any person of life, liberty, or property, without due process of law; nor deny to any person within its jurisdiction **the equal protection of the laws.**

18 U.S.C. § 1841(d) As used in this section, the term "unborn child" means a child in utero, and the term "child in utero" or "child, who is in utero" means a member of the species homo sapiens, at any stage of development, who is carried in the womb.

Appendix D:

Roe's legislative history reviewed by Alabama

Hamilton v. Scott, 97 So. 3d 728 (Ala. 2012)

A. Roe misstated the protection of the unborn child under the common law.

Roe 's viability rule was based, in significant part, on an incorrect statement of legal history. The Supreme Court in Roe erroneously concluded that "the unborn have never been recognized in the law as persons in the whole sense." 410 U.S. at 162. Roe also referred to "the lenity of the common law." 410 U.S. at 165. However, scholars have repeatedly pointed to inaccuracies in Roe 's historical account since Roe was decided in 1973.[53] "[T]he history embraced in Roe would not withstand careful examination even when Roe was written." Joseph Dellapenna, Dispelling the Myths of Abortion History 126 (Carolina Academic Press 2006).

Sir William Blackstone, for example, recognized that unborn children were persons. Although the Court cited Blackstone in Roe, it failed to note that Blackstone addressed the legal protection of the unborn child within a

---

53 See generally Joseph Dellapenna, Dispelling the Myths of Abortion History (Carolina Academic Press 2006); John Keown, Abortion, Doctors and the Law: Some Aspects of the Legal Regulation of Abortion in England from 1803 to 1982 (Cambridge University Press 1988). See also Paul Benjamin Linton, Planned Parenthood v. Casey: The Flight from Reason in the Supreme Court, 13 St. Louis U. Pub.L.Rev. 15 (1993); Dennis J. Horan, Clarke D. Forsythe & Edward R. Grant, Two Ships Passing in the Night: An Interpretavist Review of the White–Stevens Colloguy on Roe v. Wade, 6 St. Louis U. Pub.L.Rev. 229, 230 n. 8, 241 n. 90 (1987); James S. Witherspoon, Reexamining Roe: Nineteenth Century Abortion Statutes and the Fourteenth Amendment, 17 St. Mary's L.J. 29, 70 (1985) ("In short, the Supreme Court's analysis in Roe v. Wade of the development, purposes, and the understandings underlying the nineteenth-century antiabortion statutes, was fundamentally erroneous."); and Robert Byrn, An American Tragedy: The Supreme Court on Abortion, 41 Fordham L.Rev. 807 (1973).

section entitled "The Law of Persons." It also ignored the opening line of his paragraph describing the law's treatment of the unborn child: "Life is an immediate gift of God, a right inherent by nature in every individual." 1 William Blackstone, Commentaries on the Laws of England *129.[54] As Professor David Kadar noted in 1980, "Rights and protections legally afforded the unborn child are of ancient vintage. In equity, property, crime, and tort, the unborn has received and continues to receive a legal personality." David Kadar, *The Law of Tortious Prenatal Death Since Roe v. Wade,* 45 Mo. L.Rev. 639, 639 (1980) (footnotes omitted).

B. Roe misstated the protection of the unborn child under tort law and criminal law.

Professor Kadar and others have pointed out "the mistaken discussion within Roe on the legal status of the unborn in tort law." Kadar, 45 Mo. L.Rev. at 652. The Court's discussion in Roe of prenatal-death recovery "was perfunctory, and unfortunately largely inaccurate, and should not be relied upon as the correct view of the law at the time of Roe v. Wade." 45 Mo. L.Rev. at 652–53. See also William R. Hopkin, Jr., *Roe v. Wade and the Traditional Legal Standards Concerning Pregnancy*, 47 Temp. L.Q. 715, 723 (1974) ("[I]t must respectfully be pointed out that Justice Blackmun has understated the extent to which the law protects the unborn child.").

Roe 's adoption of the viability standard in 1973 did

---

54 See Dellapenna, at 200:"[M]odern research has established that by the close of the seventeenth century, the criminality of abortion under the common law was well established. Courts had rendered clear holdings that abortion was a crime, no decision indicated that any form of abortion was lawful, and secondary authorities similarly uniformly supported the criminality of abortion. The only difference among these authorities had been the severity of the crime (misdemeanor or felony), an uncertainty that, under Coke's influence, began to settle into the pattern of holding abortion to be a misdemeanor unless the child was born alive and then died from the injuries or potions that led to its premature birth."

not reflect American law. Viability played no role in the common law of property, homicide, or abortion. Clarke D. Forsythe, *Homicide of the Unborn Child: The Born Alive Rule and Other Legal Anachronisms*, 21 Val. U.L.Rev. 563, 569 n. 33 (1987). And there was no viability standard in wrongful-death law because the common law did not recognize a cause of action for the wrongful death of any person. *Farley v. Sartin*, 195 W.Va. at 674, 466 S.E.2d at 525 ("At common law, there was no cause of action for the wrongful death of a person."); W. Page Keeton et al., *Prosser and Keeton on the Law of Torts* § 127, at 945 (5th ed. 1984) ("The common law not only denied a tort recovery for injury once the tort victim had died, it also refused to recognize any new and independent cause of action in the victim's dependants or heirs for their own loss at his death.").

The viability standard was introduced into American law by Bonbrest v. Katz, 65 F.Supp. 138 (D.D.C.1946), the first case to recognize a cause of action for prenatal injuries. Bonbrest implied that such a cause of action would be recognized only if the unborn child had reached viability. 65 F.Supp. at 140.

Viability was initially adopted by courts in prenatal-injury law, but its influence was waning by 1961. See Daley v. Meier, 33 Ill.App.2d 218, 178 N.E.2d 691 (1961) (holding that an infant born alive could recover damages for injuries suffered before viability); see also Note, *Torts—Extension of Prenatal Injury Doctrine to Nonviable Infants*, 11 DePaul L.Rev. 361 (1961–62). One thorough legal survey of prenatal-injury law a decade before Roe was decided concluded that "[t]he viability limitation in prenatal injury cases is headed for oblivion. Courts are coming to realize that it is illogical and unjust to the children affected and not readily amenable to scientific proof." Charles A. Lintgen, *The Impact of Medical Knowledge on the Law Relating to Prenatal Injuries*, 110 U. Pa. L.Rev. 554, 600

(1962).

....Since Roe was decided in 1973, advances in medical and scientific technology have greatly expanded our knowledge of prenatal life. The development of ultrasound technology has enhanced medical and public understanding, allowing us to watch the growth and development of the unborn child in a way previous generations could never have imagined. Similarly, advances in genetics and related fields make clear that a new and unique human being is formed at the moment of conception, when two cells, incapable of independent life, merge to form a single, individual human entity.[55] Of course, that new life is not yet mature—growth and development are necessary before that life can survive independently—but it is nonetheless human life. And there has been a broad legal

---

55 See, e.g., Bruce M. Carlson, Human Embryology and Developmental Biology 3 (1994) ("Human pregnancy begins with the fusion of an egg and a sperm ."); Ronan O'Rahilly & Fabiola Muller, Human Embryology and Teratology 8 (2d ed. 1996) ("Although life is a continuous process, fertilization is a critical landmark because, under ordinary circumstances, a new, genetically distinct human organism is thereby formed. This remains true even though the embryonic genome is not actually activated until 4–8 cells are present, at about 2–3 days."); Keith Moore, The Developing Human: Clinically Oriented Embryology 2 (8th ed. 2008) (The zygote "results from the union of an oocyte and a sperm during fertilization. A zygote or embryo is the beginning of a new human being."); Ernest Blechschmidt, The Beginning of Human Life 16–17 (1977) ("A human ovum possesses human characteristics as genetic carriers, not chicken or fish. This is now manifest; the evidence no longer allows a discussion as to if and when and in what month of ontogenesis a human being is formed. To be a human being is decided for an organism at the moment of fertilization of the ovum."); C.E. Corliss, Patten's Human Embryology: Elements of Clinical Development 30 (1976) ("It is the penetration of the ovum by a sperm and the resultant mingling of the nuclear material each brings to the union that constitutes the culmination of the process of fertilization and marks the initiation of the life of a new individual."); and Clinical Obstetrics 11 (Carl J. Pauerstein ed. 1987) ("Each member of a species begins with fertilization—the successful merging of two different pools of genetic information to form a new individual.").

consensus in America, even before Roe, that the life of a
human being begins at conception.[56] An unborn child is a
unique and individual human being from conception, and,
therefore, he or she is entitled to the full protection of law
at every stage of development.

---

56 See Paul Benjamin Linton, Planned Parenthood v. Casey: The
    Flight From Reason in the Supreme Court, 13 St. Louis U.
    Pub.L.Rev. 15, 120–137 (1993) ("Appendix C: The Legal Consensus
    on the Beginning of Life," citing caselaw and statutes from 38 states
    and the District of Columbia stating that the life of a human being
    should be protected beginning with conception).

Appendix E:
Scriptures SCOTUS must address before saying Christianity supports abortion

Introduction: Roe accepted validation of its alleged ignorance of whether unborn babies of human mothers are humans from the fact that many savage religions of ancient times had no problem murdering unborn babies. Which seems an undesirable precedent for a free people, since those religions had no problem with murdering adults, either, or savagely "sacrificing" them. But Roe thought its ignorance vindicated by elements within Christianity and Judiasm too.

When those trained in the respective disciplines of medicine, philosophy, and theology are unable to arrive at any consensus, the judiciary, at this point in the development of man's knowledge, is not in a position to speculate as to the answer....There has always been strong support for the view that life does not begin until live birth....It appears to be the predominant, though not the unanimous, attitude of the Jewish faith.[57] It may be taken to represent also the position of a large segment of the Protestant community, insofar as that can be ascertained; organized groups that have taken a formal position on the abortion issue have generally regarded abortion as a matter for the conscience of the individual and her family.[58] The Aristotelian theory of "mediate animation," that held sway throughout the Middle Ages and the Renaissance in Europe, continued to be official Roman Catholic dogma until the 19th

---

57 Lader 97-99; D. Feldman, Birth Control in Jewish Law 251-294
   (1968). For a stricter view, see I. Jakobovits, Jewish Views on
   Abortion, in Abortion and the Law 124 (D. Smith ed.1967).
58 Amicus Brief for the American Ethical Union et al. For the position of
   the National Council of Churches and of other denominations, see
   Lader 99-101.

century, despite opposition to this "ensoulment" theory from those in the Church who would recognize the existence of life from the moment of conception. Roe v. Wade, 410 U.S. 113, 159-161

Roe's treatment of Christianity and Judiasm notes how men choose to respond to the Truth, and ignores what the Bible says is true.

Neither Judaism nor Christianity are understood by taking a poll of how well Christians and Jews *live up to* their standards. They are understood by reading the Scriptures they claim *are* their standards. (I hope the views of "secular Jews" who reject Jewish Scriptures is not part of Roe's evidence of Jewish positions!)

Limiting understanding of any religion to human opinion is like a judge not looking up a law or a case for himself but taking lawyers' word for what it says. It is like hearsay, compared with cross examining an eyewitness. Citing a book about The Book, as Roe did, is a poor substitute for reading The Book.

You will find varying opinions in various churches about how Christians ought to respond to abortion. But you will not find, even where those statements conflict, *significant* disagreement about what various verses say about the unborn. Those who base their positions on a careful reading of Scripture pretty much agree. Those who don't, are no guide to understanding Christianity. SCOTUS can't rule analysis of the Bible irrelevant, and expect to understand the religions who revere it.

Iowa will be totally surprised if SCOTUS conducts an appropriate analysis of Scripture in order to correct Roe's vague reliance on religion for its alleged uncertainty whether the babies of human mothers are humans/persons. But this analysis must be done or SCOTUS must retract any implication that its legalization of abortion finds any support in any religion.

Psalm 139 says David's human life began before his

tiny body had arms and legs. *Before* conception.[59] He was God-recognized before he was legally recognized.

> Psalm 139:13-16 You created every part of me; you put me together in my mother's womb. I praise you because you are to be feared; all you do is strange and wonderful. I know it with all my heart. When my bones were being formed, carefully put together in my mother's womb, when I was growing there in secret, you knew that I was there---you saw me before I was born. and in thy book all *my members* were written, *which* in continuance were fashioned, when *as yet there was* none of them. GNB/KJV

Luke 1 says that in the womb, a baby (1) can hear voices; (2) can sense the difference between a voice sweet with blessing and a voice coarse with cursing; and (3) can choose which kind of voice to get excited about. In other words, (4) an unborn baby can choose between good and evil.

> Luke 1:39 And Mary arose in those days, and went into the hill country with haste, into a city of Juda; 40 And entered into the house of Zacharias, and saluted Elisabeth. 41 And it came to pass, that, when Elisabeth heard the salutation of Mary, the babe [John the Baptist] leaped in her womb; and Elisabeth was filled with the Holy Ghost: 42 And she spake out with a loud voice, and said, Blessed *art* thou among women, and blessed *is* the fruit of thy womb. 43 And whence *is* this to me, that the mother of my Lord should come to me? 44 For, lo, as soon as the voice of thy salutation sounded in mine ears, the babe leaped in my womb for joy. KJV

A few verses before that tell us that even from the womb, a baby has a soul for the Holy Spirit to fill:[60]

> Luke 1:15 For he shall be great in the sight of the Lord, and shall drink neither wine nor strong drink; and he shall be

---

59 Jeremiah 1:5 likewise affirms that our souls begin *before* conception: "Before I formed thee in the belly I knew thee; and before thou camest forth out of the womb I sanctified thee, *and* I ordained thee a prophet unto the nations."

60 This, along with Jeremiah 1:5, supports the capacity of an unborn baby to choose good or evil.

filled with the Holy Ghost, even from his mother's womb.

Saline abortions, which burn babies alive with acid that blackens over half their skin while eating out their lungs, are our cultural equivalent of the pagan god Molech, into whose red hot brass arms worshipers threw their children, whose screams were covered by the priests' drums. Today we similarly have what was given as the name of the first video of an ultrasound of an abortion: "The Silent Scream." God said this is so barbaric that He never even imagined such a thing. This is a remarkable idea for those who believe God foresees every detail of what evils men will do, but all translations and commentators seem to agree that's what the verse means. Of no other evil in the entire Bible does God say this was so evil that He did not foresee it.

> Jeremiah 32:35 And they built the high places of Baal, which *are* in the valley of the son of Hinnom, to cause their sons and their daughters to pass through *the fire* unto Molech; which I commanded them not, neither came it into my mind, that they should do this abomination, to cause Judah to sin.

God also has something to say about *how we should respond* to abortion. This verse was in Operation Rescue's masthead, until 1993 when the first abortionist was shot. The scenario is where murderers have so much power over their victims that they can "lead them away" to kill them where they choose, and by a schedule known to others. That pretty much limits the scenario to government-protected murders.

> Proverbs 24:10 If you faint in the day of adversity, your strength is small. 11 Rescue those who are being taken away to death; hold back those who are stumbling to the slaughter. 12 If you say, "Behold, we did not know this," does not he who weighs the heart perceive it? Does not he who keeps watch over your soul know it, and will he not repay man according to his work? ESV

The only citation of any Bible verse in Roe is to Exodus 21:22, in footnote 22. Roe says the verse *"may* have" influenced Augustine! What was the point of adding such a speculation if it can't even be documented that Augustine *thought* about it? Was it an attempt to stick a verse into the record that some have thought minimizes the value of the unborn, even though most do not? Cults use obscure, ambiguous verses as a wedge to get Doubt's foot in the door. Here is the verse:

> Exodus 21:22 And when men fight, and they strike a pregnant woman, and her child goes forth, [literally "so her children come out" according to an NLT note] and there is no injury, being fined he shall be fined. *As much as* the husband of the woman shall put on him, even he shall give through the judges. [That is, he can sue in a court of equity and a jury will decide any award.] (Literal Translation of the Holy Bible)

The uncertainty is whether "there is no injury" means "no injury to either the mother or the child", or only "no injury to the mother – who cares about the child?" Commentator John Gill (1690-1771) notes places in the talmud that say the verses are concerned only for women, but he says the verse itself applies also to babies:

> **and yet no mischief follow**: to her, as the Targum of Jonathan, and so Jarchi and Aben Ezra restrain it to the woman; and which mischief they interpret of death, as does also the Targum of Onkelos; but it may refer both to the woman and her offspring, and not only to the death of them, but to any hurt or damage to either.... *John Gill's Exposition of the Entire Bible*

Adam Clark (1715-1832) understands it to protect mother and child alike:

> But if mischief followed, that is, if the child had been fully formed, and was killed by this means, or the woman lost her life in consequence, then the punishment was as in other cases of murder - the person was put to death.... *Adam*

The Bible Knowledge Commentary is emphatic that the child's life is revered as much as the mother's. Commentaries since 1973 take a position on abortion.

> 21:22–25. **If ... a pregnant woman** delivered her child prematurely as a result of a blow, but both were otherwise uninjured, the guilty party was to pay compensation determined by **the woman's husband** and **the court**. However, **if there** was **injury** to the expectant mother or her child, then the assailant was to be penalized in proportion to the nature of severity of the injury. While unintentional life-taking was usually not a capital offense (cf. vv. 12–13), here it clearly was. Also the unborn fetus is viewed in this passage as just as much a human being as its mother; the abortion of a fetus was considered murder.[61]

Wiersby sees no uncertainty that the unborn are as revered as the born:

> Verses 22–23 are basic to the pro-life position on abortion, for they indicate that the aborting of a fetus was equivalent to the murdering of the child. The guilty party was punished as a murderer ("life for life") if the mother or the unborn child, or both, died. See also Ps. 139:13–16.[62]

Tyndale's commentary sermonizes about it:

> In the case of mothers and children, special laws were given to protect the helpless and innocent (21:22–25). If a man caused a woman to give birth prematurely but the infant was not harmed, then a simple fine was to be levied. If the child or mother was harmed, then the law of retaliation was applied. Punishment was restricted to that which was commensurate with the injury. In these verses God shows clear concern for protecting unborn children, a concern that people today would do well to heed. Surely the abortion of

---

61 Hannah, J. D. (1985). Exodus. In J. F. Walvoord & R. B. Zuck (Eds.), *The Bible Knowledge Commentary: An Exposition of the Scriptures* (Vol. 1, p. 141). Wheaton, IL: Victor Books.
62 Wiersbe, W. W. (1993). *Wiersbe's Expository Outlines on the Old Testament* (Ex 21:12–36). Wheaton, IL: Victor Books.

millions of unborn babies will fall under God's condemnation.[63]

But the *NIV FaithLife Study Bible,* copyright 2012, on the eve of legal abortion's 40th birthday, seems to be pro-abortion:

> **21:22 as the judges determine** Describes a situation where the woman who is injured survives the attack but her child does not. The penalty in such a case is a fine. However, v. 23 says that if the woman is killed, the death penalty is prescribed. Consequently, the life of the adult woman was deemed of greater value than the contents of her womb. This passage is frequently used to justify abortion: the woman was viewed as a person; the child was not.[64]   [Wow!]

The Hebrew text simply doesn't specify whether "if there is no injury" applies to both child and mother, or to only one of them. Nor does the Hebrew say whether "the baby comes out" means healthy or dead. The disagreement of translators and commentators is possible because of this textual ambiguity. Commentaries since 1973 face societal pressure to stay out of Roe's way. Ancient Talmud entries likewise faced the social pressure of the ever present Molech worship surrounding Israel, and too frequently invading Israel. Jesus' metaphor for Hell was the "valley of Tophet" just outside Jerusalem where children were once burnt alive to Molech.

I would submit that while the *text* may be unclear, the *context* is certainly clear. From "be fruitful and multiply", Genesis 1:28, to "As arrows in the hand of a mighty man, so *are* the sons of the young. Blessed *is* the man who has filled his quiver with them....", Psalm 127:4-5,

---

63 Hughes, R. B., & Laney, J. C. (2001). *Tyndale concise Bible commentary* (p. 39). Wheaton, IL: Tyndale House Publishers.
64 Barry, J. D., Heiser, M. S., Custis, M., Mangum, D., & Whitehead, M. M. (2012). *Faithlife Study Bible* (Ex 21:22). Bellingham, WA: Logos Bible Software.

and all the laws in between about the importance of descendants, it is inconceivable that any jury in Moses' time could be apathetic about an unnatural miscarriage! The translations that leave this idea implied but not specified are MKJV, RV, YLT, GW, ISV, JPS, KJV, ABP, ASV, ESV, NLT, NIV84, NASB95, HCSB, NCV, TNIV, CPB, NirV. However, these translations limit concern to the mother: BBE, "causing the loss of the child, but no other evil comes to her"; CEV, if she "suffers a miscarriage" but "isn't badly hurt"; DRB "and she miscarry indeed, but live herself"; ERV "If the woman was not hurt badly"; and Message "so that she miscarries but is not otherwise hurt". As noted before, "miscarriage" is a poor translation since the Hebrew word as easily means a healthy birth.

The Brenton translation expresses concern *only for the baby:* "And if two men strive and smite a woman with child, and her child be born imperfectly formed, he shall be forced to pay a penalty...."

Theologians are less likely than lawyers to consider in this verse the difficulty of assessing criminal intent in this situation. Two men are fighting, and a woman gets hit. What is she doing there? What responsibility did she have for getting out of the way? When the man hit her, was he actually aiming at her or was he just struggling against the other man? If he deliberately hit her, was he just defending himself against her attack, or was he deliberately aiming at the womb? These are questions for a jury. They are factors that could make a penalty greater for harm to the mother than for the child, *or vice versa,* depending not on their relative human worth but on where any culpability was focused.

WEB translation: "If men fight and hurt a pregnant woman so that she gives birth prematurely, and yet if no harm follows, he shall be surely fined as much as the woman's husband demands and the judges allow. But if any harm follows, then you must take life for life...

Appendix F:
Errors in abortion prevention cases

The opinion below documents how universally courts in abortion prevention cases wrongly think *Roe* says abortion's "constitutional protection" makes irrelevant any facts established by court-recognized fact finders about who abortion harms.

> "The rationale utilized by '[t]he majority of courts. . . [was] that because abortion is a lawful, constitutionally protected act, it is not a legally recognized harm which can justify illegal conduct.'" (p. 19 of Opinion Below, quoting *City of Wichita v. Tilson,* 855 P.2d 911 (Kan. 1993)

Error #1: *Tilson* ignored *Casey* which had ruled just the year before. *Casey*[65] abandoned "constitutional protection" for abortion in 1992.[66]

Error #2: *Tilson* ignored *Roe's* open door to fact finders, and closed it.
Didn't Roe say in so many words "we can't even *speculate* whether these babies we let mothers kill are humans/persons – of course if that is ever *established*, then we will stop it"?[67] By saying doctors and preachers know more about it than SCOTUS, didn't Roe defer to fact

---

65 Planned Parenthood v. Casey, 505 U.S. 833, 945, 954 (1992)

66 Justice Scalia's dissent in *Lawrence v. Texas* 539 U.S. 558, 595, 123 S. Ct. 2472, 2493 (U.S., 2003), explaining how the Supreme Court, in 1992, abandoned Roe's position that the right of a woman to choose to hire someone to kill her unborn child was a "fundamental right": "We have since rejected Roe' s holding that regulations of abortion must be narrowly tailored to serve a compelling state interest, see *Planned Parenthood v. Casey,* 505 U.S., at 876,....-and thus, by logical implication, Roe' s holding that the right to abort an unborn child is a 'fundamental right.'

67 "If this suggestion of personhood [of unborn babies] is established, the...case [for legalizing aborticide], of course, collapses, for the fetus' right to life is then guaranteed specifically by the [14th] Amendment." *Roe v. Wade,* 410 US 113, 156

finders,[68] treating personhood as a fact question?

Certainly by the principle "actions speak louder than words" it is reasonable for courts below, and Americans in general, to infer that SCOTUS has ruled that unborn babies are in fact *not* human beings and have no value other than for their "potential" to *become* human beings. Or that their personhood is irrelevant. But aren't SCOTUS's *words* also important? Haven't these courts "decided an important federal question in a way that conflicts with relevant decisions of this Court"?[69]

Error #3: **Roe never said abortion's *legality* makes its *reality* irrelevant.** Tilson assumes "saving the lives of unborn humans/persons" was made legally unrecognizable by *Roe,* but the reality is that *Roe's* "collapse" clause makes unborn lives a strong enough legally recognizable interest to not only "justify" saving them, but to "collapse" the entire abortion industry.

> "The evil, harm, or injury sought to be avoided, or the interest sought to be promoted, by the commission of a crime must be legally cognizance [should be "cognizable", or recognizable] **to be justified as necessity.** '[I]n most cases of civil disobedience a lesser evils defense will be barred. This is because as long as the laws or policies being **protested** have been lawfully adopted, they are conclusive evidence of *the community's view* on the issue.' 2 P. Robinson, *Criminal Law Defenses* 124(d)(1), at 52. Abortion in the first trimester of pregnancy is not a legally recognized harm, and, therefore, prevention of abortion is not a legally recognized interest to promote." (*City of Wichita v. Tilson,* 253 Kan. 295) quoting *State v. Sahr,* 470 N.W.2d 185, 191 (1991)

---

68 "We need not resolve the difficult question of when life begins. When those trained in the respective disciplines of medicine, philosophy, and theology are unable to arrive at any consensus, the judiciary, at this point in the development of man's knowledge, is not in a position to speculate as to the answer." *Roe v. Wade* 410 US 113, 159

69 Supreme Court rule 10c.

Error #4: ***Tilson*** **quoted** ***Robinson*** **out of context.** *Robinson* explained why the Necessity Defense shouldn't be invoked by protesters against nuclear missile sites, at which there is no certainty that even one life will be harmed if the action is not taken, there is no danger is "imminent" by any definition, and there is time and real opportunity for more peaceful alternatives.

Error #5: ***Tilson*** **labeled as the "community view'** **the view that every community had criminalized.** *Tilson*, quoting *Sahr* and *Robinson,* labeled as a "community view" what almost all state legislatures had criminalized since their founding but were forced to legalize by eight unelected men who said they were "in no position to speculate" on the position now being labeled "the community view".

It is circular reasoning for courts to force all states to legalize what they had criminalized since their founding, forcing communities across America to reverse their definition of abortion as murder, under protest more vigorous than America saw during the Civil Rights Movement, and then say it is only honoring "the community view" to rule that abortion cannot be recognized as murder!

A lesson from Nazi Germany is that some things which are legal are evil. Murder can be made legal, but not harmless. The slaughter of millions whose only offense is their existence has often been encouraged by laws, and justified by ruthless governments based on ruthless religions, but never justified by American legal principles or by the religion after which they were patterned.

Another lesson is the power of evil laws to intimidate "the community" into tolerating terrible evils which poison its "community values" into what "the community" itself recognizes as an abomination, both before, after, and even during the reign of those laws. One measure of how far laws depart from historical "community values" is the number of martyrs compelled to act by the departure.

Even apart from the poison of evil laws, the history of slavery that necessitated the 14th Amendment should remind us that not all "communities" have "values" that always protect the least among us. America is founded on higher law than "community values". The Declaration of Independence, which officially articulates the foundation of American Freedom, explains some of the Fundamental Rights embedded in that Higher Law, and Who gave it, and the right of the people to alter, as necessary, usurpations of it.

Another device common in abortion prevention precedents is Straw Man arguments: substituting, for the actual defense of the defendant – saving life, something way easier to ridicule – like "interfering with another person's lawful activity".[70]

Below is another "straw man" replacement of "saving lives" with "interfere with the exercise of constitutional rights by others", followed by the misguided assumption that *Roe* prejudices the inquiry whether abortion is in fact a "significant evil":

> "Appellants **may not criminally interfere with the exercise of constitutional rights by others,** and then escape punishment for their criminal conduct by asserting

---

70 Tilson summarized several other appellate rulings which employed the same Straw Man, such as: "...the 'injury' prevented by the acts of criminal trespass is not a legally recognized injury." *People v. Krizka*, 92 IILApp.3d 288, 48 III.Dec. 141, 416 N.E.2d 36, "... a claim of necessity cannot be used to justify a crime that simply interferes with another person's right to lawful activity." *State v. Sahr*, 470 N.W.2d at 191-192. *Krizka* is correct, if the "injury prevented" is merely abortions of unloved soul-less "blobs of tissue" whose humanity is uncertain. Krizka is cruelly corrupt, if the "injury prevented" is the mass slaughter of human beings who are "persons in the whole sense" as documented by triers of fact! *Sahr* is precise, if the only reason for breaking a law is to "interfere with another person's right to lawful activity". *Sahr* is foolishly sad, if saving human lives was the real reason a relatively minor law was broken, and it was to obscure that real reason that *Sahr* contracted with a Straw man.

the defense of necessity....A **pregnant woman's decision to exercise her right under the Constitutions** of the United States and of the State of California to terminate a pregnancy is not and cannot be held to be a 'significant evil.'"
People v. Garziano 230 Cal. App. 3d 242 (1991) 244

This next case characterizes an acquittal of abortion preventers as allowing "strangers" to deprive mothers of their right to kill. But the defendants only asked that their case be judged by a jury. By calling juries "strangers", the judge deprived defendants of a trial by jury.

"If the legislature cannot delegate a 'veto power' to the patient's ... spouse .... we think it unlikely that a state court could delegate such a 'veto power' to strangers, to be exercised in such an obstrusive manner." *Cleveland v. Municipality of Anchorage,* 631 P.2d 1073, 1080 n. 15 (1981) [This was essentially quoted in] *Pursley V. State,* 21 Ark.App. 107, 730 S.W.2d 250 (1987), rev. refused July 22, 1987

Is the "equal protection" clause of the 14th Amendment violated by assembling the historically ambiguous elements of the Necessity Defense in abortion prevention contexts in a way that makes it illegal to save the lives of a discrete class of persons?

Can "imminence", in the context of self defense or defense of others, be defined as a given number of minutes or seconds away, even in situations where the window of opportunity to save life is farther away than that, making it impossible to both save life and comply with that definition? Or is it enough that the window of opportunity to prevent absolutely certain harm is about to close with no less alternative use of force in view?

Numerous courts say Roe said abortion is "constitutionally protected" so its harmfulness can't be "legally recognized" as a question of law, which is the opposite of Roe's statement that abortion is "constitutionally protected" *only until its harmfulness is "established"* as a *fact* question about which "the judiciary...is not in a position to speculate...." *Roe v. Wade* 410 US 113, 159. For example:

> "...the justification defense [is still] unavailable because abortion is lawful by virtue of the United States Constitution." *Allison v. City of Birmingham,* 580 So. 2d 1377 (1991)
>
> "...the defense of necessity asserted here cannot be utilized when the harm sought to be avoided (abortion) remains a constitutionally protected activity and the harm incurred (trespass) is in violation of the law."[71] *State v. O'Brien,* 784 S.W.2d 187, 192 (1989)
>
> "Because the harm sought to be prevented is not recognized as an injury under the law, the defense of necessity is insufficient as a matter of law and the court properly refused to allow the defendant to raise it." *State v. Clarke,* 24 Conn.App. 541, 590 A.2d 468, cert. denied 219 Conn. 910, 593 A.2d 135 (1991);

Or, abortion is constitutional, which makes irrelevant the evidence that *Roe* says would challenge its constitutionality. The opposite is true. The legality or "constitutional protection" of abortion is entirely irrelevant to legal recognizability of abortion as a "harm", because Roe specifically said[72] its ruling was without prejudice[73] to that fact question. Roe says saving lives trumps abortion's "constitutional protection", once a conflict is "established". Roe's "of course" treats the fact as important, implicitly demanding that triers of fact be heard.

Lower courts say Necessity's "comparison of harms"/"choice of evils" is subject to Roe v. Wade as a

---

71 The opinion also says abortion harms no legally protected interest. Isn't human life a legally protected interest?

72 In its "collapse" clause

73 Roe of course didn't use the phrase "without prejudice", but the effect of Roe's "collapse" clause has precisely the same meaning and effect. It specifically declares the absence of a decision on the merits of "when life begins" and leaves future defendants free to litigate the matter in subsequent cases, as if *Roe* had never been decided.

matter of *law*, making factual evidence irrelevant. This violates Roe, which made *itself* subject to future factual evidence of personhood. *Roe invites* fact finders to resolve "when life begins". Roe's invitation is blocked by lower courts saying Roe *prohibits* triers of facts *from even learning there is a question.*

It would be presumptuous, and odd, for any lower court to say they can know something that SCOTUS said no court is qualified to know,[74] but no lower court has weighed in on whether abortion is in fact a "harm", either, other than, ignoring *Roe*, to rule the fact "irrelevant" to Necessity's "comparison of harms".

Not all authorities agree with Wharton and Robinson that Necessity is available when the threat to the harm prevented is legal. But not every past formulation of Necessity elements fits the facts before us today.

Any formulation of legalisms for a particular situation that make it a crime to save lives of a discrete class of human beings[75] violates the "equal protection" clause, and fails the "absurd result" test[76] and the "smell" test.

Our ultimate litmus ought to be what is right, and what is good. "Is it lawful to do good...or to do evil? to save life, or to kill?" a great lawmaker once asked.[77]

---

74 We need not resolve the difficult question of when life begins. When those trained in the respective disciplines of medicine, philosophy, and theology are unable to arrive at any consensus, the judiciary, at this point in the development of man's knowledge, is not in a position to speculate as to the answer. Roe v. Wade, 410 U.S. 113, 160

75 Discrimination against a discrete class is a civil rights violation. Dehumanization to the extent of alleged uncertainty whether people are "persons" and thus protected from slaughter by our laws is the ultimate discrimination.

76 "...where the language of a statute is clear, our normal rule is that we are bound by it. A legitimate exception exists, however, when that language leads to absurd results. The United States Supreme Court agrees. See *Public Citizen v. Department of Justice,* 491 U.S. 440...." [The rest of the quote is found in *State v. Kirkpatrick,* Kansas, No. 93,465, May 30, 2008)]

77 Mark 3:4, Luke 6:9

We are talking about the most controversial ruling in the United States since slavery. We are talking about a ruling based on alleged ignorance of the factual nature of the unborn, whose humanity/personhood, over the past 43 years, have been unanimously affirmed by court-recognized finders of fact. This exposes formulations of Necessity that make it impossible to save millions of lives as legalistic quibbling, at the most charitable.

The "choice of evils" has the character of an equitable inquiry, where statutes do not specifically apply, yet justice must be discerned. It perverts the defense to attach book definitions/elements to the defense which were not designed for the situation at hand, and treat them as if they were inviolable statutes.

The longer any question reasonably raised remains unanswered, the more potential it acquires to undermine confidence in those questioned. Especially when it involves the very legal definition of which Human Beings have a right to live long enough to ask.

Appendix G:
No backup for Roe is possible
No other rationale than alleged ignorance can excuse killing babies

This section reviews several of the wannabe replacement rationales waiting to take Roe's place when it "collapses", to show that none of them – nor any possible rationale – can survive Roe's "collapse". They are:

In oral arguments in Roe v. Wade, Justice Potter Stewart asked Sarah Weddington "If it were established that an unborn fetus is a person, you would have an almost impossible case here, would you not?" Weddington audibly laughed and acknowledged "I would have a very difficult case." Stewart pursued, "This would be the equivalent to after the child was born...if the mother thought it bothered her health having the child around, she could have it killed. Isn't that correct?" Weddington answered, "That's correct."

This exchange is what presumably prompted Justice Blackmun to write "[If the] suggestion of personhood is established, the case, of course, collapses, for the fetus' right to life is then guaranteed specifically by the [14th] Amendment."

Since 2004, the "suggestion of personhood" was "established" by federal law. The 14th Amendment right to life of unborn human beings has been "guaranteed". Abortion has been no longer legal.

These facts can certainly be ignored. They cannot be squarely addressed and still refuted.

Is it true that abortion's fragile "legality" must "collapse" along with *Roe*? Can it be sustained, after *Roe's* burial, by SCOTUS rationales added after *Roe*, to *Roe's* "outer shell"?

What is Roe's "outer shell"? Can any rationale hanging on it stand alone, without it?

Since it does not appear to be identified anywhere, it must be taken as a metaphor of whatever it is about Roe that keeps abortion legal despite the shifting sands of legal rationales for it.

There is only one skeletal sustaining principle Iowa can think of in Roe, to which a succession of rationales may attach in turn: *alleged uncertainty whether the unborn babies of human mothers are human.*

This alleged uncertainty is articulated in Roe's "collapse" clause where it is explicitly identified as Roe's sustaining principle, in the sense that without it, Roe cannot stand.

This uncertainty as a matter of law cannot still seriously be alleged. Granting that the unborn babies of humans are humans, making their killing murder, will this Court still insist their murder is some kind of "private and personal right", a "sacred choice" with which courts and lawmakers ought not interfere? Once this "outer shell" of alleged uncertainty who is human "collapses", no rationale attached to it can stand by itself.

Let us be clear that *Roe* does not merely "collapse". The terms of Roe's "collapse" clause make it clear that *Roe* becomes unconstitutional, along with every law and court ruling which violates the 14th Amendment by obstructing protection of the Right to Life in the course of protecting abortion's fragile "legality".

Yet there are wannabe Roe replacements. First:

1. Should abortion remain legal, even after legal personhood of the unborn is established, because women have come to "rely" on murder?

Planned Parenthood v. Casey explains that mothers have for two generations relied on the right to kill their babies in order to advance their careers, so it would simply be too costly to mothers to suddenly punish them for killing the human beings whom they so urgently want to kill.

> The inquiry into reliance counts the cost of a rule's repudiation as it would fall on those who have relied reasonably on the rule's continued application. *(Cont'd)*

Translation: We have to look into the terrible cost of outlawing abortion to mothers who have come to reasonably rely on the legal right to kill their own babies.

> Since the classic case for weighing reliance heavily in favor of following the earlier rule occurs in the commercial context, see Payne v. Tennessee, [505 U.S. 833, 856] supra, at 828, where advance planning of great precision is most obviously a necessity, it is no cause for surprise that some would find no reliance worthy of consideration in support of Roe. *(Cont'd)*

Translation: since the "reliance interests" principle has peviously been applied only to laws that affect business contracts, where businessmen need to be able to rely on a contract in order to plan, we shouldn't be surprised that some folks think the principle has no application to "reliance" on the right to kill.

> While neither respondents nor their amici in so many words deny that the abortion right invites some reliance prior to its actual exercise, one can readily imagine an argument stressing the dissimilarity of this case to one involving property or contract. (Cont'd)

Translation: Although even prolifers agree women have come to rely on legal abortion, it wouldn't be hard to argue what a stretch it is to give that any legal weight.

> Abortion is customarily chosen as an unplanned response to the consequence of unplanned activity or to the failure of conventional birth control, and except on the assumption that no intercourse would have occurred but for Roe's holding, such behavior may appear to justify no

reliance claim. (Cont'd)

Translation: The only way you can argue that women rely on Roe *is if you can believe* Roe *is the only reason they fornicate, which creates the babies which mothers need to kill. The increase in fornication caused by* Roe *might not seem like a strong justification to continue the killing.*

> Even if reliance could be claimed on that unrealistic assumption, the argument might run, any reliance interest would be de minimis. [minimal] This argument would be premised on the hypothesis that reproductive planning could take virtually immediate account of any sudden restoration of state authority to ban abortions. (Cont'd)

Translation: even if abortion could be justifed because women have gotten so used to fornication, prolifers would say that is a weak argument since as soon as abortion is outlawed, women are able to immediately stop fornicating.

To eliminate the issue of reliance that easily, however, one would need to limit [re]cognizable reliance to specific instances of sexual activity. But to do this would be simply to refuse to face the fact that, **for two decades of economic and social developments, people have organized intimate relationships and made choices that define their views of themselves and their places in society, in reliance on the availability of abortion in the event that contraception should fail. The ability of women to participate equally in the economic and social life of the Nation has been facilitated by their ability to control their reproductive lives.** See, e.g., R. Petchesky, Abortion and Woman's Choice 109, 133, n. 7 (rev. ed. 1990). The Constitution serves human values, and while the effect of reliance on Roe cannot be exactly measured, neither can the certain cost of overruling Roe for people who have ordered their thinking and living around that case be dismissed. [505 U.S. 833, 857]

Translation: But if that objection to killing the babies of fornication were a good argument, it would be an argument against killing babies of fornication, but married couples should still be free to kill their babies. The fact is now that "murderer" has now become Americans' self image. It is Who We Are. That is a sacred trust which law ought never violate, to self-identify as whatever you want. The Constitution allows no discrimination against any adult for how he sees himself – murderer, rapist, terrorist, sexually undecided, little child – so long as he doesn't see himself as a Christian. Crime even helps Americans become rich, and we can't just dismiss that economic benefit of legalized killing.

Americans United for Life summarizes this argument:

> The *Casey* plurality ultimately justified its adherence to *Roe* and *Doe* on the foundation of the "reliance on the availability of abortion in the event that contraception should fail."...The bottom-line rationale of *Casey* is that "reliance interests" in abortion—as a backup to failed contraception—justified retaining the rule of *Roe*. ... The assertions of the plurality opinion in *Casey*, its reliance interests justification, and its "undue burden" standard were adopted by the majority in *Stenberg v. Carhart* in 2000.120 (An argument found at www.trolp.org/main_pgs/issues/v10n1/Forsythe.pdf.)

Such reasoning can only escape public ridicule to the extent it remains uncertain whether unborn babies of human mothers are humans. This issue, upon which abortion's legality hangs, has still not been addressed by any court.

Roe acknowledged a balance between the mother's right to *privacy*, and the baby's right to life. *Casey* alleged the mother's *"reliance interests" but not* the baby's right to life. Here is *Roe's* statement:

> As we have intimated above, it is reasonable and appropriate for a State to decide that at some point in time another interest, that of health of the mother or that of potential human life, becomes significantly involved. The woman's privacy is no longer sole and any right of privacy she possesses must be measured accordingly. (Roe v. Wade)

Now that the humanity of the unborn is established as a matter of undisputed, unchallenged, unanimous legal recognition, it is impossible to credibly argue that we need to be able to rob or enslave any group of American humans if it will benefit us, once we "have come to rely on" oppressing them "in order to achieve...equality". If the legal right to rob or enslave any human group is repugnant to American sensibilities, how much more the legal right to brutally kill them?

No doubt it will be hard for some mothers to break their habit of murdering human beings even after learning it is legally "established" that that is what they will have been doing.

But most Americans still, fortunately, find it unthinkable to *knowingly* murder. Most Americans, upon learning that the right to kill human beings has no legal justification and in fact is murder, will back away from any thought of such behavior as readily as a child backs away from pouring pop in the fish tank upon learning that it kills a living goldfish. They will back away from political parties founded on murder. They will impeach and vote out judges who continue to protect murder.

Legal abortion, after legal establishment of the humanity of those aborted, is legally unthinkable under any pretense, because of its unacceptable cost: reversal of our 14th Amendment, and of our laws against murder.

The *Casey* reasoning was only possible before federal law legally established the fact that all unborn babies are human beings. The "reliance interests" of mothers to kill can't stand against federal establishment of the fact that those whom mothers "rely" on killing are human beings with full 14th Amendment Rights to Life. Fortunately no Court has said otherwise.

Were that indeed to become the Court's formal position, let the courts say so! Let them put in writing that even though the unborn are human beings, so that aborting them is infanticide – the legal and moral equivalent of mass murder, mothers have developed such a habit of murdering them – such a blood lust – that the blood letting must go on! Such a ruling would very likely cause its injustice and error to become so apparent to everyone, that political solutions [i.e., voting against state judges and impeaching federal judges] would find more support.[78]

Americans will no more tolerate the doctrine that getting into the habit of depriving others of fundamental rights creates a Constitutional Right to legal protection while you do so, than they will tolerate a ruling that America must again permit slavery. Again, to set aside the 14th Amendment outlawing of murder, would definitely set aside its outlawing of slavery. But if Iowa is wrong – if Americans are truly ready to legalize murder and slavery

---

78   (Second dissent in Planned Parenthood v. Casey): "As long as this Court thought (and the people thought) that we Justices were doing essentially lawyers' work up here - reading text and discerning our society's traditional understanding of that text - the public pretty much left us alone. Texts and traditions are facts to study, not convictions to demonstrate about. But if in reality, our process of constitutional adjudication consists primarily of making value judgments; if we can ignore a long and clear tradition clarifying an ambiguous text, as we did, for example, five days ago in declaring unconstitutional invocations and benedictions at public high school graduation ceremonies, Lee v. Weisman, 505 U.S. 577 (1992); if, as I say, our pronouncement of constitutional law rests primarily on value [505 U.S. 833, 1001] judgments, then a free and intelligent people's attitude towards us can be expected to be (ought to be) quite different. The people know that their value judgments are quite as good as those taught in any law school - maybe better."
    Also see Matthew 23:21-27.

again – Ezekiel 3:18-20 still requires that Americans be clearly informed that that is where they are going.

Now that federal law has legally recognized the fact that the unborn are just as human as blacks, a northern state like Iowa that still knowingly, deliberately, consciously permits, protects, and even funds abortion can no more be tolerated than a southern state whose laws still protect slave owners.

2. We have to keep abortion legal because it is impossible to know whether the very young or the very old are human beings.

> There is, of course, no way to determine [whether]...the human fetus is in some critical sense merely potentially human...as a legal matter; it is, in fact, a value judgment. Some societies have considered newborn children not yet human, or the incompetent elderly no longer so. (Planned Parenthood v. Casey, dissent by Scalia, White, Thomas.)

This fatalistic view that there is "no way to determine" who is human "as a legal matter" undoubtedly did not foresee 18 U.S.C. 1841(d), since it was articulated before the first efforts to insert Personhood language into the U.S. Code.

But for the sake of argument let's suppose the argument fails, that 18 U.S.C. 1841(d) has resolved Roe's alleged uncertainty about unborn humanity, and instead there is a future precedent that indeed it *is* impossible to know whether the unborn or the elderly are human beings. That excuse for such critical ignorance would just as easily stretch to include Blacks, Jews, Christians, or "illegals", and/or return us to the days of slavery, so long as the majority within a state vote for it.

This is not so remote a danger in the case of "illegals", where there is a significant movement in

Congress and in conservative media to redefine who is under the "jurisdiction" of state laws. For centuries the word has indicated those whom state police can arrest. Some want it to mean some sort of undefined "allegiance" to America, which is measured by one's place of birth rather than by one's actions and is judged by people who have never met the people whose "allegiance" is questioned. No one has recommended enslaving "illegals" yet, fortunately, but legalization of slavery would be the direct legal effect of that redefinition, since it was that "jurisdiction" clause in the 14th Amendment which closed the loophole in the 13th Amendment through which slavery continued.

The doctrine that it is "impossible to know" who is human "as a legal matter" must be driven out of our legal discourse, where it threatens all our freedoms.

Roe acknowledged the 14th Amendment Right to Life of all human beings, at least with lip service. Many believe that through Roe's alleged uncertainty about who is human, judicial disregard of human life has become *implicit*. To whatever extent that may be so, *we cannot allow judicial disregard of human life to become explicit.*

3. We need to keep abortion legal because the unborn are not human, as proved by how cruelly we mistreat them.

What if someone argues that lack of protection of a group of humans proves they are not, in fact, humans after all? That is very close to what *Roe v. Wade* argued. Roe argued, "In short, the unborn have never been recognized in the law as persons in the whole sense. (So why should the law so recognize them now?)"

How different is that from the reasoning that blacks are 3/5 of a person so they have no fundamental right to freedom, and that's how it's been from America's founding? (That wasn't the *Scott v. Sandford* reasoning. That ruling described blacks as "persons" but noted two clauses in the

Constitution in which they were treated as property.)[79]

Roe reasons that if certain population groups have been dehumanized in past centuries, that raises doubt whether they ever have been, in fact, human. Who is safe from that caliber of "justice"? "Illegal" immigrants today are objects of discrimination. In America's past, it has been Catholics, blacks, Chinese, Japanese, Slavs, Southern Europeans, Irish, and Germans.

It is theoretically impossible to make any *progress* against discrimination, to the extent we embrace *Roe's* reasoning that objects of past dehumanization are actually not "persons in the whole sense" so they are actually "endowed by their Creator" with no rights whatsoever.

One example of *Roe's* "evidence" was that Texas' law criminalizing abortion had an exception when the pregnancy threatened the life of the mother. (As if SCOTUS was unaware of the legal principle of "self defense.")

> When Texas urges that a fetus is entitled to Fourteenth Amendment protection as a person, it faces a dilemma. Neither in Texas nor in any other State are all abortions prohibited. [There is always at least an exception] for the purpose of saving the life of the mother.... But if the fetus is a person who is not to be deprived of life without due process of law, and if the mother's condition is the sole determinant, does not the ... exception appear to be out of line with the Amendment's command?" (Roe v. Wade, Footnote 54 of the Opinion)

Not that striking the exception for the "life of the

---

79 *Scott v. Sandford,* 60 U.S. (19 How.) 393-394 (1856) "6. The only two clauses in the Constitution which point to this race treat them as persons whom it was morally lawfully to deal in as articles of property and to hold as slaves. 7. Since the adoption of the Constitution of the United States, no State can by any subsequent law make a foreigner or any other description of persons citizens of the United States, nor entitle them to the rights and privileges secured to citizens by that instrument. ...9. The change in public opinion and feeling in relation to the African race which has taken place since the adoption of the Constitution cannot change its construction and meaning, and it must be construed and administered now according to its true meaning and intention when it was formed and adopted.

mother" would make a law against abortion court-proof. As justice Rehnquist pointed out,

> If the Texas statute were to prohibit an abortion even where the mother's life is in jeopardy, I have little doubt that such a statute would lack a rational relation to a valid state objective under the test stated in Williamson, supra. (Dissent by Rehnquist, section II)

It is hard to be sure whether to take Blackmun's logic seriously, or as some kind of sarcasm, in view of the eminent sense which the "life of the mother" exception makes. Our Necessity Defense barely *allows* a hero to save others, typically at considerable risk to his own freedom if not to his life; we have no law which *requires* people to be life-saving heroes. We admire parents who put themselves in harm's way for their children. We are not about to require it as a matter of law!

On the other hand, maybe Blackmun was right. Actively killing somebody whose threat to you is only his existence, goes beyond normal self defense scenarios. But to whatever extent Blackmun was right, it was evil hypocrisy for him to use America's abandonment of a percent of a percent of America's babies as his pretext for forcing Americans to abandon all of them.

Another example of Blackmun's evidence against considering unborn babies "persons" is that penalties against mothers who abort are historically lighter than penalties for murdering adults. It does not overstate the strangeness of his argument to say he literally argues that legal mistreatment of a group of people casts doubt, not on whether laws and courts are just, but on whether their victims are even human.

We can't deny fundamental rights to people, and then take our own wicked mistreatment of them as proof that they are not people after all so we are free to enslave them, as we used to treat blacks. Or torture and kill them, as we still treat over a fifth of our unborn babies.[80] That is not the kind of reasoning that has made America a "shining city on a hill". It is the tarnish that has reduced the brightness God made available to us.

4. No one would ever believe the Supreme Court again, if they updated their precedents to keep up with updated facts.

> (i) Overruling Roe's central holding would not only reach an unjustifiable result under stare decisis principles, but would seriously weaken the Court's capacity to exercise the judicial power and to function as the Supreme Court of a Nation dedicated to the rule of law. Where the Court acts to resolve the sort of unique, intensely divisive controversy reflected in Roe, its decision has a dimension not present in normal cases, and is entitled to rare precedential force to counter the inevitable efforts to overturn it and to thwart its implementation. *Only the most convincing justification under accepted standards of precedent could suffice to demonstrate that a later decision overruling the first was anything but a surrender to political pressure and an unjustified repudiation of the principle on which the Court staked its authority in the first instance. Moreover, the country's loss of confidence in the Judiciary would be underscored by condemnation for the Court's failure to keep faith with those who support the decision at a cost to themselves.* **A decision to overrule Roe's essential holding under the existing circumstances would address error, if error there was, at the cost of both profound and unnecessary damage to the Court's legitimacy and to the Nation's commitment to the rule of law.** Pp. 864-869. *[Casey, 505* U.S. 833, 836]

It would end America's "Rule of Law" to correct error?!!

America would suffer "loss of confidence in the

---

80 " The abortion rate for 2012 was 13.2 abortions per 1,000 women aged 15–44 years, and the abortion ratio was 210 abortions per 1,000 live births." http://www.cdc.gov/reproductivehealth/data_stats/

judiciary" if it ruled correctly?

The American public has so much confidence in the justice and lawfulness of the Supreme Court now, that any deviation from its rulings towards reality would be a blow to "the Court's legitimacy"?!!

Of course this firm stand would make sense if it were on principle – if it were limited to positions based on reality, with a readiness to withdraw support of positions shown to be wrong. But this opening statement in *Casey* pledges commitment to positions even after they are exposed as wrong, and says that is necessary to preserve confidence in the Supreme Court. That is crazy talk.

5. Moms must murder to preserve their dignity.

Stenberg v. Carhart 530 U.S. 914 (2000), which perpetuates "partial birth abortion" by striking down a law of Congress that bans it, begins:

> "We again consider the right to an abortion. We understand the controversial nature of the problem. Millions of Americans believe that life begins at conception and consequently that an abortion is akin to causing the death of an innocent child; they recoil at the thought of a law that would permit it. Other millions fear that a law that forbids abortion would condemn many American women to lives that lack dignity, depriving them of equal liberty and leading those with least resources to undergo illegal abortions with the attendant risks of death and suffering. Taking account of these virtually irreconcilable points of view, aware that constitutional law must govern a society whose different members sincerely hold directly opposing views, and considering the matter in light of the Constitution's guarantees of fundamental

individual liberty, this Court, in the course of a generation, has determined and then redetermined that the Constitution offers basic protection to the woman's right to choose. *Roe v. Wade,* (1973); *Planned Parenthood of Southeastern Pa. v. Casey,* (1992). We shall not revisit those legal principles.

Notice a few things about this opening. "causing the death of an innocent child" is treated as a matter of "belief" and a "view". No attempt is made to consider whether the deaths taken by abortion are a *fact*.

The "opposing view", that not being allowed to kill their babies would rob women of "dignity", is treated as if it is equal in weight to the "view" that "abortion causes the death of an innocent child", and as if two "virtually irreconcilable...sincerely held...points of view" cancel each other out by their mere weight of popularity, like two chess pieces of similar value "traded" and discarded, cleared out of the way so they no longer distract us from the battle before us, leaving our decisions simpler, uncomplicated by their nagging cries.

The Court could not treat opposing views as capable of canceling each other out if the Court felt qualified to determine which "view" is supported by the *facts*. If, in *fact*, aborticide "causes the death of innocent children", then it is absurd to count such bloody carnage as an ingredient of "dignity". It is absurd to treat such murders as any kind of legally acceptable "choice". If the Court weighed the *facts*, then the two "views" would not be irreconcilable at all. The "view" that children die would govern the case, and the "view" that mothers cannot have dignity without murdering their babies would simply be laughed out of the courtroom.

ALTERNATIVES TO SCOTUS RATIONALES

A number of analogies have arisen in the veritable cottage industry of Roe replacement wannabes, offering to supplant Roe's rationales when they fall, in order to keep abortion's fragile "legality" on life support.

Care must be taken before using an analogy as the basis for obstructing the 14th Amendment Right to Life of millions of unborn U.S. citizens, who are called "posterity" by the Constitution's Preamble. Care must be taken that both legs of the analogy, the illustration and the reality, at least match. Otherwise law limps along, as described in Proverbs 26:7 "The legs of the lame are not equal: so is a parable in the mouth of fools."

6. **We should kill unborn babies for kidnapping mothers.**

Judith Jarvis Thomson wrote *"A Defense of Abortion".* She published this in 1971, justifying infant murder before it was cool. This summary is taken from "Abortion: the Irrepressible Conflict" by Eric Rudolph.[81]

> ...M.I.T. Philosophy Professor Judith Jarvis Thomson['s] "A Defense of Abortion" is probably the most talked about pro-abortion essay. Using a series of examples, Thomson insists that a woman has an unqualified right to an abortion, even if the fetus is a human being. ...Because even if a person, **the fetus has no right to use a woman's body without her consent.** To make her argument, Thomson asks you to imagine waking up in a hospital back-to-back with a famous violinist, who has a fatal kidney ailment. Because you are the only one with a matching blood type, the Society of Music Lovers has kidnapped you and hooked you up to the famous fiddler to "extract the poisons from his blood." The hospital director tells you it will be another nine months before the violinist's kidneys are in good shape and they can unhook you.

---

81 That's right, *the* Eric Rudolph, the one still in a Colorado prison for bombs, who managed to elude federal officers for years in a forest. The summary in his book of *Roe* wannabe rationales is a lot more scholarly than his manner of addressing the problem.

Even though it was immoral for the Society of Music Lovers to kidnap you and put you in this predicament, unhooking you, the hospital director says, would be doubly immoral, because it would kill the violinist. *Judith Jarvis Thomson, "A Defense of Abortion," in* <u>*The Abortion Controversy: Twenty-Five Years After Roe v. Wade,*</u> *(Belmont, CA: Wadsworth Publishing, 1998) Poijman And Beckwith ppl. 117-118*

The first problem with this parable is that mothers are not kidnapped into having babies. The analogy should have begun with you volunteering to hook yourself to the violinist, in return for the most exhilarating pleasure as you are being hooked up.

Even in the case of rape or incest, the analogy should emphasize that the violinist was an unwilling, unwitting participant in the scheme. The baby is as innocent as the violinist. If anyone merits retribution, it would not be the baby.

Second, the parable leaves out the consolation prize of the 9 months' "captivity": the sweetest music imaginable! Babies are even more adorable than violinists!

In fact, way more, because there are many people who don't like violins, but there is nobody who doesn't like babies. Well, if there actually are, it is questionable whether they are "persons in the whole sense."

Now if the analogy had featured a trumpet player, it would have been a different matter. But it is too late now to mend mistakes: we are stuck with a violinist, and no violinist is pretty, compared with a baby. Unless of course it is a baby violinist. Babies cry and wet, but they also smile smiles of purer joy than any adult can comprehend, reminding young adults newly free from parents and from the overwhelming influence of peers in school, how to love. How to really love. How to glimpse Heaven.

Calling it "captivity" brings us to the third problem. Mothers do not lose their freedom just because they are pregnant. Most pregnancies cause almost no curtailment of activity for the whole nine months. Certainly nothing remotely as restrictive as being hooked up to a violinist!

In those few pregnancies where doctors advise mothers to remain in bed much of the time or risk losing the baby, it remains the mother's legal choice whether to follow that advice, partly because any doctor's analysis of the precise limits to mom's activities which are safe for the baby is a guess: no one would accuse the mother of killing the baby if she had to get up and work.

And even in the most medically risky cases, the mother probably won't even know she is pregnant for several weeks, and at about 7 months the child could be surgically removed and still live, with less medical risk to the mother, not to mention the child, than that of an abortion in a clinic which courts have protected from modern medical standards — so even the worst case would probably involve 6 months of voluntary restricted activity.

Fourth, to keep Thompson's analogy honest, our alternative is not to merely detach the violinist and walk away, leaving him at the mercy of God to perhaps heal him. No, we must chop the violinist into tiny pieces, and then lay the pieces on a table and count them to be sure we did not miss any. And should our plans be interrupted by the violinist's miraculous healing before we can take our first slice, we must not let him walk away unscathed, but must strap him down and finish chopping.

When a man is dying and it is time to give up on the tubes and monitors, we just withdraw them as gently as we can and let the man die as peacefully as we can. We don't rip out the plastic like we are pulling kittens out of a house fire, and then go in with machetes, acids, and poison gas to dispatch the poor slob as brutally as we can! American law calls that "cruel and unusual punishment". How dare this Thomson woman compare very real, very prevalent, and very brutal infanticide with the peaceful separation of the mythical violinist!

Fifth, the violinist is a "parasite" in a true sense, which no baby can be. God gave me my kidney for my sole use. I *may choose* to lend it out or give it away, but no one would imagine an *obligation* to encumber my body in this way.

By contrast, the baby is using an organ for which the mother has absolutely no personal use. The organs the baby is using were made specifically for another person besides the woman to use. The baby is not "out of place" in her body. He is exactly where unborn babies belong. A woman's body, in a way quite unlike a man's body, is not "hers". It is specifically engineered to act as temporary life support for the exact kind of being that is threatened by an abortion. She sees her kidneys as thus "mine" and "for me" in a way that her uterus is not.

Sixth, if the duty of a mother to nourish the Gift of God whom she has received into her Heaven-designed life support system cannot be presumed, what duty of any mother can be presumed? What duty is greater? Can the care of a born toddler be half as urgent, when the toddler is so much more capable of living safely with others? Can faithfulness to a husband be half as urgent, when her faithlessness will not cause her husband to die? Can financial responsibility seem a fraction as important? Can obedience to laws and court rulings be said to be one speck of her responsibility for her baby?

No! Telling a mother she owes no responsibility to nourish the life cradled within her is telling her she owes no responsibility to anyone for anything! She may, with no pang of conscience, no legitimate legal consequences, kill her toddler, her husband, her creditors, and her judge! Any defense of abortion is a legal theory of Anarchy!

Seventh, the violinist is not "mine" in any sense, but a baby is "mine" to its mother, genetically, built from the very substance of her own body and blood. We owe a higher level of responsibility towards what we call "mine", than to a stranger. It is not as much that we "owe" more responsibility to our "own", but that when our laws side with those whose hearts can't motivate them to forbear destroying the most precious thing that is "theirs", we should not be surprised when hearts harden to the laws that govern our legal responsibilities to strangers. As the will to take and to hurt rises, so does the cost of security and the losses from lawlessness.

Eighth, in the case of rape, the child of rape is the good that God draws out of evil. To destroy the child is to reject the incredible mercy and generosity God has shown.

Far from showing that God either does not love, or is not powerful, the child of rape is the whisper of God, "Look how powerful and good I am! Even out of this supreme horror for you, dear woman, I can create a dazzling miracle of joy: another human being, whole and entire, made in my likeness, made to praise and glorify and love and be loved by Me, who will console you for your suffering in his conception!"

Rape victims who bear their babies are offered the gift of healing through them. Indeed, it is the more horrible when a rapist is sterile, so that the abuse is "for nothing".

Ninth, in healthy societies, even during the pregnancy, the miracle of motherhood is universally celebrated as a source of joy for the mother, the siblings, the father, the extended family, the neighbors, and the community, as expressed in customs like "Baby Showers", passing out cigars (is that still legal?), "It's a boy/girl!" balloons, infant dedication ceremonies in churches, and the "new baby" section of Hallmark Card displays. What sickness, what ingratitude, can spin this Gift from Heaven into "kidnapping" and "imprisonment"?

Much in our culture establishes this joy as beginning during pregnancy. "Baby showers" are celebrations, not times of mourning – not wakes. Broad happy smiles are often seen on expectant mothers as they announce their

Gift from God to friends. Mothers prepare by reading books about how to be the best mother possible. They hold Mozart up to their bellies to begin their child's education early.

The tenth problem with this parable is that, personal notions of morality aside, under a world government which socialists like Thomson dream about, the secret police would hook you up to the fiddler, or more likely, the dictator, and no one would complain. (Publicly.) Instead, you would be publicly admired, and counted as fortunate to be so valuable to the State! "The State" would as easily hook you up to anyone else, for its own alleged best interests, calculating your value by your benefit to it.

What keeps America from falling headlong into this nightmare government scenario is the Laws of God that proclaim our liberty. But these are the same Laws of God which proclaim life and liberty for the unborn. The same Laws of God which protect the unborn, protect the born.

History is full of states abandoning God's Laws, after which states have no restraint against enslaving and murdering whomever they please, whether babies or violinist donors.

In fact, the farther American law "evolves" away from God's Laws in which it is an unthinkable crime to destroy your own baby, Jeremiah 19:5, the *less* legal right you will have to unhook yourself.

Thompson wants our support for unhooking the violinist to extend to support for killing our baby. But it is our recession from God's laws that will make it illegal to unhook ourselves, while it will remain legal to kill our babies; the protection she wants for the right to unhook ourselves comes from God whose Laws against our own kidnapping also outlaw us murdering others.

"Duty to Assist" laws, and mothers' responsibilities

The loss of freedom a mother experiences through pregnancy is infinitesimal compared to the kidnap victim in

Thomson's analogy; but is even an hour's loss of freedom an unreasonable expectation of a mother? In other words, is there any precedent in law for forcing anyone, in any situation, to be a Good Samaritan?

Yes, according to "Good Samaritan" laws:

> Good Samaritan statutes in the states of Minnesota and Vermont do require a person at the scene of an emergency to provide reasonable assistance to a person in need. This assistance may be to call 9-1-1. Violation of the duty-to-assist subdivision is a petty misdemeanor in Minnesota and may warrant a fine of up to $100 in Vermont. At least five other states, including California and Nevada, have seriously considered adding duty-to-assist subdivisions to their good Samaritan statutes. (Wikipedia, under "Good Samaritan", 2011)

A "Duty to Assist" is most clear when one's actions have contributed to the dependency which another now has upon you. For example, hitting and injuring someone with your car will not send you to jail if you can prove you could not help it; but if you "hit and run" in any state, the penalties will be severe.

Of course, in 98% of cases, the mother's participation in conception is voluntary. Her actions have contributed to the dependency of her baby.

American laws - indeed, the laws of what we call "civilization" - are full of "duties to assist". But especially in America.

If we have a retail store, we don't have a legal right to pick and choose which customers we want to serve, refusing to serve racial groups we don't want.

We can't put up a sign, "Every customer a wanted customer", as a pretext for throwing out customers we don't "want" because of their color, IQ, religion, weight, legal training, looks, etc.

Public school teachers don't have a right to stop teaching students who don't learn fast, or who challenge teacher patience. No principal, no school board, has a legal right to refuse education to any remotely educable child.

Hospitals can't turn away patients based on whims, to let them die because they aren't "wanted". Federal law requires hospital emergency rooms to care even for undocumented immigrants rather than let them die on the hospital doorsteps. Nursing homes can't put residents out on the curb who are not "wanted" any longer.

Landlords can't instantly remove tenants who won't pay, or who even damage property! Landlords must give tenants a reasonable time to find other housing.

No parent has a legal right to simply stop caring for a child because the parent doesn't like the child any longer. Minor child neglect that causes no harm to the child is grounds for removing the child and severing custody, and placing the parent on the Child Abuse Registry which bars that parent from future employment involving children. Neglect that causes injury is grounds for criminal charges that put parents in jail.

Contracts require commitments which must be kept even if a party to the contract no longer "wants" to keep their end of the bargain.

Thomson's logic fails. Our laws simply do not recognize any absolute right not to help those who depend on us. If her logic governed our laws, the same logic would end everyone's responsibility to whoever becomes dependent upon them to be responsible.

In no human relationship is a human being more dependent on another human being who has done more to create the dependency, than in childbirth.

The bonds of responsibility that bind together what we call "Western Civilization" would dissolve into utter anarchy, if responsibilities less than those of mothers for their unborn babies were stripped of legal support!

We can at least be grateful that Jarvis confines her

logic to babies, so that it does not take the entire rest of civilization down with the unborn. For now.

7. **Babies should die for breaking and entering.**

Here is another analogy of Judith Jarvis Thompson, again summarized by Eric Rudolph:

> Thomson says even where sex was consensual, the child's right to use his mother's body is still dependent on the mother's consent. ...If you opened your window "to let the air in" (had sex for pleasure) and a burglar (baby) climbed in instead, are you obligated to let him stay? What if you "installed burglar bars" (contraception) on your windows and a burglar came through anyway? A mother is no more obligated to let the unwanted child stay in her womb than the homeowner is obligated to let the burglar stay in his home. It may be "indecent and self centered" to deny the child the use of her body "for one hour," but it's not "unjust." Ibid, p. 129-130. "It would be indecent in the woman to request an abortion, and indecent in a doctor to perform it, if a fetus is in her seventh month, and she wants the abortion just to avoid the nuisance of postponing a trip abroad." Such an abortion would be immoral. The state, however, has no legal basis to interfere. Rudolph, Ibid,, p. 130.

To make this analogy honest, the "burglar bars" need to be made out of tissue, to reflect the well known failure rate of contraception, and there needs to be a vacuum in our bedroom so powerful that innocent, unwilling, unwitting babies minding their own business outside are sucked in without any action on their part.

What callousness, to compare a Messenger from Heaven with a "burglar"! What anarchy, to see no responsibility to honor even humanity's most sacred of trusts!

Thomson at least acknowledges that this logic applies as well after birth! As it inevitably must.

But it really applies far longer than that! It applies to an adult guest in your home. Thomson would have us free to boot out a guest into the cold, even if the guest is sick and needs hospitalization!

> Orlando Depue was awarded damages after he was literally kicked out in the cold. It was a cold January night in Minnesota - we're talking Eskimo weather. Depue had eaten dinner with a couple, the Flateus. Feeling sick after the dinner, he asked the couple if he could sleep over. But the Flateus refused to give him board and told him to leave. Too sick to drive, Depue was forced to sleep in the backseat of his car. In the morning his fingers were popsicles, and later had to be amputated. ...The Court said:... "The law as well as humanity required that he not be exposed in his helpless condition to the merciless elements." [John T. Noonan, "How to Argue About Abortion," in Morality in Practice(Belmont, CA: Wadsworth Publishing, 1998) p. 150] An obligation is assumed once you "understand and appreciate" the conditions of your fellowman, even if he is a stranger. What goes for strangers goes double for family members. (Rudolph, Ibid.)

Thomson's logic applies to a tenant whom you, the landlord, no longer "want", and justifies you breaking the law if you don't "want" to give him time to leave safely.

Thomson's logic justifies a prisoner who no longer "wants" to remain in jail, and thinks he can be free by killing a few guards. Sure, the guards had a "right to life", and it was "immoral" to kill them, but the prisoner was under no "obligation" to permit his body to be "kidnapped" any longer.

How about the husband who no longer "wants" his wife? And who sees no reason to give her time to pack?

How about the guy who doesn't "want" anyone traversing his sidewalk in winter anyway, so what harm is there if he does not shovel it?

How about the guy who WANTS junk in his yard? Or ragweed in his front lawn?

If Thomson is willing to open up a law firm to defend every criminal which her logic justifies, she is going to be busy!

What about a surgeon who, half way through surgery, decides he doesn't "want" to stay in medicine and quits?

Is a man a murderer who refuses to hold out his hand, allowing another man to drown? The facts may be difficult to establish: would the man indeed have been saved? Or was it at least reasonable to have anticipated he would have been? Did the defendant know that? Did the defendant have any better reason, than hatred of the deceased, to not hold out his hand? But to the extent such facts are clear, the defendant is likely to be prosecuted in civil court, if not criminal. But Thomson will at least visit him in jail, if not marry him.

What if the police no longer "want" to protect people in a particular slum? And what if the city council approves that policy, and voters agree?

What if society no longer wants to protect the 14th Amendment fundamental rights of "Illegal Aliens", and votes to sell them into slavery to meet the "legitimate state purpose" of balancing the budget? Or authorizes citizens to enslave any Illegal Alien whom they can find and catch?

What if a state no longer "wants" to be subject to the U.S. Supreme Court?

We are all little sovereign autonomous entities with no prior social obligation. We dole out rights on a voluntary basis. But we don't owe anybody anything, says Thomson.... Libertarian liberals like Thomson get their current definition of individual liberty from John Stuart Mill. Back in 1859, Mill wrote a book entitled <u>On Liberty</u>. Its purpose was to expound the principle that "the sole [justification for] interfering with the liberty of action of any [citizen] is self protection... The only purpose for which power can be exercised over any member of a civilized community, against his will, is to prevent harm to others. ...the conduct from which it is desired to deter him must be calculated [by him] to produce evil to someone else. The only part of the conduct of anyone, for which he is amenable to society, is to which concerns others. In the part which concerns himself, his independence is, of right, absolute. Over himself, over his body and mind, the individual is sovereign." (Rudolph, p. 77, 75, characterizing Thomson. His quote from Mill comes from John Stuart Mill, <u>Autobiography,</u> (Penguin Classics, 1989) pp. 66-69)

Iowa would not recommend any deference to this policy to any Supreme Court justice who would like his rulings to be obeyed! In addition to all the previously mentioned disregard of laws Thomson's legal principles would cause, courts would no longer be able to compel witnesses to testify! Subpoenas would be ignored! Because Thomson thinks we have no responsibility to help anyone who depends on us, so long as we do not actively hurt them. (But if they are babies we can actively hurt them.) Setting a murderer free to resume his spree, by refusing to testify against him, is not *actively* hurting anybody!

In fact, if a woman is free to hire a butcher to carve up her own flesh and blood, because she has no obligation to help her own flesh and blood, how much less does a witness have a moral obligation to obey a subpoena to help strangers, which in a notorious case or where defendants are threatening, is dreaded more than the birth pangs of ten babies?!

My recommendation to the Supreme Court is that if Thomson ever wants to go to law school and apply to your bar, reject her! She is going to be trouble!

This reasoning is as applicable to aborting a nation's Rule of Law as it is to aborting a Gift from God! Our "rule of law" means our American legal principle that laws are applied to everybody equally. No lawmaker, and no voting majority, is exempt from the laws imposed on a minority. Even if the minority is not yet born. "Rule of law" prohibits laws protecting dismemberment of a fifth of the unborn population, from which voters, lawmakers and judges are exempt.

In American law, the Rule of Law is most succinctly encapsulated in our 14th Amendment: "No State shall ...deny to any person within its jurisdiction the equal protection of the laws."

The model for that was God's principle that a nation must "have one manner of law, as well for the stranger [immigrant], as for one of your own country", Leviticus 24:22. Also Exodus 12:49.

Incredibly, Thomson knows babies are human beings with a Right to Life. She does not dispute babies are made in the Image of God.

It is irrational for anyone with this knowledge to say mothers can pull babies into their homes and then butcher them rather than wait until the baby can depart in peace and safety, because mothers have a sovereign choice whether to help another whose life depends on their help; but then to say it is unlawful for a nursing home to stab Grandma to death or put her out on the street in December, because the nursing home no longer "wants" her and does not want to wait until another home, or charity, can take her in peace and safety!

It is irrational to say a mother has no responsibility towards her most sacred obligation and occasion for joy, and then to say any other citizen has any responsibility whatsoever towards infinitely lesser societal obligations which occasion far less joy!

It is irrational for anyone who knows babies are human beings to believe in both a Right to Abortion, and the Rule of Law. Both because Thomson's reasoning undermines obedience to any law defining our responsibilities towards each other, and because Rule of Law, by definition, does not impose burdens upon one group of human beings, such as the unborn, from which other groups are exempt. All of us were residents in our mothers' wombs: we lay upon the unborn burdens we are not willing to touch with one of our fingers, Luke 11:46, if we deprive our successors of the legal protection from maternal responsibility which we insist was properly binding upon our own mothers.

8. Unborn babies are humans but don't force moms to nurture them.

Lawrence Tribe is Professor of Constitutional Law at Harvard Law School. He is a frequent guest on network television and National Public Radio. (According to the back of his book, "Abortion: The Clash of Absolutes". Norton & Company, 1992.) One normally takes such credentials as a measure of intelligence.

But here is how he offers to solve the Infanticide madness:

> ...perhaps the Supreme Court's opinion in Roe, by gratuitously insisting that the fetus cannot be deemed a "person," needlessly insulted and alienated those for whom the view that the fetus is a person represents a fundamental article of faith or a bedrock personal commitment. Perhaps, as Yale Law School Dean Guido Calabresi has suggested, the Roe opinion for no good reason said to a large and politically active group, "[y]our metaphysics are not part of our Constitution." The Court could instead have said: Even if the fetus is a person, our Constitution forbids compelling a woman to carry it for nine months and become a mother. (p. 135)

What? "Even if the fetus is a person", a mother can slaughter her infant limb from limb? That's a *solution?*

Let's expose the Straw Men here. The mother who doesn't want to be "burdened" with a Gift from God has an alternative to brutally torturing him to death: when the baby is big enough to show very much, and cause very much discomfort, the baby will be big enough to be delivered safely and grow to maturity, safely, in a maternity ward, until the baby can go home to a loving adoptive family. It may be an expensive way to do it, and it isn't the best for the health of the baby, but it's a lot healthier than tearing him limb from limb, and thousands of parents are in line for the opportunity to pay all those bills in return for their own Gift from God!

Tribe imagines he can solve the world's problems by authorizing the slaughter of legally recognized Human Beings "even if the fetus, no less than Judith Thomson's violinist, is regarded as a person"! (Rudolph, ibid)

Tribe tells how the famous Infanticidist Kate Michelman, in 1970, at 33, was pregnant with her 4th child when her husband left her for another woman. No car, no credit because she hadn't worked, no child support because she didn't know where he was, her only choice was to murder her fourth, in order to have a shot at providing for the other three. Tribe overlooks the Adoption Option: instead of going deeper in debt to hire a hit man, she could have found adoptive parents who would have paid her bills with a handsome bonus that would have helped her other children!

Why is it that resisting murder never seems to enter the minds of these people, as they go over their options?

9. We are worth saving, but not babies – there is that much difference between us

The myth that there is a clear line of humanity distinguishing us adults from our unborn offspring is the same charade slave owners once played with Blacks.

It is funny to follow **Mary Ann Warren's** creative criteria of "personhood" by which unborn babies are *not* "human" or "persons", but she *is*. From her book, "On the Moral and Legal Status of Abortion":

> (1) Consciousness (of objects and events, external and internal to the being, and the capacity to feel pain);
>
> (2) reasoning (the developed capacity to solve new and relatively complex problems);
>
> (3) self-motivated activity (activity that is relatively independent of either genetic or direct external control);
>
> (4) the capacity to communicate, by whatever means, messages of indefinite variety of types, that is not just with

an indefinite number of possible contexts, but of many possible topics;

(5) the presence of self-concepts, self-awareness, either individual or racial, or both. Mary Ann Warren, "On the Moral and Legal Status of Abortion," in <u>The Ethics of Abortion,</u>(New York: Prometheus Books, 2001) Baird and Rosenbaum

Well, #4 (capacity to communicate on many topics) rules out children younger than 4, depending on how fussy you are about clarity of communication. Newborn babies can communicate about many topics with eye movements, smiling, and crying. Experiments are done with babies in the womb, trying to give them an educational head start. The younger the child, the more perceptive the adults must be to communicate. The Bible records a time when a 6-month unborn baby leaped at the sound of the voice of Jesus' mother in a clear communication of joy. Luke 1:39-44. Will that testimony persuade Mary Ann Warren if we tell her?

#5, the presence of self concepts or self awareness, how would you test that in a child much under 7? Even then it could be difficult. It's one thing to be self aware; it's quite another thing to convince a skeptic that you are! And that is what Warren demands before she relinquishes her right to kill you! If there is a test available to prove a newborn is self aware, I would like to see it prove that a preborn is not!

#3 self-motivated activity free of genetic control; until we can get scientists to agree how much of *adult* behavior is genetic, maybe we better lop off the "free of genetic control" and stick with "self-motivated activity". One would think the attempts of preborns to escape scalpels and suction machines, documented in the very first ultrasound video titled "Silent Scream", is pretty overwhelming evidence of their capacity for self-motivated activity.

#1, Consciousness is proved by the reactions of preborns to many stimuli; from the suction machine to loving educational information. Ability to feel pain by 20 weeks is clearly enough established to be a threshold in Nebraska law, since 2010, beyond which abortion is a crime – not that anyone has proved that preborns feel no pain before that.

#2, reasoning that can "solve...complex problems" kind of rules out the author.

Had she settled for "ability to *think about* ...relatively complex problems" she might have escaped. But she had to insist on the "ability to *solve* ...relatively complex problems". I think everyone can agree her essay argues against her being human.

Warren criticizes Thomson for allowing that murdering your own baby to avoid postponing a trip might at least be immoral: "...it would not, in itself, be immoral, and therefore it ought to be permitted." Ibid.

Having assumed she has satisfied skeptics that the unborn are not human but she is, she next switches to an analogy that assumes everyone accepts Roe's view of the unborn as merely "potential life". As if there are people who insist on constitutional protection for life before conception which is only "potential", she sets out to refute these fanatics.

Warren's bizarre analogy has space aliens capturing you to clone your body. Is it right for you to escape, when that would keep innumerable people from being created out of you? "...one ACTUAL person's right to liberty outweighs whatever right to life even a hundred thousand POTENTIAL persons have." Ibid.

The contested issue was never whether "potential life" has any constitutional rights. It was always, in *Roe's* world, whether life in the womb is human or merely "potential". So Warren's analogy is irrelevant to abortion of human beings after conception. So where *is* such a strange analogy relevant?

Well, perhaps it could justify laws against pimps

forcing women into prostitution where pregnancies recur continually. Perhaps it could justify laws against Moslems *forcing* their daughters into marriage. Perhaps it could justify laws against rape.

Oh, wait, we already have those laws.

Warren's analogy doesn't fit much of anything, so it is difficult to imagine how to repair it. The mother would be pregnant by the normal human means, and then the picketers outside Planned Barrenhood were actually space aliens in disguise, who beamed her up as she was headed inside and strapped her down to keep her from killing her own child. That would make a lot more sense. Aliens could provide us a much needed service by doing that.

10. Abort born children, whose personhood is almost as much in doubt.

[Michael] **Tooley's** definitions of personhood are pretty narrow. He admits that "even newborn humans do not have the capacities in question....it would seem that infanticide during a time interval shortly after birth must be viewed as morally acceptable." Michael Tooley, *"In Defense of Abortion and Infanticide," in* The Ethics of Abortion, *(New York: Prometheus Books, 2001),* [and] Mary Ann Warren - adopt a very narrow definition of personhood, which allows them to deny the unborn child's humanity, and therefore exclude him from legal protections. Their narrow definitions don't hold water though because they end up excluding most of mankind, both born and unborn. *[As reported in "Abortion: The Irrepressible Conflict" by Eric Rudolph.]*

11. Wouldn't handicapped babies rather be tortured to death?

Surely a handicapped baby does not want to live! Surely he or she would be grateful for assisted suicide! Of course, since the baby is "incompetent" to express his own wishes, the decision must be made by the baby's legal guardian, the mother. Right? To assume, as a matter of law, that a baby would want to live, even with a handicap, is surely "establishing religion" "because it enforces a particular religiously inspired moral choice and lacks a countervailing secular justification". (Edward Rubin, writing for the Vanderbilt Law Review[82]. He argues for assisted suicide for adults; his argument is applied here to abortion.)

Fortunately, our laws still charge a guardian of a handicapped person with murder, who kills his dependent, and it isn't a defense to say "my dependent was unable to express his preference, so I assumed on his behalf that since she was handicapped, she would rather I kill her."

A website for the disabled says the greatest pressure on them is not the disability, but the attitude among the rest of us that surely handicapped people would rather be dead.

> The challenges faced by people who experience forms of disabilities are influenced more by negative social expectations and tacit ideas concerning disability than by any emotional, physical, or cognitive impairment a person may experience. Each day, organizations work to educate the public about what life with a form of disability is like. For these organizations, that often times means assisting non-disabled neighbors and friends to understand that people with disabilities are not ill and that **our lives are not without happiness or meaning.**
>
> The fact is - research on disability and depression has consistently shown that when people with disabilities report dissatisfaction with their lives they are not nearly as concerned with things such as reliance on machines or medications as they are with their relationships, financial security, or difficulties while at work. Despite this, the social message repeatedly presented is that life with a form of disability is miserable and when the people around us believe that without questioning it, it may become very hard for people with disabilities to think anything different. - *www.disabled-world.com/disability/awareness/suicide.php*

12. Medical evidence does NOT suggest "life begins at conception." Although expert witnesses in

---

82 http://www.vanderbiltlawreview.org/2010/04/assisted-suicide-morality-and-law-why-prohibiting-assisted-suicide-violates-the-establishment-clause/

court are settled that "life begins at conception", a few outliers, whose credentials afford them no court-recognized legal value, grumble their dissent.

One example is Arthur Caplan, *When does life begin?,* Council for Secular Humanism, July 10 2014.[83]

Part of his quibble is that the word "conception" is not precise enough. If we are going to give an embryo constitutional rights, we need to know whether to do so when the sperm reaches the egg, or when it penetrates, or when genes start to recombine:

> Put aside the fact that those who advocate for personhood never say when personhood precisely begins—when a sperm reaches an egg, when it penetrates the egg, when genetic recombination begins, or when a new genome is formed. There is plenty about personifying an embryo that makes no empirical sense.

The "problem" is irrelevant to any legal need we have today because we do not have the technology anyway to monitor when any of these changes occur. We can't even tell for several more days if there is a body there at all, and we have to wait longer to be sure.

We are like the situation of our ancestors, so poorly understood by *Roe,* in which "quickening" – the baby's first kicks that the mother can feel – was the first mothers could be certain they were pregnant. Before that, their clues were missed periods and nausea, but those could have been caused by other things; the kicks were the first proof. Before there was evidence of a human life, how could there be legal penalties for murder? The only possibility of penalties was for intent, not for actual killing. *Roe* completely missed this point and wrongly assumed that because penalties were less before quickening than afterward, therefore babies before quickening were not considered "persons in the whole sense."

It was not until after the War Between the States that

---

83 https://www.secularhumanism.org/index.php/articles/5639

legislation began generally to replace the common law. Most of these initial statutes dealt severely with abortion after quickening but were lenient with it before quickening. Most punished attempts equally with completed abortions.... In short, the unborn have never been recognized in the law as persons in the whole sense.

Caplan also quibbles that while every adult human began at conception, whenever that is, not every baby survives to adulthood or even birth.

Those who argue that personhood begins at conception base their claim on the assertion that every human life begins with conception. That is true. But what they fail to acknowledge is that conception does not always create an embryo life, much less a baby. In fact, it usually does not.

? Is that an argument for denying human beings fundamental rights until they *do* die? Caplan continues the same puzzling point for a page:

The biggest empirical problem with the view that personhood begins at conception is the scientific fact that a large percentage of embryos lack the capacity, under any circumstances, to become human beings. During the period of embryonic development that begins with fertilization and ends a few days later with successful implantation of the blastocyst into the uterine wall—the period known as "preimplantation development"—up to 50 percent of human conceptions fail to survive, most likely due to genetic errors in the embryo.

Miscarriage is the most common type of pregnancy loss, according to the American College of Obstetricians and Gynecologists. Studies show that anywhere from 10 to 25 percent of all clinically recognized pregnancies (meaning that an embryo has implanted) end in miscarriage, depending in part on the age of the woman.

The biological facts don't tell us where to draw the line as to when personhood begins. But they do show that many embryos that result from conception—indeed, the majority of them—lack the capacity to become living human beings. They do not produce disabled humans. They cannot produce any sort of human life. Science and medicine know this. They are simply too intimidated to say so.

Caplan's alternative view of "when life begins":

> When a fetus has developed a brain that can support its basic biological functions, probably at around six months of life, it can be reasonably argued that personhood has begun.

But would Caplan outlaw abortion *then?*

What about Chimeras?[84] Where fraternal twins – separate eggs fertilized by separate sperm – combine into a single person? If they were two "persons" at fertilization, what happened to the other one? Does the combined "person" have *double* Constitutional rights? How about identical twins, where there is one fertilization that results in two persons? Are each of them half a "person"?

These objections are as silly as they sound. As Psalm 139 says, God knits us together in our mother's wombs and knows all our members before there are even any. If God wants to be especially creative with some of us, that is no justification for the rest of us to become murderers.

Although any concession is legally unnecessary, perhaps we prolifers may concede, if it will help these doubters understand our position, that when we say "life begins at conception/fertilization", we mean this as a precise legal position, but we do not mean it as an encylopedic review of all the ways God creates "in secret", as the Psalm says – that is, where we cannot monitor.

Our legal position is that we must stop destroying what God creates. Whether through contraception that kills before implantation, or pills that kill weeks afterward, or surgery that kills months afterward. Whether God makes two persons out of one, or one person out of two, is irrelevant to our legal duty to welcome and protect every person that God sends us.

13. Shouldn't we oppose all laws whose origins are exclusively Christian?

Reverence for all human life has a "religious

---

84 https://en.wikipedia.org/wiki/Chimera_(genetics)

motivation". In fact, it has a specifically Christian "religious motivation". Only Judeo-Christianity, of all the world's religions, asserts that God made *all* men in His own image, Genesis 1:27, making the killing of *any* legally innocent man "murder". Other religions worship idols – all kinds of images other than human, but Judeo-Christianity directs our reverence to human life itself, regarding it as a terrible thing to divert our reverence to anything less.

Certainly reverence for human life (as opposed to some kind of "self" obscured by the human body) is not found in Hinduism, which asserts that human life is not worth living, and the goal of a Hindu is to deaden his desire to every good thing on Earth so when he dies he won't have to come back.

It is not found in the B'hagavad Gita, where Arjuna is told by Krishna that he must fight and kill even though the other side is largely his own family, because he is a Kshatria, a warrior by birth, so it is his "duty" to do the work of the class into which he was born; and besides, killing people doesn't hurt their souls anyway. It just sets them free from their bodies.

Certainly man as "the image of God" is not found in Islam which dehumanizes "disbelievers" as "the worst of men" (Surah 98:6) and Christians and Jews as "apes and pigs". (2:63-66; 5:59-60; 7:166)[85]

And certainly not in Atheism, where there is no God, no God-given human rights beyond what you can seize for yourself, whose Darwinian and Marxist religious principle is "survival of the fittest", justifying whatever raw lawless power is available.

Only Judeo-Christianity demands "equal protection of the laws", as our 14th Amendment calls it, or "no respect of persons", as the Bible calls it, for even society's least influential – as epitomized in the Bible, the orphans, widows, poor, and immigrants ("strangers"). Jesus calls

---

85 For a little more detail, http://unravelingislam.com/blog/?p=113

them "the least of these my brethren (brothers)" in Matthew 25:39-46, where He warns that mistreating these "least" is mistreating God, and will send you to Hell. This theology certainly violates Hinduism's "caste system" with its brutal oppression of "untouchables". Or Islam's slaughter of "disbelievers".

The day "religious motivation" becomes grounds for overturning America's laws, respect for human life must disappear. Our "due process" and "equal protection" clauses will wither. What "secular purpose" do they serve?

What will keep us from enslaving "illegals"? Or executing everyone with a life sentence? Or abandoning "unwanted" or orphaned children? Or letting people die whose medical treatments would be expensive?

Will not a wit too dull to see the connection between (1) what reverence for life is left in our laws, and (2) the economic landscape our laws make possible in which brains are free to create, invent, and serve without fear of snipers, government torturers, etc., justify an unlimited central government (dictatorship) as more "efficient"?

What "legitimate state purpose" is served by The Due Process clauses and the Equal Protection clause which ended slavery? Only in retrospect is it clear that peace and freedom for all are the foundations of national prosperity, but what "legitimate state purpose" does national prosperity serve? Democrats openly argue that "the rich" are a national evil and must be accordingly taxed. Democrats also argue that wealth itself is evil, at least insofar as it is built upon energy consumption whose fumes will destroy our ecosystem in a century or two. The Population Control wing argues that human life itself is an evil, and must be reduced by two thirds to restore Mother Earth's ecosystem. Communists say "the rich" are such a national evil that they must be killed, and their goods confiscated and distributed.

What "legitimate state interest" can be asserted in

opposition to these philosophies, without resorting to Judeo-Christian reverence for all human life as having equal value? Should not the Due Process and Equal Protection clauses be repealed? Are they not inconsistent with a "secular" legal system? What "legitimate state interest" do they serve?

Why do we need a Constitution? Why do we need courts? Dictators, preferred by atheists, don't need them. Justice just gets in their way. It is too "inefficient".

"Globalists" are a breed of people who do not even think the survival of America as a sovereign, autonomous government is good, because the world will be better under a "world government", or a "New World Order". Against such thinking, who can justify Freedom as a "legitimate state interest" without resort to principles which are exclusively Judeo-Christian?

The "Lemon Test" utterly, tragically, ignorantly fails to address these questions.

> ...the *Lemon* test, which provides that a statute is constitutional only if it has a secular purpose, neither advances nor inhibits religion as its primary effect, and does not foster excessive government entanglement with religion."
> (From Edward Rubin's article)

This "test" does not resolve the issue whether prosperity, freedom, or national security itself are a "legitimate state interest", in opposition to the prevalent political philosophies and world religions which say they are not.

This "test" does not resolve whether legal values such as giving the right to vote to every adult, or freedom of speech even to criticize either church or state, count as a "secular purpose" even though they are supported by no world religion or anti-religion other than Judeo-Christianity.

The earliest record of a "Republic" in which all the people elect representatives to govern them was not in 600

BC in Athens, as encyclopedias say, but in about 1460 BC when Moses confirmed the "judges" whom the people elected.

> Numbers 1:16 These were the tribal leaders elected from among the people.
>
> Deuteronomy 1:9, 13 At that time I told the people...choose some men from each tribe who are wise, experienced, and understanding, and I will appoint them as your leaders. (The Book translation)

Josephus makes this interpretation explicit.

> *"[the leaders were] such as the whole multitude have tried, and do approve of, as being good and righteous men".* *Antiquities of the Jews,* Book 3, Chapter 4, Section 1.

An 1828 translator's note adds that this selection followed campaign speeches, and then an election, making Moses' government the first Republic, or representative Democracy.

> *"This manner of electing the judges and officers of the Israelites by the testimonies [campaign endorsements] and suffrages [votes] of the people, before they were ordained by God, or by Moses, deserves to be carefully noted, because it was the pattern of the like manner of the choice and ordination of bishops, presbyters, and deacons, in the Christian church."*

Calvin's *Institutes of the Christian Religion* corroborate in detail the elections of Christian church leaders for several centuries.[86] Here is Calvin's analysis of elections in the New Testament:

> 15. The next question is, Whether a minister should be chosen *by the whole Church*, or only by *colleagues* and *elders*, who have the charge of discipline; or whether they may be appointed by the authority of one individual? 546546 See chap. 4 sec. 10, 11; chap. 5 sec. 2, 3. Also Calv. in <u>Acts 6:3</u>, and Luther, tom. 2 p 374. Those who attribute this right to one individual quote the words of Paul to Titus "For this cause left I thee in Crete, that thou shouldest set in order the

---

86 Calvin's *Institutes,* Book 4, Chapter 3 and 4.

things that are wanting, and ordain elders in every city" (<u>Tit. 1:5</u>); and also to Timothy, "Lay hands suddenly on no man" (1 Tim. 5:22).

But they are mistaken if they suppose that Timothy so reigned at Ephesus, and Titus in Crete, as to dispose of all things at their own pleasure. They only presided by previously giving good and salutary counsels to the people, not by doing alone whatever pleased them, while all others were excluded. Lest this should seem to be a fiction of mine, I will make it plain by a similar example.

Luke relates that Barnabas and Paul ordained elders throughout the churches, but he at the same time marks the plan or mode when he says that it was done by suffrage. The words are, χειροτονησαντες (Gr: hand stretcher, or voter) πρεσβυτερους και εκκλησιαν (Acts 14:23).

They therefore selected (creabant - [Latin: third-person plural imperfect active indicative of creo]) two; but the whole body, as was the custom of the Greeks in elections, declared by a show of hands which of the two they wished to have. Thus it is not uncommon for Roman historians to say, that the consul who held the comitia elected the new magistrates, for no other reason but because he received the suffrages, and presided over the people at the election. Certainly it is not credible that Paul conceded more to Timothy and Titus than he assumed to himself. Now we see that his custom was to appoint bishops by the suffrages of the people. *Calvin's Institutes of the Christian Religion, Book 4, Chapter 3, Section 15*

"The Works of John Robinson", about 1,000 pages published by the pastor of the "Pilgrims" (specifically, the Separatists) trace the Scriptural origins of the Pilgrim vote given to every man, beginning with the signature of every man on the Mayflower on the 1620 Mayflower Compact, Western Civilization's first instrument of self-government. In a world where the freest existing government gave a vote to maybe 5% of the population, the vote in Plimoth was not only for the church members, but all men; not only free men, but servants. And when Elizabeth Warren became head of household in 1627 upon the death of her husband Richard, she was authorized to vote.[87]

Freedom of Speech to criticize both church and state was recognized as extending even to the right to respectfully criticize leaders of both church and state, creating the first expression of our First Amendment in a thousand years:

> "[In our Prophesying Service we are] briefly to speak a word of exhortation as God enableth, and ... **questions also about things** delivered, [**preached**] and with them, **even disputations,** as there is occasion, being part, or appurtenances of that exercise. Acts xvii. 2 and xviii. 4. *(Book 3, Chapter 8, "On the Exercise of Prophecy", Argument Tenth.) [We all prophesy to/reason with each other so] that things* **doubtful** *arising in teaching may be* **cleared***, things* **obscure opened***, things* **erroneous** *convinced [***refuted***]; and lastly, that as by the beating together of two stones fire appeareth, so may the light of the truth more clearly shine by* **disputations, questions, and answers modestly had** *and made, and as becomes the church of saints, and work of God.† Luke ii. 40; iv. 31, 32; Acts xvii. 2; xviii. 24, 26, 28.*

It is legally reckless to allow a precedent for overturning a law to proceed one inch, just because it happens to conform with exclusively Judeo-Christian principles to the detriment of competing principles, before examining how much of our laws and constitutions would be left were such a precedent turned loose.

What if it is proved that the very institution of courts of law was established only in the Bible and not in the governments surrounding Israel where kings acted as lawmaker, judge, jury, and executioner? What if the very concept of "rule of law", or "lex rex" itself – meaning "the law is king" - with rules equally binding upon everyone from whom not even the lawmakers are exempt, as opposed

---

to "rex lex" where the king is the law, was established by Christians during the Reformation out of their Bible studies of the political governments of Moses and the church governments of Jesus and is found in no other world religion?

In that case, any precedent for justifying abortion as constitutionally protected because prohibiting it would "establish religion", turned loose, would eventually close down all courts of law and replace our freedoms to vote, speak, and worship, with the form of government which preceded the Bible: dictatorship.

Our "rule of law", applying to everyone equally, came from Ex 12:49, Lev 24:22, Num 15:15-16.

Corroborating witnesses came from Deu 17:6, 19:15, 18:16, 2 Cor 13:1, 1 Ti 5:19, Heb 10:28.

Sequestering witnesses was implied in the Bible but made explicit in Susanah, a 1st to 2nd century BC apocryphal book usually appended to the beginning of Daniel, a history cited in *Virgin Islands v. Edinborough*, 25 F.2d 472, footnote 3. Sequestering witnesses had to be practiced at Jesus' trial; that assumption is the only explanation for why the witnesses had such difficulty agreeing. Mark 14:59.

American law has until now favored Biblical legal precedents which not only "disfavor" the legal systems of competing systems like Sharia law, the human sacrifices of the Mayans and Aztecs, and some other Native Americans, etc., but make criminals of their practitioners. Shall we abandon American law for that reason?

This is not an idle question. A growing number of Muslims in America want their communities, if not all America, to be ruled by Sharia law. If we are afraid to officially discern that American law, regardless of the extent to which it favors Biblical principles over competing systems, is better for America and for Americans and indeed for the whole world than any alternative, we will give it away and our children will read about it only in underground history books whose reading makes them traitors to the state, criminals worthy of torture and death, as it is in many countries in the world today.

> Deuteronomy 4:5 "I have taught you all the laws, as the LORD my God told me to do. Obey them in the land that you are about to invade and occupy. 6 Obey them faithfully, and this will show the people of other nations how wise you are. **When they hear of all these laws, they will say, 'What wisdom and understanding this great nation has!'** 7 "No other nation, no matter how great, has a god who is so near when they need him as the LORD our God is to us. He answers us whenever we call for help. 8 **No other nation, no matter how great, has laws so just as those that I have taught you today.** 9 Be on your guard! Make certain that you do not forget, as long as you live, what you have seen with your own eyes. Tell your children and your grandchildren. (GNB)

Edward Rubin argues that reverence for all human life should be dismissed as "represent[ing] a choice of the traditional morality of higher purposes [than any individual's changing feelings about right and wrong] over the modern morality of self-fulfillment". Such laws should be suspect when "The traditional morality thus favored is specifically Christian".

"Self fulfillment" is the morality of Psychiatry, which in many respects is a religion[88] which is state-established. (It is given police powers in cases of adoption, alleged insanity or child abuse, and in criminal investigations. Its practitioners are given access to children in school.)

William Daubert, et ux., etc., et al., Petitioners v. Merrell Dow Pharmaceuticals, Inc., No. 92-102, 61 LW 4805. This case changed the courtroom definition of a scientific discipline whose practitioners may qualify as "expert witnesses" from whether its articles are published in peer-reviewed journals to whether the findings are

---

88 See http://saltshaker.us/BibleStudies/PsychologyVBible.htm for a comparison of seven fundamental incompatibilities between psychiatry and the Bible.

testable, saying, "One can sum up all this by saying that the criterion of the scientific status of a theory is its falsifiability, or [in other words] refutability, or testability." The Court's footnote on that quote was to a book[89] that gives psychoanalysis as an example of a pseudo-scientific [scientific in appearance only] discipline that is more like religion than science – more like astrology than astronomy.

But if "self fulfillment", the goal of psychiatry, is a "modern morality" which is a fit foundation for law, how can any law against narcotics be Constitutional? Or smoking, or consensual sex with minors, or children skipping school, or sitting down when the judge enters the courtroom? Or disobeying a court ruling which does not satisfy or "fulfill" a litigant? Where are any bounds to such a legal theory?

Edward Rubin says:

> "...arguments...that...prohibitions on abortion should be struck down because of their religious origins...have foundered on the awkward fact that many laws originate in religious thought.129 No one would argue that we should hold that laws against murder violate the Establishment Clause because the prohibition is found in the Ten Commandments, or that we should declare the prohibition of slavery unconstitutional because it was first advanced by the Quakers and carried forward by evangelical Christians....
>
> "The argument advanced in this Article does not rely on a general claim that laws against assisted suicide have religious origins. Rather, it rests on an analysis that in this society, at this historical time, these laws are based on one particular, specifically religious concept of morality and specifically reject rival concepts of morality. They thus align with one side in an ongoing debate within society and employ the coercive force of the state to impose that side's view upon the other. This is simply not true for laws against murder or slavery."

---

89 Karl R. Popper, Conjectures and Refutations (The Growth of Scientific Knowledge) published by Routledge, London and New York, 1963. For selections from Popper's book, see www.Saltshaker.US/American Issues/ChildAbuse/ Popper.htm.

Edward Rubin thus argues that it's OK to retain those laws supported by all religions; it's just the laws whose origins are exclusively Judeo-Christian which we should jettison. Rubin's ignorance of the exclusively Judeo-Christian origins of most of our laws, institutions, and freedoms is shared by most Jews and Christians, but it is still ignorance. His ignorance is, literally, breath-taking.

Moslems own slaves! Moslems justify "honor killings", [ie. if your daughter is raped and pregnant, or worse yet converts to Christianity, you kill her to preserve the family "honor"] conducted by families and mobs without investigation by police or courts. These "honor killings" are lawful, by Sharia Law. By American law, they are are murders.

Hindus burned widows alive on their husbands' funeral pyres as part of their religion until restrained by Christian Englishmen! Hindus have a "caste system" by which, in India, especially in rural areas to this day, a huge portion of the population are "untouchables" and treated as badly as slaves. (It exists less in cities, which are more likely to enforce the Indian Constitution's prohibition of the caste system, which exists because of Ghandi, whose autobiography says half his religious inspiration came from Christianity.)

The mass murders and "labor camps" of Atheism's Communism are legend. Only Communism, of the world's despotisms, has slain more adults during its bloody career than Americans have slain their babies. (That doesn't count the unborn babies slain under Communism.) Communist China's slave labor keeps some of our prices low. Atheism offers no rationale against it, (that has any authority for any other atheist other than the power of one's personal opinion), and much for it.

Slavery, as practiced anywhere outside ancient Israel, was a crime by Moses' laws,. "Manstealing" was a capital crime, and the closest to slavery under Moses' laws was "bondservice" where someone works a maximum of 6 years to pay off a debt, (a little like our multi-year contracts for teachers, athletes, actors, soldiers, etc.,) during which time a permanent injury caused by the master is grounds for immediate release. Prisoners of war could be "enslaved" a maximum of 49 years, and they were kept in the custody of Levites who were in charge of enforcing the laws against cruelty to slaves. Exodus 21:16, 26-27, Leviticus 25

American laws against slavery and murder definitely "are based on one particular, specifically religious concept of morality and specifically reject rival concepts of morality. They thus align with one side in an ongoing debate within society and employ the coercive force of the state to impose that side's view upon the other." If this is to become the basis for repealing American law, out must go our laws against murder and slavery.

Here is the real problem: life *is* sacred, at least in the sense that it is profoundly in our own best interests to treat it so. "Western civilization" as we know it rests on the foundation of this truth which is affirmed exclusively by Judeo-Christian Scriptures. Civilization must inevitably regress into Barbarism to the extent this foundation is discarded.

One who seeks to move our laws outside the bounds of "due process" laid out in those same Scriptures and reflected fairly accurately in American law, doesn't understand life's purpose, or lacks faith in God to realize it.

It is serious enough when occasional individuals don't understand. But for society to heartily join such ignorance threatens the fabric of society.

This purpose is found in Christianity and nowhere else. Hinduism doesn't teach that life is sacred, but profane, and our purpose is to escape its cycles, and indeed to escape individual consciousness for all eternity. Hinduism's "self realization" turns out to be the "oblivion" sought by drunks – the complete cessation of anything left of "self".

But the fact human purpose as understood in America is not understood outside Christianity does not make it any less true, than the fact that Freedom of Speech, religion, and a vote for all are Biblical principles found nowhere else, makes these institutions unfit for American experience. Abortion therefore, besides its irreconcilability with current American law, ravages the very foundation of civilization. It has brought America to the brink of collapse, and given enough more time, will inevitably finish her off.

Appendix H:
Judge Clark's Case against Abortion

First, a summary of the ruling: then, several pages of excerpts. For the complete ruling, see www.saltshaker.us/SLIC/1992%20-07-20PaulClarkWichita.pdf

SUMMARY: Judge Clark said the evidence of Elizabeth Tilson's world-renowned expert witnesses established that life begins at conception, so that killing life before birth is a great harm:

> I will find Mrs. Tilson's evidence proffered through witnesses Lejeune, Hilgers, McMillan and Rue relevant to the issue here. The entire evidence of her experts is admitted. The evidence proves that the medical and scientific communities dealing with the subject matter on a daily basis are of opinion that life in homo sapiens begins at conception; and harm is the result of termination of life under most circumstances.
>
> That opinion—as a proposition based on intuition in earlier years—has always been foundation for the public policy in Kansas (*State vs. Harris, Supra; Joy vs. Brown, Supra*).

Judge Clark conceded that "*Roe* and its progeny" made a woman's choice to kill her baby legal, and gave a killing corporation a right to do its business without interference.

> P. 8: <u>Roe vs. Wade</u> (401 U.S. 113, 35 L.Ed 147, 93 S.Ct. 705) set the law whereby the Constitution guarantees a right whereby a pregnant woman, during the first trimester, may make a decision whether to terminate her pregnancy without governmental interference in that decision.
>
> P. 10: The City of Wichita's ordinance prohibiting "criminal trespass" (Ex. 4, Supra) protects the right of a corporation and its business invitees to do lawful business without interference.
>
> P. 20-21: Roe, Supra, and Doe, Supra, declared a

qualified constitutional right protecting a woman "from unduly burdensome interference with her freedom to decide whether to terminate her pregnancy," (Casey vs. Planned Parenthood....

P. 24: Any corporation authorized to do business and its clientele still have a right to do lawful business without interference under the law of this state.

BUT "*Roe* and its progeny" did not reverse the policy of Kansas, that abortion other than to save the life of the mother is a "wrongful act", making termination of pregnancy normally a "harm".

[P. 23] Neither *Roe vs. Wade, Supra;* its companion case *Doe vs. Bolton, Supra*; nor their progeny (*Webster vs. Reproductive Services et al, Supra; Casey vs. Planned Parenthood of Southeastern Penn., Supra*) worked to abrogate the public policy of the state of Kansas that the voluntary act of prematurely terminating a pregnancy without qualifications is a wrongful act.

[That is, none of those cases undermined Kansas' policy that abortion is a "wrongful act" - a "harm" - except when it is to save the life of the mother.]

(Cont'd) Those federal cases only qualified that policy by constitutionally guaranteeing to each woman in Kansas or elsewhere a "qualified right" (Roe, Doe, Webster, Casey) to decide whether to terminate her pregnancy.

[That is, those cases gave women a legal right to do it, but it's still legally recognizable as wrong.]

In other words, just because it is legal, that doesn't make it harmless. Harms are made legal all the time.

The City argues (Page 4, above) that *Roe vs. Wade, Supra,* declares that the voluntary termination of pregnancy cannot be a harm because it is legal. That is too broad an application.

In other words, the Supreme Court made abortion legal – the Court stopped *states* from stopping abortion with criminal laws. But the Court could not make abortion *harmless* (in fact *Roe* explicitly declined to rule on whether abortion is a "harm", saying the justices were "in no position to speculate" about that) – and thus *Roe* has no effect on the right of *individuals* to prevent abortions. The "harm" of abortion is legally recognizable as serious enough to justify stopping it.

Another argument for the inapplicability of *Roe* to the restraint of individual life-saving is that the Bill of Rights, in whose "penumbra" the *Roe* court imagined they spotted a right to kill babies, has not one provision that restrains any *individual*. All its provisions protect *individuals* from their *government!*

> P. 9-10: The Bill of Rights, federal and state, is law that protects the people from their government. Neither was meant to protect people from fellow citizens (<u>Burdeau vs. McDowell</u>. 41 S.Ct. 574, 65 L.Ed. 1048, 256 U.S. 465).

So the Necessity Defense justifies Tilson's interruption of the corporation's business, *without affecting the law that makes that business legal.*

> [P. 25] Mrs. Tilson's wrongful act is forgiven in the eyes of the law under the doctrine of justification by necessity. She is discharged from further responsibility in the case.
>
> The City's ordinance is still the law....

Judge Clark disposed of the objection that Elizabeth Tilson had political alternatives to breaking the law to save lives:

> She has peacefully assembled to petition her government for a redress of what she felt to be a grievance. She has exhausted her alternative remedies. The City's point is not well taken.

Although Judge Clark doesn't develop the point, he insinuates that the abortionist does not have "clean hands" in the matter, being himself beyond the protection of *Roe v.*

147

Wade:

> I will find that the City's evidence (Through Ms. Riggs) meant to show that the corporation's services were sold only to those pregnant women in the first trimester of pregnancy is not credible. The same is disbelieved.

FAIRLY COMPLETE EXCERPTS:

Excerpts from Wichita District Judge Paul Clark's ruling in favor of Elizabeth Tilson, July 21, 1992, Case No. 91 MC 108, "Memorandum of Opinion Following Bench Trial". (The complete ruling is posted at www.Saltshaker.US/SLIC/PaulClark)

(While blocking the abortionist's doors) she did not say nor do anything except perhaps participate in a song of praise for or a prayer to the same "Supreme Judge of the World" upon which Messrs. Hancock, Adams, Jefferson, Franklin, Clark and their colleagues at Philadelphia in 1776 relied "for the rectitude of [their] intentions..." (The Declaration of Independence, Kansas and United States Constitution Pg. 159 @ 160, 1988). The police say that they heard such activity....

Mrs. Tilson takes umbrage at any attempt to label her an "abortion protester." She says that she was not there to protest anything. Her goal was to "rescue" the unborn, their progenators and the families of both from the ill effects that might follow termination of pregnancy.

...She admits [what she did but] asks for a ruling of not guilty, however, claiming at Page 3 of her trial brief that:

> "...she was justified to go on the property ... as such entrance was necessary to protect human life and health. ... such entry ... is a lesser evil than either the taking of the lives of the babies ... or the potential harm to the mothers, and other affected persons ..."

The defense of justification relieves her of criminal responsibility under the facts here, she says.

The city contests the applicability of the defense of justification by necessity. At page 12 of its trial brief, the reason is stated in this way:

> "... because the harm (abortion) sought to be prevented is not a legally recognized injury ..., there were legal alternatives available to the defendant. ... the legislature has effectively excluded the prevention of abortion as a justification for the commission of a crime. ..."

At common law, justification by necessity developed as a doctrine whereby under certain factual situations, the perpetrator is forgiven an act otherwise criminal.

The mindset supporting the doctrine is set out in a part of Magna Carta (15 June 1215) where those men, who for one brief moment of time were charged with administering the government, reaffirmed by mutual agreement that:

> "No free man shall be seized, or imprisoned or dispossessed, or outlawed, or in any way destroy; nor will we condemn him, nor will we commit him to prison excepting by the legal judgment of his peers, or by the law of the land. To none will we sell, to none will we deny, to none will we delay right or justice."

The first ten amendments to the Constitution of the United States (25 September 1789) are but affirmation of these basic principles of freedom following more than 500 years of practice. All 16 amendments following find root there.

...The common law is whence our jurisprudence evolved in North America. In Kansas our Supreme Court said:

> "From the beginning of our history, the common law of England has been the basis of the law... and except as modified by constitutional or statutory provisions, by judicial decisions, or by the wants and needs of the people, it has continued to remain the law of this state." ....

In <u>Perkins on Criminal Law</u> (Foundation Press, Inc., 1957) at Page 848, justification by necessity is explained in this manner:

> "Where the act done was necessary or reasonably seemed to be necessary, to save life or limb or health, and did not in itself in any way endanger life or limb or health, the exculpatory effect of the necessity is too clear for argument; but where the offense charged is not one of particular gravity, the courts have not hesitated to recognize necessity as an excuse where the danger, or apparent danger to be avoided was less serious in its nature. Thus one unavoidably caught in a traffic jam is not guilty of violating the law which forbids stopping at that place, and a carrier has not violated the statute which requires a specified coach if the failure to provide that coach on a particular trip was due to an unavoidable accident which ordinary prudence could not have guarded against. These are not situations, it should be noted, where no choice was possible. The driver elected to stop rather than proceed until his vehicle was brought to a halt by actual contact with the one ahead, and the carrier could have avoided sending the train without the specified coach by sending no trial [sic] at all. The harm threatened in these cases, moreover, is not to life or limb or health. The motorist is excused for stopping even if proceeding so slowly that the bumper-to-bumper contact would cause neither personal injury nor appreciable property damage, and the carrier would have suffered only only financial loss by complying with the letter of the law. In another case, it may be added, the court reversed a conviction of killing a deer in violation of the game laws because it was shown this killing was reasonably necessary to prevent substantial damage to defendant's propertly."

The federal courts recognize the doctrine (<u>U.S. v. Simpson</u>, 460 F.2d 515, 9th Cir. 1972; <u>U.S. vs. Seward</u>, 687 P.2d 1270, 10th Cir. 1983)

Neither party cites Kansas case law treating the doctrine....

[P. 7] The City claims that "the legislature has

effectively excluded the prevention of abortion as a justification for the commission of a crime...." (Page 12, trial brief) At closing argument, the City pointed to H.B. 2646 Sec. 6(a)(2) where the legislature did in part define criminal trespass as:

> "...(2) entering or remaining on private and or structure in a manner that interferes with access to or from any health care facility ..."

That law (H.B. 2646) is effective from and after July 1, 1992. It does not have the effect on this case that the City would give it.

[P. 8] I will this day hold that the doctrine of justification by necessity was legally recognized in the State of Kansas on August 3, 1991. The roots are anchored in common law. The purpose is to protect the people from their government by an assurance that in all matters right will be done and justice rendered.

The doctrine is found at A.L.I. Model Penal Code Sec. 3.02. It is instructive as a guide for practical application. These are the elements:

> "(1) Conduct which the actor believes to be necessary to avoid a harm or evil to himself or to another is justifiable, provided that: (a) the harm or evil sought to be avoided by such conduct is greater than that sought to be prevented by the law defining the offense charged; (b) neither the Code nor other law defining the offense provides exceptions or defenses dealing with the specific situation involved; and (c) a legislative purpose to exclude the justification claimed does not otherwise plainly appear."

As aforesaid, Mrs. Tilson admits violation of the ordinance. No "legislative purpose to exclude" the offense is applicable to this set of facts. No exceptions or defenses are set out in the ordinance or other law.

The provisions of (b) and (c) above contain no exclusion of the doctrine. We will then turn to the provisions of (a).

The "harm or evil" sought to be avoided by Mrs. Tilson through her violation of law on August 3, 1991 was the premature termination of pregnancy and the harm that may flow therefrom.

The City argues that premature termination of pregnancy is not "harm or evil" nor is it a wrong to be compared with Mrs. Tilson's defiance of a police order because <u>Roe vs. Wade</u> (401 U.S. 113, 35 L.Ed 147, 93 S.Ct. 705) set the law whereby the Constitution guarantees a right whereby a pregnant woman, during the first trimester, may make a decision whether to terminate her pregnancy without governmental interference in that decision.

Those are the positions. To resolve the issue, we need to explore some general concepts of constitutional law, the history of law in Kansas and apply the same to the facts.

Every female at the sige of occurrence on August 3, 1991 had a right to make an individual decision whether to terminate pregnancy (<u>Roe vs. Wade, Supra</u>). Any member of the public there that day had a right to purchase a service from the corporation.

The corporation had a right to do business there on that day. It was so authorized by the State of Kansas.

Mrs Tilson had a 1st Amendment (United States Constitution) and Section 11 (Kansas Constitution) right to express her opinion on any subject concerning governmental action or nonaction. Her opinion could be expressed by action, nonaction or words (<u>Texas vs. Johnson,</u> 491 U.S. 397, 105 L.Ed.2d 342, 109 S.Ct. 2533; <u>U.S. vs. Eichman, et al</u>, 496 U.S. , 110 L.Ed.2d 287, 110 S.Ct.).

None of these individual rights are subservient to others. As with all constitutionally protected rights, each here involved has parameters (<u>Burson vs. Freeman</u>, 504 U.S.   , 119 L.Ed.2d 5, 112 S.Ct. Decided May 26, 1992; <u>Michigan Department of Police vs. Sitz, et al</u>, 496 U.S.   , 110 L.Ed.2d 412, 110 S.Ct.   (1990); <u>Roe vs. Wade, Supra;</u>

State vs. Cleveland, 205 Kan. 426, 469 P.2d 251; State vs. Great American Theatre, 227 Kan. 633, 608 P.2d 951; State vs. Crouch, 192 Kan. 602, 389 P.2d 824). The Bill of Rights, federal and state, [P. 10] is law that protects the people from their government. Neither was meant to protect people from fellow citizens (Burdeau vs. McDowell. 41 S.Ct. 574, 65 L.Ed. 1048, 256 U.S. 465).

The City of Wichita's ordinance prohibiting "criminal trespass" (Ex. 4, Supra) protects the right of a corporation and its business invitees to do lawful business without interference. In this particular case, the ordinance can be viewed as establishing parameters on Mrs. Tilson's right to be on business property for the purpose of expressing an opinion.

When Mrs. Tilson remained on the corporate property "in defiance of an order ... to leave such premises ... personally communicated to ..." her by the police, she violated the law. The question then becomes is her violation excused by the doctrine of justification by necessity under the facts here presented?

Mrs. Tilson points out that her act of defiance "did not in itself in any way endanger life, limb or health" (Perkins, Supra).

The City's evidence proves that the corporation did busines on August 3, 1991, but only after Mrs. Tilson was removed by the police.

The defense evidence shows that the corporation lost business that day, perhaps indirectly by Mrs. Tilson's conduct. A Ms. Tina McLaughlin gave evidence at trial. She said that she went to the scene of the occurrence on the day Mrs. Tilson was there. She was a member of the public, there to have a medical procedure done for the purpose of terminating her pregnancy. Ms. McLaughlin left scene because of the activity there before she had the medical procedure. She later made contact by telephone with Mrs. Tilson's colleagues and [P. 11] made an appointment to talk. After the talk, she reversed her decision to terminate her pregnancy prematurely. Her pregnancy went to term, whereupon a normal, healthy girl was delivered. The girl is named Destiny. She sat on her mother's lap during the testimony of her mother.

The overall evidence proves that those members of the public there that day as business invitees were at the least inconvenienced and at the most, obstructed because of Mrs. Tilson's act. No one was prevented from carrying out a decision to terminate a pregnancy that day, so far as the evidence shows.

Mrs. Tilson was on that day a housewife and mother from Wichita, Kansas, whose formal education terminated prior to the 12th grade, but who has been awarded a Kansas State High School Equivalencey Diploma (K.S.A. 72-4530; K.A.R. 91-10-1). Her training in obstetrics and gynecology is limited to the practical gained through experiences as a mother and woman, so far as the evidence here shows. As to the field of human genetics and histogenesis of homo sapiens while en ventre sa mere, her knowledge comes from a magazine article (Life Before Birth, ULifeU, April 30, 1965; Defense Exhibit B). Practical experience gained by personal actions and observations in human relationships constitute her pychological knowledge. So far as the evidence here proves, she probably has limited knowledge of and little interest in concepts of constitutional law evolving as American jurisprudence from the common law of England.

She sees through her heart. Her inner voice tells her that the premature termination of pregnancy by surgical procedure terminates life. By intuition, she maintains that it can also cause great psychological harm to "the woman, the father of the baby, the grandparents, and brothers and sisters involved." It was intuition that drove her actions on August 3, 1991. She did what she thought was right, but it is the law of the land from where the light comes to judge whether or not her actions were justified under law.

To prove her point that the service offered by the corporation on that day terminated life, she offered the testimony of experts. From Paris, France, she called to testify one Dr. Jerome Lejeune. He holds doctorate degrees in medicine and science. He has for the last 40 years divided his time between the practice of medicine and research of human genetics in a teaching environment. His credentials prove that he is at this time recognized by the scientific community as the world's expert in the field of human genetics. Pathology of the chromosome is his particular specialty.

Dr. Lejeune is of the opinion that human beings (homo sapiens) begin life at conception. He gave as reason for his opinion certain scientific facts. A few are set out here. When the ovum donated by the woman is fertilized by the sperm from the man, all ingredients and all instruction necessary to make a human being are therein contained. The new human has a unique genetic organization. The mother is the sole source of shelter and vital fluids for the term of the pregnancy. This need not be the biological mother; any woman's body will do so long as the recipient's body is in the same stage of ovulation as the donor. The new being forms all its own body systems, to include circulatory. It is "a little man in a space capsule," Dr. Lejeune says.

[P. 13] In further support of his opinion, Dr. Lejeune points out that tests done after the fertilized ovum has divided one time shows the protein of the new being is distinct from its progenitors.

The "D.N.A. bar code" - now popular in criminal identification (K.S.A. 1991 Supp. 21-2511) is present after the eighth division from fertilization. At 90 days from fertilization, all systems are fully developed. The fingerprints and palmprints are present and could be taken and recorded at that time. Those will be the same forever. Growth of the new being and its various organs continue for

25 years after fertilization, the doctor testified.

Dr. Thomas Hilgers was called from Nebraska to give evidence. He is a medical doctor, certified as trained in obstetrics and gynecology. His specialty is reproductive medicine. He has 20 years experience in his profession. He has authored several books and scientific papers of significance in his field.

Dr. Hilgers opines that life for the human being begins at conception. Through him, certain exhibits were brought as evidence, meant to prove his point.

Exhibit D is a video tape made by the witness. It was nine years in production. It depicts scenes meant to demonstrate development of homo sapiens in utero from conception through a few minutes after normal, live birth. Sonogram is the primary tool used for the depiction of Exhibit D. All the subjects where sonography is used are live patients, pregnant at the time. It shows, among other things, considerable embryonic movement before the mother can feel it within her body. It shows fertilization, then heart beat at 16 days following.

[P. 14] The witness says that brain waves have been demonstrated at 42 days after fertilization in humans. His experience is that 12 weeks from fertilization, all normal, well-baby reflexes are present in the new being and at approximately 22 weeks gestational (20 weeks after fertilization) the body of the mother is not necessary for further life of the new human being, given modern medical techniques, Dr. Hilgers explains.

Vincent Montgomery Rue, Ph.D. was called by Mrs. Tilson. His qualifications fill 13 pages (Defendant's Exhibit O). He is recognized in his field as one of the world's leading experts on the post-psychological ramifications, diagnosis of mental illness arising therefrom and treatment therefore of those persons so affected following the voluntary premature termination of pregnancy. His patients over the years have included mothers, fathers, siblings and grandparents suffering in the symptoms ascribed to a diagnosis of post-traumatic stress disorder (D.S.M. 111 309.81 Axis IV (Pg. 26) – Physical Injury or Illness as a Stressor). It follows a feeling of guilt or a sense of loss, Dr. Rue says, both natural occurrences in the psyche of human beings.

From Jackson, Mississippi, Mrs. Tilson called a physician named Beverly McMillan, who specializes in obstetrics-gynecology. She has performed numerous procedures that result in the premature termination of pregnancy. By testimony and demonstrative is, [sic] she explained the four medical procedures used to terminate pregnancy. She testified that each procedure results in termination of life at the time or within minutes of the time of the procedure. According to Mrs. Tilson, the purpose of this evidence is to show the threatened harm she was [P. 15] trying to stop was imminent.

What Mrs. Tilson has proven by her witnesses LeJeune, Hilgers and McMillan is that genetically, histologically, obstetrically, and gynecologically, the scientific community is of opinion that life in homo sapiens bgegins at conception and continues on for an average life span unless interrupted by trauma or disease.

With witness Rue, Mrs. Tilson roves the scientific community is of opinion that great harm can occur to any number of persons joined in interest following termination of pregnancy other than by natural birth.

This scientific evidence of Mrs. Tilson's demonstrates that the scientific community has proved throug research and discovery what Mrs. Tilson believes by intuition.

The City's objection thereto is that this evidence is not relevant to the issue being litigated (K.S.A. 60-401(b)). **The City does not contest the truth thereof.**

To determine the relevancy of Mrs. Tilson's evidence, as well as the validity of her defense, it is necessary to note the law applicable on August 3, 1991 at the place of occurrence, particularly that pertaining to the issue of whether or not the voluntary premature termination of pregnancy is a wrong or harm with which Mrs. Tilson's defiance can be compared.

The voluntary premature termination of pregnancy was at common law deemed a criminal act. William Blackstone (1723-80) wrote that:

> "To kill a child in its mother's womb is now no murder, but a great misprision..." (W. England 198).

At 1 Hale's P.C. 429 (cited in <u>State vs. Harris</u>, 90 Kan. 807, P.), the law of England in the year 1670 is stated in this way at Page 812:

> "But if a woman be with child and any gives her a potion to destroy the child within her, and she takes it and it works so strongly that it kills her, this is murder ..."

The Kansas Supreme Court in <u>State vs. Harris</u> was interpreting a statute thathad been the law of Kansas since territory days whereby the legislature made "it a misdemeanor willfully to administer to any pregnant woman any medicine, drug or substance or use any instrument or means with intent thereby to produce abortion or the miscarriage of such woman, unless necessary or medically advised to be necessary to preserve her life," (Terr. Stat. 1855, Ch. 48, Sec. 39; G.S. 1868 Ch. 31, Sec. 44; R.S. 1923 21-437; G.S. 1949 21-437).

Our Supreme Court reasoned in <u>Harris</u> that the act of intentionally terminating a pregnancy was one mala in se. [Evil all by itself, even if it weren't illegal.] In support of such reasoning, other cases were cited with the opinion. Here is a part:

> "The act was not only immoral, violative of the law of nature and deliberate in character, but reckless of life and wrongful <u>per se</u>" (At Page 814)

> "**At common law life is not only sacred but it is inalienable.** To attempt to produce an abortion or miscarriage, except when necessary to save the life of the

mother under advice of medical men, is an unlawful act and has always been regarded as fatal to the child and dangerous to the mother."

[P. 17] It is instructive to note the court's reference to the beginning of life at Page 817:

> "The arbitrary refusal of the common law to regard the fetus as alife in such cases until quick was based on no sound physiological principles. Beck makes it plain that the movement recognized by the mother, and which is supposed to prove that her unborn child is alive, is merely one evidence of life, whereas unless life had existed long before the most diastrous consequences to the mother must have already been suffered (1 Beck Medical Jurisprudence 464-467).

Mrs. Tilson's scientific evidence seems to prove what the Supreme Court of Kansas believed in 1913.

The same statutory law interpreted in <u>Harris</u>, <u>Supra</u>, became G.S. 1923, 21-437.

Here is the statute defining Kansas state policy:

> "Every physician or other person who shall willfully administer to any pregnant woman any medicine, drug or substance whatsoever or shall use or employ any instrument or means whatsoever with intent thereby to procure abortion or the miscarriage of any such woman, unless the same shall have been necessary to preserve the life of such woman, or shall have been advised by a physician to be necessary for that purpose, shall upon conviction be adjudged guilty of a misdemeanor and punished by imprisonment in the county jail not exceeding one year, or by fine not exceeding five hundred dollars or by both such fine and imprisonment."

The same state policy was codified at G.S. 1949, 21-437.

The Supreme Court of Kansas in 1953 at <u>Joy vs. Brown</u> (173 Kan. 823, 252 P.2d 889 @ Page 839) noted that the above statute was one of three enacted:

> "For the purpose of protecting the life not only of the unborn child, but that of the mother ..."

"The state has a vital interest" in both, the court said [P. 18] in the same opinion.

The statute was repealed in 1969 (Chap. 180, Page 503, 1969 Ses. Laws of Kansas).

July 1, 1970 (Ses. Laws of Kan. 1969, Chap. 180, Sec. 21-3407) is the effective date of the legislative enactment that replaced G.S. 1949 21-437, _Supra_. The replacement statute provided that:

> "(1) Criminal abortion is the purposeful and unjustifiable termination of the pregnancy of any female other than by a live birth. (2) A person licensed to practice medicine and surgery is justified in terminating a pregnancy if he believes there is substantial risk that a continuance of the pregnancy would impair the physical or mental health of the mother or that the child would be born with physical or mental defect, or that the pregancy resulted from rape, incest or other felonious intercourse; and either: (a) Three persons licensed to practice medicine and surgery, one of whom may be the person performing the abortion, have certified in writing their belief in the justifying circumstances, and have filed such certificate prior to the abortion in the hospital licensed by the state board of health and accredited by the joint commission on accredidation of hospitals where it is to be performed or in such other place as may be designated by law; or (b) an emergency exists which requires that such abortion be performed immediately in order to preserve the life of the mother. (3) For the purpose of this section pregnancy means that condition of a female from the date of conception to the birth of her child (2) Of this section all illicit intercourse with a female under the age of sixteen (16) years shall be deemed felonious. (5) Criminal abortion is a class D felony."

K.S.A. 65-443 is of interest. It goes to the general policy of the State of Kansas. There it is provided that:

> "No person shall be required to perform or participate in medical procedures which result in the termination of a pregnancy and the refusal of any person to perform or participate in those medical procedures shall not be a basis [P. 19] for civil liability to any person. No hospital,

hospital administrator or governing board of any hospital shall terminate the employment of, prevent or impair the practice or occupation of or impose any other sanction on any person because of such person's refusal to perform or participate in the termination."

Another statute illustrative of state policy in the area is K.S.A. 65-2837. That part pertinent here is this:

"(b) 'unprofessional conduct' means:
(5) performing, procuring or aiding and abetting in the performance or procurement of a criminal abortion."

The statute applies to all persons licensed by the State Board of Healing Arts (K.S.A. 65-2812).

In 1972 the United States District Court for the District of Kansas declared (339 F.Supp.986) Section 2(a) of K.S.A. 21-3407 violative of the equal protection clause of the 14th Amendment to the U.S. Constitution.

It is not necessary t decide here what, if any, ramifications the federal district court's opinion may have had on prosecutions for violation of the statute in Kansas, because in January, 1973, the Supreme Court of the United States handed down <u>Roe vs. Wade</u>, <u>Supra</u>, and its companion case, <u>Doe vs. Bolton</u>, (410 U.S. 179, 35 L.Ed.2d 201, 93 S.Ct. 739, reh den 410 U.S. 959, 35 L.Ed.2d 694, 93 S.Ct. 1410).

Insofar as concerns the resolution of the issue here, the ruling in <u>Roe</u> is best summarized by the reporter of decisions at Page 155, Paragraph 3, where it is written that:

"State criminal abortion laws, like those involved here, that except from criminality only [p. 20] a life-saving procedure on the mother's behalf without regard to the stage of her pregnancy and other interests involved violate the Due Process Clause of the Fourteenth Amendment, which protects against state action the right to privacy, including a woman's qualified right to terminate her pregnancy. Though the State cannot ovride that right, it has legitimate interests in protecting both the pregnant woman's health and the potentiality of human life, each of which interests grows and reaches a "compelling" point at various stages of the woman's approach to term. ...(c) For the stage subsequent to viability the State, in promoting its interest in the potentiality of human life, may if it chooses, regulate and even proscribe, abortion except where necessary, in appropriate medical judgment, for the preservation of the life or health of the mother."

<u>Doe</u>, <u>Supra</u>, rendered unconstitutional any attempts by the legislature to impose into the decision to terminate a pregnancy the concurrence of physicians or groups other than the pregnant woman's personal physician and herself.

When K.S.A. 21-3407 is viewed in light of <u>Doe</u>, <u>Supra</u>, with the guidance of that rule of statutory construction laid down in <u>State vs. Trudell</u> (243 Kan. 29, 755 P.2d 511) where, in part, at Syl. 2, the court said that "... a criminal statute with its punitive effect must be strictly construed against the state ..." it is clear that the statute is unconstitutional on its face.

The legal history of Kansas teaches that as a matter of public policy, the act of voluntarily terminating a pregnancy prior to term has been considered a wrongful act except when done under strict guidelines. The purpose is to protect the life of the unborn child and the mother (<u>Joy vs. Brown</u>, <u>Supra</u>). <u>Roe</u>, <u>Supra</u>, and <u>Doe</u>, <u>Supra</u>, declared a qualified constitutional right protecting a woman "from unduly [P. 21] burdensome interference with her freedom to decide whether to terminate her pregnancy," (<u>Casey vs. Planned Parenthood of Southeastern Penn., et al</u>, 1992 W.L. 14546, decided June 29, 1992); but left the state government with a legitimate interest in both the woman and the premature life during the entire period of pregnancy (<u>Roe</u>, <u>Supra</u>; <u>Webster vs. Reproductive Health Serv.</u>, 492 U.S. 490, 106 L.Ed.2d 410, 109 S.Ct. 3040 (1989); <u>Casey</u>, <u>Supra</u>; see also <u>Joy vs. Brown</u>, <u>Supra</u>).

It may be said that on August 3, 1991, a pregnant woman in the state of Kansas had an unqualified right to undergo a medical procedure meant to terminate her pregnancy at any time prior to term. <u>Roe vs Wade</u>, <u>Supra</u>, and <u>Doe vs. Bolton,</u> <u>Supra</u> (1973) rendered K.S.A. 21-3407, Supra, constitutionally void. Perhaps that is why there were no reported cases of prosecution thereunder during the 20 year life of the statute. The legislature took no action during the 18 years following. The Supreme Court of Kansas, during the same time period, did not act on the particular issue but did find that the unborn are not human being at any stage of pregnancy so far as the law of criminal homicide is concerned (<u>State vs. Green</u>, 245 Kan. 398; 781 P.2d 678; <u>State vs. Trudell</u>, <u>Supra</u>).

Mrs. Tilson says that this unqualified right to terminate a pregnancy at any stage contradicted the state's historical public policy. That is the wrong with which her defiance ofhe City's criminal trespass ordinance must be compared, she maintains.

In addition to the argument that the woman's right to terminate is not a wrong, the City argues (Tr. brief, <u>Supra</u>) that alternatives to law-breaking were available to Mrs. Tilson on that day. [P. 22]

Mrs. Tilson's evidence on that point proves that she had, prior to August 3, 1991, made contact with the legislature, federal and state, by telephone, writing and lobbying. She has protested the government's action in <u>Roe vs. Wade</u>, <u>Supra</u>, and the Kansas state government's nonaction following. **She has peacefully assembled to petition her government for a redress of what she felt to be a grievance. She has exhausted her alternative remedies. The City's point is not well taken.**

I will find that the City's evidence (Through Ms. Riggs) meant to show that the corporation's services were sold only to those pregnant women in the first trimester of pregnancy is not credible. The same is disbelieved.

I will find Mrs. Tilson's evidence proffered

through witnesses Lejeune, Hilgers, McMillan and Rue relevant to the issue here. The entire evidence of her experts is admitted. The evidence proves that the medical and scientific communities dealing with the subject matter on a daily basis are of opinion that life in homo sapiens begins at conception; and harm is the result of termination of life under most circumstances.

That opinion—as a proposition based on intuition in earlier years—has always been foundation for the public policy in Kansas (<u>State vs. Harris</u>, <u>Supra</u>; <u>Joy vs. Brown</u>, <u>Supra</u>).

The City argues (Page 4, above) that <u>Roe vs. Wade</u>, <u>Supra</u>, declares that the voluntary termination of pregnancy cannot be a harm because it is legal. That is too broad an application.

[P. 23] Neither <u>**Roe vs. Wade**</u>, <u>**Supra**</u>; its companion case <u>**Doe vs. Bolton**</u>, <u>**Supra**</u>; nor their progeny (<u>**Webster vs. Reproductive Services et al**</u>, <u>**Supra**</u>; <u>**Casey vs. Planned Parenthood of Southeastern Penn.**</u>, <u>**Supra**</u>) worked to abrogate the public policy of the state of Kansas that the voluntary act of prematurely terminating a pregnancy without qualifications is a wrongful act. *[That is, none of those undermined Kansas policy that abortion is a "wrongful act" - a "harm" - unless it is to save the life of the mother.]* Those federal cases only qualified that policy by constitutionally guaranteeing to each woman in Kansas or elsewhere a "qualified right" (<u>Roe</u>, <u>Doe</u>, <u>Webster</u>, <u>Casey</u>) to decide whether to terminate her pregnancy. *[That is, those cases gave women a right to do it, but it's still wrong.]*

The act of termination of pregnancy without qualification, always violative of state policy as mala in se, was not by statute prohibited on August 3, 1991, given the peculiar state of affairs caused by the action of federal government (<u>Roe vs. Wade</u>), combined with the inaction of the state government.

The wrongfulness of the act (i.e. unqualified termination of pregnancy) is what must be compared with the wrongfulness of Mrs. Tilson's act of interfering with the right of a corporation and its invitees to engage in lawful business.

The courts in Kansas by tradition have been a place where citizens find a forum at which all with grievances can be heard, their actions measured by proper application of law, under an assurance that right be done and justice administered in every instance.

I will find that the doctrine of justification by necessity is applicable to the facts of this case. The facts of the case must be viewed in light of the law on August 3, 1991.

[P. 24] The doctrine is applied by weighing the two wrongs, while comparing the harm each seeks to avoid. The weighing must be done while balancing constitutionally guaranteed activites associated with these acts. The weighing and balancing must be done in light of the peculiar facts of the individual case.

The legislature of our state has acted since and perhaps in part because of Mrs. Tilson's defiance. It has by House Bill No. 2646 (effective July 1, 1992) reaffirmed the state's policy discussed above by exercising control of and regulating the act of voluntarily terminating a pregnancy prior to live birth. The legislature addressed the situation where citizens might do the same act as Mrs. Tilson did here.

Since Mrs. Tilson's defiance, the Supreme Court of the United States has reaffirmed the constitutional right of a woman to "decide whether to terminate her pregnancy," (<u>Casey</u>, <u>Supra</u>) prior to viability of the new life.

Any corporation authorized to do business and its

clientele still have a right to do lawful business without interference under the law of this state.

Insofar as concerns the present matter, keeping the tradition that in all matters, right be done and justice administered, Mrs. Tilson's wrongful act done by violating the ordinance (<u>Supra</u>) was done to prevent a greater "harm" to society at large than that harm those running the city government for a time sought to prevent by enactment and enforcement of the ordinance.

[P. 25] Mrs. Tilson's wrongful act is forgiven in the eyes of the law under the doctrine of justification by necessity. She is discharged from further responsibility in the case.

The City's ordinance is still the law, even though certain application of it may be subject to interpretation in light of the provisions of H.B. 2646, but that is a subject for another day.

As in all legal matters, this case is decided on the peculiar facts of this particular case. It is not dispositive of any other matter whatsoever.

The length of this opinion can be attributed to the important [sic] of the subject matter addressed.

Judge Paul W. Clark, July 20, 1992.

Appendix I:
Dorland's Illustrated Medical Dictionary cited in *Roe*

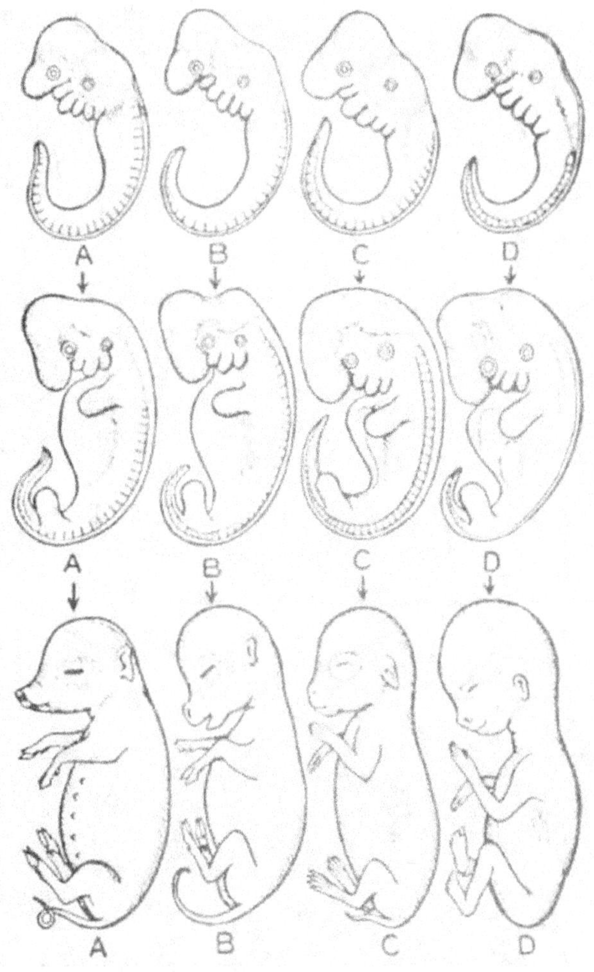

Roe v. Wade, p. 157: "B. The pregnant woman cannot be isolated in her privacy. She carries an embryo and, later, a fetus, if one accepts the medical definitions of the developing young in the human uterus. See Dorland's Illustrated Medical Dictionary 478-479, 547 (24th ed. 1965)."

Four mammalian embryos at various stages of development: A, hog; B, calf; C, rabbit; D, human. (Villee: from Romanes' "Darwin and After Darwin," after Haeckel, with the permission of the Open Court Publishing Company.)

embryo (em-bre-o) [Gr. *embryon*]. 1. The early or developing stage of any organism, especially the developing product of fertilization of an egg. In the human, the embryo is generally considered to be the developing organism from one week after conception to the end of the second month. 2. The element in the seed of plants which develops into a new individual. **hexacanth e.,** the embryo of *Taenia saginata* as found in the intestinal tract of cattle. **presomite e.,** the embryo at any stage prior to the appearance of the first somite. **previllous e.,** the embryo at any stage prior to the appearance of the chorionic villi. **somite e.,** the embryo at any stage between the appearances of the first and the last somites. **Spee's e.,** an embryo described by Spee as being between one and two weeks old. **Wilms's e.** See under *tumor*.

p. 547

fetus (fe'tus) [L.]. The unborn offspring of any viviparous animal; the developing young in the human uterus after the end of the second month. Before 8 weeks it is called an embryo; it becomes an infant when it is completely outside the body of the mother, even before the cord is cut. **f. acardi'acus,** acardius. **f. amor'phus,** holoacardius amorphus. **calcified f.,** lithopedion. **f. compres'sus,** f. papyraceus. **harlequin f.,** a fetus with congenital ichthyosis. **f. in fe'-tu,** a small, imperfect fetus, incapable of independent life, contained within the body of another fetus, the autosite. **mummified f.,** a shriveled and dried-up fetus. **paper-doll f., papyraceous f.,** f. papyraceus. **f. papyra'-ceus,** a dead fetus pressed flat by the growth of a living twin. **parasitic f.,** an incomplete minor fetus attached to a larger, more completely developed fetus, or autosite. **f. sanguinolen'-tis,** a dead fetus which has undergone maceration. **sireniform f.,** a sirenomelus, or sympus.

Dorland's Diagrams: Frauds

The following background on these diagrams, which were a key rationale for Roe to doubt that the unborn are "recognizably human", is posted at www.wayoflife.org/free_ebooks/downloads/Lying_Evolutionary_Art.pdf

(p. 8) Haeckel's Embryo Chart

It was Ernest Haeckel, Charles Darwin's most enthusiastic disciple in Germany, who devised the iconic embryo chart "proving" that at the embryonic stage man looks almost exactly like various types of animals.

He based this on his "law of recapitulation" (also called the biogenetic law) which stated that the human embryo goes through an evolutionary cycle during which it resembles a single-celled marine organism, then a worm, then a fish with gill slits, then a monkey with a tail, and finally a human. According to recapitulation, each creature repeats or recapitulates the entire alleged evolutionary history. Thus, the human embryo progresses from a single cell to a fish to an amphibian to a reptile to a mammal to an ape to a human.

Haeckel's embryo chart first appeared in print in 1866 in his book Generalle Morphologie der Organismen and in 1868 in The Natural History of Creation, and since then it has been republished in various forms in countless textbooks, journals, popular reports, and museums. It is still appearing in textbooks in the 21st century. One teacher said, "I have taught Jr. High Science for over 35 years. Every textbook from every major publisher I have ever seen has had Haeckel's embryos pictured and the text usually claims this as a proof for evolution" (http://creation.com/fraudrediscovered).

The influence of the embryo chart has been incalculable. Dr. Carl Werner testifies that he was confronted with Haeckel's embryo chart in his first class in medical school in 1977, and this convinced him that evolution is true.

> (p. 9) "These drawings were extremely compelling to me, especially the 'fact' that humans had gills and a tail. After this lecture, I found myself rapidly accepting evolution" (Evolution: The Grand Experiment, Vol. 2, p. 2).

The problem is that it is a grand scientific fraud, and it has been known by scientists to be a fraud since the 19th century!

Haeckel mislabeled embryos; he changed the size of embryos; he deleted parts; he added parts; he changed parts. For example, Haeckel took a drawing of a monkey embryo and removed its arms, legs, navel, heart, and yolksac to make it look like a fish embryo. He then labeled it "Embryo of a Gibbon in the fish-stage." In fact, it wasn't a gibbon even before it was doctored; it was some other type of ape.

For his "embryo of man in the fish-stage," Haeckel either removed or doctored more than half of the embryos' essential organs.

> "His piece de resistance was his manipulation of the drawing of a human embryo by Ecker. He changed the details of the human eye significantly, made the human posterior twice its actual length, took 2 mm off the head, and like the Macaque, removed the arms, legs and heart" ("The Life of Ernst Haeckel," Creation Worldview Ministries, http://www.creationworldview.org/ articles_view.asp?id=29).

Haeckel also brazenly ignored every facet of embryology that directly disproved his theory.

Haeckel's deception was exposed by Ludwig Rutimeyer, a professor at the University of Basel, who brought the matter to the attention of the university at Jena. Rutimeyer called the drawings "a sin against scientific truthfulness." Rutimeyer demonstrated that Haeckel had used the same

(p. 10) woodcut of a dog embryo three times to depict the supposed wormlike stage of what he called the embryos of a dog, a chicken, and a tortoise. Haeckel was convicted at a university tribunal and made a "confession" of sorts, but even his confession was a lie. He claimed that his draughtsman made the blunder, not acknowledging that he was the draughtsman (Russell Grigg, "Fraud Rediscovered," http://creation.com/fraud-rediscovered).

Haeckel's embryo fraud was also exposed early on by Wilhelm His, Sr., professor of anatomy at the university of Leipzig. His showed how that Haeckel had doctored his embryo charts to make them fit his theory and concluded that "anyone who engaged in such blatant fraud had forfeited all respect and that Haeckel had eliminated himself from the ranks of scientific research workers of any stature" (cited from Shawn Boonstra, Out of Thin Air, p. 47).

In spite of his deception and in spite of having been exposed, Haeckel continued as a professor at Jena for another 30 years and continued to promote his evolutionary deception far and wide.

In 1915 Haeckel's fraud was publicized in the book Haeckel's Frauds and Forgeries by Joseph Assmuth and Ernest Hull, which cited 19 authorities, but this carefully documented work was largely ignored by Darwinian scientists and educators in their zeal to disprove the Bible.

In the late 1990s, a team led by Michael Richardson, embryologist at St. George's Hospital Medical School, London, did extensive research into the embryo to test Haeckel's chart. Richardson gathered an international team of scientists who examined and photographed embryos of 39 different species at stages comparable to those depicted in

(p. 11) Haeckel's chart. Richardson concluded that Haeckel was "an embryonic liar." In a 1997 interview with Nigel Hawkes, Richardson said,

> 'THIS IS ONE OF THE WORST CASES OF SCIENTIFIC FRAUD. It's shocking to find that somebody one thought was a great scientist was deliberately misleading. It makes me angry … What he [Haeckel] did was to take a human embryo and copy it,

pretending that the salamander and the pig and all the others looked the same at the same stage of development. They don't ... These are fakes" (Nigel Hawkes' interview with Richardson, The Times, Aug. 11, 1997, p. 14).

A major error of Haeckel's embryo chart is the misidentification of "gill slits" on the human embryo. In fact, they are not gill slits at all. They have no respiratory function. "The so-called 'gill slits' are really wrinkles in the throat region. This body tissue becomes the palatine tonsils, middle ear canal, parathyroid gland, and thymus. ... These folds in the neck region of the mammalian embryo are not gills in any sense of the word and never have anything to do with breathing. They are merely inward folds, or wrinkles, in the neck region resulting from the sharply down-turned head and protruding heart of the developing embryo" (Alan Gillen, Body by Design, p. 33)

Child psychologist Benjamin Spock promoted Haeckel's doctrine of recapitulation in his popular books: "Each child as he develops is retracing the whole history of mankind, physically and spiritually, step by step. A baby starts off in the womb as a single tiny cell, just the way the first living thing appeared in the ocean. **Weeks later, as he lies in the amniotic fluid of the womb, he has gills like a fish...**" (Baby and Child Care, 1957, p. 223).

(p. 12) Haeckel's myth that the developing human embryo is animal-like has encouraged the modern abortion industry. Dr. Henry Morris wrote:

"We can justifiably charge this evolutionary nonsense of recapitulation with responsibility for the slaughter of helpless, pre-natal children--or at least for giving it a pseudo-scientific rationale" (The Long War against God, 1989, p. 139).

We have seen that Haeckel believed that the embryo is still in the evolutionary stage and not fully human. He said that it is "completely devoid of consciousness, is a pure 'reflex machine,' just like a lower vertebrate" (Weikart, p. 147). Thus, killing an unborn baby would be like killing an animal.

Haeckel taught that even the newborn child has no soul and therefore infanticide "cannot rationally be classed as murder" (Haeckel, The Wonders of Life, 1904, p. 21). For physically or mentally handicapped infants, Haeckel r e c o m m e n d e d " a s m a l l d o s e o f m o r p h i n e o r cyanide" (Weikart, p. 147).

In 1990, Carl Sagan and his wife, Ann Druyan, argued that abortion is ethical on the grounds that the fetus is not fully human until the sixth month. Taking Haeckel's recapitulation theory as fact, they claimed that the embryo begins as "a kind of parasite" and changes into something like a fish with "gill arches" and then becomes "reptilian" and finally "mammalian." By the end of the second month, the fetus "is still not quite human" ("The Question of Abortion: A Search for the Answers," Parade, April 22, 1990).

Biology textbooks continue to use the embryo chart as a major evidence for evolution. In some cases, they repeat Haeckel's doctrine of recapitulation, while it is more

(p. 13) common for the embryo chart to be used as an example of homology.

Biology: The Dynamics of Life by Merrill Publishing (1991) goes full bore for the doctrine of recapitulation:

"The fossil record indicates that aquatic, gill-breathing vertebrates preceded air-breathing land forms, and comparisons of embryos of different classes of vertebrates support this view of evolutionary change. An embryo is an organism in its earliest stages of development. In the early stages of embryo development of reptiles, birds, and mammals, a tail and gill slits can be observed. As you know, fish use gills to breathe under water. Fish embryos retain these structures; reptile, bird, and mammal embryos lose them as their development continues. In the human embryo, a tail is visible up to the sixth week of development. In humans, the tail disappears, but in fish, reptiles, and birds the tail is retained into maturity" (Biology: The Dynamics of Life, p. 202).

Modern Biology by Holt, Rinehart, and Winston (1999) features the chart on page 291 with the accompanying text: "Although modern embryologists have discovered that Haeckel exaggerated some features in his drawings, it is true that early embryos of many different vertebrate species look remarkably similar."

(Observe how casually this textbook whitewashes Haeckel's deception!)

The Prentice Hall *Biology* textbook of 2002, edited by Kenneth Miller and Joseph Levine, is another example of the use of the embryo chart as homology. On page 385 there are photos of the embryos of a chicken, turtle, and rat, with this statement: "In their early stages of development, chickens, turtles, and rats look similar, providing evidence that they shared a common ancestry."

(p. 14) While some evolutionists are using modified editions of Haeckel's embryonic chart, others have removed his name and attributed the chart to Karl Ernst von Baer, the discoverer of the female egg cell. This is a great error, because von Baer taught against Darwinian evolution as well as against Haeckel's doctrine of recapitulation!

This error of attributing embryonic recapitulation to von Baer actually started with Charles Darwin, who quoted him in On the Origin of Species.

"Darwin cited von Baer as the source of his embryological evidence, but at the crucial point Darwin distorted that evidence to make it fit his theory. Von Baer lived long enough to object to Darwin's misuse of his observations, and he was a strong critic of Darwinian evolution until his death in 1876" (Jonathan Wells, Icons of Evolution, p. 86).

In a 2008 documentary, Oxford atheist Richard Dawkins was still using the Haeckel embryo chart. Entitled "The Genius of Charles Darwin," the documentary was a three-part television production written and presented by Dawkins. It was first shown in August 2008 on British channel 4. The Haeckel chart appears in episode 1.

Science is self-correcting, we are told. But deceptive evolutionary icons such as the embryo chart, the horse chart, and the peppered moth have continued to be used decade after decade even though they have been debunked. In fact, the embryo chart was debunked more than a century age.

Great spiritual and moral damage can be done by the perpetuation of myths

Lying Evolutionary Art Copyright 2011 by David W. Cloud This edition February 3 2012 ISBN 78-1-58318-139-3 This book is published for free distribution in eBook format. It is available in PDF, MOBI (for Kindle, etc.), and ePUB formats from the Way of Life web site. We do not allow distribution of this book from other web sites. Published by Way of Life Literature PO Box 610368, Port Huron, MI 48061 866-295-4143 (toll free) - fbns@wayoflife.org www.wayoflife.org Canada: Bethel Baptist Church 4212 Campbell St. N., London Ont. N6P 1A6 519-652-2619

Part Three

Truth, Rhetoric, and the Bible

Contents

*About the Author <> That other stuff you've heard <>
A Singular Answer <> Interaction with Randall Terry*

Iowa's Heartbeat Defense

In 2018, Iowa became the third state, after Arkansas and North Dakota in 2013, to enact a Heartbeat Law which prohibits abortions after there is a detectable heartbeat, which abortionists complained to District Judge Huppert is about as soon as there is a detectable baby. (25 states have at least begun considering heartbeat laws as of April 2019.)

That would outlaw virtually all abortions, the abortionists whined. Which is exactly what prolifers had led each other to believe, which is why they worked so hard to get the law passed.

Yet in court, Iowa's defense was that its heartbeat law will not prevent one single abortion! It will simply make moms kill their babies before their babies' heartbeats are detected – before it is certain that their babies are people! ("Persons")

Two mysteries that day: Why did a prolife lawyer present a defense so contrary to what prolifers believed? and, Why didn't the 100 or so prolifers in the courtroom riot upon hearing that claim for the first time?

(To read the briefs, notes on the oral argument, and the ruling, see www.Saltshaker.US/SLIC/IowaHeartbeatArguments.pdf)

The Legal Labyrinth. Mr. Cannon had to deal with the "fundamental right" status which courts have given baby killing. Legislatures can only regulate a "fundamental right" by the "least restrictive means of achieving a compelling government interest", courts say. Completely banning it probably isn't the "least restriction" of it.

The "compelling government interest" has to be something other than "saving lives", so long as "the judiciary...is in no position to speculate" about whether unborn babies are "recognizably human" (*Roe's* definition of "persons"). like clean murder rooms, a two-month murder season, or making sure moms know they are murderers.

Cannon's solution was to offer the rationale, believed

by neither abortionists, nor the judge, nor any prolifer in the room, that the Heartbeat Law would not restrict baby killing at all! (A similarly desperate argument to meet the "least possible restriction" or "undue burden" standards in other states has been that babies with heartbeats are "viable" - which *Roe* had defined to mean able to survive outside the womb – or that "viable" may be redefined by a state as meaning "having a heartbeat". For state heartbeat laws as of April 2019 See https://www.pop.org/project/heartbeat/. Ohio Governor Kasich vetoed the law in 2016 and 2018.)

Judge Huppert asked Cannon if this law is rushing mothers to murder their babies? Cannon answered that it is not asking too much, to ask mothers to determine promptly if they are pregnant, and then if they want to murder their very own babies, to do it quickly. (Not their exact words.)

When Cannon proposed that we know a baby is a "person" upon detecting his heartbeat, the judge asked if there were any "basis" for that "rhetoric". That would have been a great opportunity for Cannon to cite the overwhelming evidence of court-recognized fact finders that *Roe* said would change everything. He could have said SCOTUS has never said "when [constitutionally protected] life [in fact] begins" no longer matters, or that even after courts rule that abortion is murder we have to let mothers keep committing murder because now they "rely" on it.

But he didn't, following in the footsteps of every other attorney who has defended a prolife law in court, so far as I can determine. He did observe that a detectable heartbeat is evidence that a person has not yet died, throughout Iowa law, so reason demands it should also be evidence that a person has begun to live. Beyond that, he said the fact that a baby with a heartbeat is a "person" is just intuitively obvious. He said "no law is needed to tell people that a baby with a heartbeat is a person. That is a determination that legislatures must be free to make."

"Common knowledge" is a courtroom word for facts

which don't need to be proved because everybody already agrees. That is not a strong argument where SCOTUS has ruled that "the judiciary...is not in a position to speculate" about such mysteries, and where SCOTUS has said the word of a single state is insufficient to "establish" the fact.

It is very interesting that Judge Huppert even invited evidence that unborn babies are "persons".

But without strong court-recognized evidence that babies are humans/persons whose right to life is "guaranteed" by the 14th Amendment, Banned Parenthood's claim was virtually unchallenged that a restriction on abortion must not be an "undue burden" on mom's "choice".

So on Roe's 46th Deathday, January 22, 2019, District Judge Huppert ruled the Heartbeat Law so invalid that it didn't even deserve a trial. (Summary judgment).

Facts: The Issue. The issue in a Summary Judgment hearing is whether there is disagreement about facts. If the facts are undisputed, no trial is needed to establish them. The judge is ready to apply the law to them.

Cannon said over 20 facts were disputed, regarding ultrasounds, heartbeat time frames, and the effects of abortion on women. But Alice Clapman, representing Planned Barrenhood, said none of those disputes affect the undisputed "critical fact" that the Heartbeat Law protects babies before they are "viable", which *Roe* prohibits. Judge Huppert agreed, ruling that "viability is not only material to this case, it is dispositive...." [It, alone, determines the disposition/outcome of the case.] He ruled: overturned. No trial.

The *more* critical fact, which renders *"viability"* irrelevant, is that babies are humans/persons whose rights to life are constitutionally protected, pre- and post-viability. *The irrefutable fact that babies are humans/persons is not only material to any abortion case, it is dispositive.*

But that fact was not mentioned among the 20+ facts which Cannon said were disputed. Not that Cannon was silent about "personhood", but Cannon's statement that heartbeats certify human life throughout law was not disputed, and his statement that legislatures must be allowed to determine that babies with detectable heartbeats are people was not an alleged fact but rather a statement about law. He offered no other evidence in support of his "rhetoric", and gave no indication that if there were a trial, any other factual evidence existed that might be explored.

Out of court, The Family Leader, working with Cannon, promised petitions to Judge Huppert saying "that's a baby". Unexplained was how that claim would be formalized into an objective finding of fact admissible in court by a public petition. But juries have already done precisely that: they have formalized that claim into an established fact that was not only admissible but dispositive in court, by acquitting prolife defendants in abortion prevention cases. Why not cite them?

Had Cannon presented the uncontested evidence that protectable human life begins at fertilization, which covers babies with heartbeats, then he wouldn't have had to deal with "strict scrutiny" or an "undue burden", because, as *Roe* said would "of course" be obvious even if *Roe* had not said it, once we know those babies are humans/persons, the 14th Amendment obligation of states shifts to *protecting all* those babies by outlawing *all* baby killing once again.

Neither in Cannon's brief, nor in oral argument, did he explicitly challenge PB's claim that the Heartbeat Law must survive "strict scrutiny" analysis, but the opposite: he scrupulously argued that the law should stand because it *does* meet that standard. He even appealed, in a brief, to the recognition given in *Casey,* 1992, of "the state's interest in 'protection of *potential* life'", without the correction that the Life of an unborn baby is more than merely "potential".

22 states remain which have enacted or at least initiated heartbeat legislation which has not yet been fully reviewed by courts. Any of those future defenses *could* explicitly challenge SCOTUS' "strict scrutiny" or "undue burden" test for abortion, and could support that challenge with the evidence of fact finders.

This challenge would be clearer, surely, if all pretense were explicitly abandoned of thinking a heartbeat ban can survive "strict scrutiny" or "undue burden" analysis. It is a desperate argument anyway. The closest the defense should come to conceding the appropriateness of those standards should be, "our law *may* be the least restrictive means of achieving a compelling government interest, but our compelling government interest is to save human lives threatened by abortion! The saving of lives by outlawing abortion is the *purpose* of this law! Fully human babies' lives have a fundamental right to life from conception, so it is *legal abortion* which must be forced to survive 'strict scrutiny' or 'undue burden' analysis!"

That is the legal strategy that will force judges to address "when [constitutionally protected] life begins". Forcing judicial attention to that issue, while presenting the full range of evidence of unborn Life before the court, will surely force courts to acknowledge that abortion is murder, we now know, so therefore *no* state may be allowed to legalize it. This is surely the *only* legal strategy that can accomplish that goal.

State Constitutional Amendment: abortion is *not* a "Fundamental Right"

After Judge Huppert's ruling cited Iowa's supreme court ruling the previous summer declaring abortion a "fundamental right" in their state, Iowa prolifers dropped their "That's A Baby!" petition drive and their promised appeal and joined the move in several states to neutralize the similar rulings of their courts through an amendment to their state constitutions saying abortion is *not* a "fundamental right".

You ask, "What is accomplished by neutralizing a ruling of a state supreme court while an identical ruling of SCOTUS remains? Hasn't SCOTUS already made abortion a "fundamental right" in *every* state?"

Yes, and no. Essentially, yes; technically, no.

Technically, the states' standard *is* a greater obstacle to saving lives than SCOTUS' standard. *Roe* had declared abortion a "fundamental right" in 1973, but SCOTUS in 1992 replaced that with a less stringent standard: that a regulation could not be an "undue burden" on baby killing, and the reasons for the regulation could not include *restricting* baby killing. There has to be some *other* "compelling government interest" unrelated to saving lives.

But in 2016 SCOTUS upgraded the "undue burden" standard so much that Justice Thomas complained that he can no longer tell any difference. (*Whole Woman's Health v. Hellerstedt,* 579 U.S. ___ (2016))

Tennessee enacted its Amendment in 2014. It was challenged, but only on a technicality about the voting process. The challenge died in 2018. (https://tinyurl.com/y6fbyjwh) West Virginia and Alabama added similar amendments to their state constitutions on November 7, 2018. (https://tinyurl.com/y9sg4zzu) Iowa is trying to pass SJR21. (https://tinyurl.com/yxuefooq) Kansas lawmakers vowed to pass their Amendment after their court made abortion a "fundamental right" April 26, 2019. (https://tinyurl.com/y58jmoxn)

What could possibly go wrong? Here are four points for prolifers to consider:

* The costs/benefits of removing the state court obstacle to saving lives should count the fact that the virtually identical (according to Justice Thomas) federal obstacle will remain;

* The risk of being overturned;

* The risk of undermining the 14th Amendment if they are *not* overturned (the Amendment gives federal courts power to define and protect rights trampled by states);

• The risk of distraction from simpler, more effective ways to neutralize the *federal* obstacle. (For details about these four points, see http://savetheworld.saltshaker.us/wiki/-Four_Drawbacks_of_a_"No_Right_to_Abortion"_State_Constitution al_Amendment)

•

Alabama: Going All the Way

(See also: http://savetheworld.saltshaker.us/wiki/Abortion_Law_Alabama)

Alabama is only the second state, since Rhode Island 46 years before, to outlaw virtually all abortion with stiff criminal penalties: 99 years! HB314 (https://tinyurl.com/yyqbgekd) removes any shadow, er, penumbra of doubt that the trial turns on "when [protectable] Life begins".

It can turn on nothing else. There can be no courtroom discussion of "whether 'the purpose or effect of the (law at issue) is to place a substantial obstacle'" before abortion. No distraction remains from the defense Alabama raises: that abortion is murder of fully human beings and the Constitution requires Alabama to outlaw it.

The 11th Circuit had told Alabama, while overturning Alabama's 2015 law against dismembering unborn babies, "The question in all abortion cases is whether 'the *purpose or effect* of the (law at issue) is to place a substantial obstacle'" before abortion.

That was then. That can not be a question in *any* abortion case where a law bans virtually all abortions! And when the law, moreover, plainly states that its *purpose* is to outlaw virtually all abortions! And plainly articulates a new, very different "question" (issue) for the court: unborn babies of humans are *in fact* humans. (Persons.) Killing them is *in fact* murder.

That is the legal step I have prayed for. That is what I wrote this book, first released in October 2018, to encourage.

In Alabama's trial, the discussion will not be about whether Alabama's law can survive "strict scrutiny" or "undue burden" analysis, but about whether abortion must not be an "undue burden" on a baby's right to live. The issue will be whether Alabama's evidence that all unborn babies are fully human people is strong enough to resolve the uncertainty which SCOTUS alleged in 1973.

In lower courts, there will be additional legal questions which are addressed in the 15-point Finding of Facts proposed in the opening pages of this book:

* Is it as irrelevant as lower courts say, that abortion in fact murders fully human beings, because babies are not people "as a matter of law"?

* When *Casey* said mothers rely on abortion too much to outlaw it now, did that rationale for legal abortion displace, and nullify, *Roe's* rationale that we can't tell if babies are "recognizably human" but if we find out then "of course" abortion must be outlawed again?

* Do "exceptions", like allowing abortion to save the life of the mother, contradict and nullify the findings of states that all babies are humans/persons, as *Roe's* notorious Footnote 54 is widely interpreted as saying?

These misunderstandings are not addressed in Alabama's findings. Of course defense lawyers always bring in arguments and facts beyond legislative findings, but these misunderstandings were not addressed in Alabama's *Foundation For Moral Law* amicus in 2018 (https://tinyurl.com/y4bbq9bt) about the dismemberment ban, either. In fact, one point FFML was able to make and did make in 2018 about *Roe's* n. 54 is aganst FFML now. The dismemberment ban did not have a "life of the mother" exception, which FFML presented as evidence that Alabama's position on the Life of all unborn babies satisfies n. 54's logic. FFML implicitly endorses n. 54's logic. But 2019's HB314 *does* have a "life of the mother" exception. So the need now will be to explain why n. 54, as widely interpreted, is patently absurd. (See p. XXI.)

As for evidence that all babies are humans, the only evidence presented in Alabama's findings is the conclusion of Alabama's own legislature, its state constitutional amendment, and medical authorities within Alabama's own borders.

Not mentioned are the 37 other state legislatures

with "unborn victims of violence" laws, Congress with its similar 18 USC 1841(d), the many uncontradicted expert witnesses in abortion prevention trials who have affirmed life from fertilization, or the several juries who have acquitted prolifers because they were saving lives, most of whom were outside Alabama.

One state can't "establish" the FACT that babies are people as decisively as 38 states can!

> Deuteronomy 17:6 At the mouth of two witnesses, or three witnesses, shall he that is worthy of death be put to death; but at the mouth of one witness he shall not be put to death.

Clarke Forsythe, counsel for and founder of *Americans United for Life,* responded to my theories at the request of Chuck Hurley, founder of and counsel for the *Iowa Family Leader.* He said states can't outlaw abortion; only an amendment to the U.S. Constitution can do that.

> [Prolifers think if you] "pass 'personhood' legislation in your state, as a bill, or as a constitutional amendment, and according to the U.S. Supreme Court Roe v. Wade decision itself, [so-called] 'legal' [sic] abortion is over in that jurisdiction. [That hope is] futile...(because of our system of federalism) it will not – it cannot – establish 14th Amendment personhood or set up a test case to overturn Roe."

Notice that the goal he is refuting is where "abortion is over *in that jurisdiction."* It was the argument of Alabama's *Foundation for Moral Law* "Amicus" in 2016 that Alabama could, indeed, make abortion go away within Alabama's jurisdiction even if it remained legal everywhere else. That appeared to be the reason fact finding authorities outside Alabama were not cited. Forsythe says the obstacle to that goal is "federalism".

I believe the obstacle is the 14th Amendment, which gives courts jurisdiction over states which trample fundamental rights – a power which encompasses the power to *define* fundamental rights. If babies were not people, courts would be right to make states allow women the management of their own bodies. When prolifers support a case that forces judges to address the evidence that babies *are* people, courts will not be able to allow *any* state to keep abortion legal. There will not be life and death differences from one jurisdiction to another.

Forsythe is correct if he means that states can't dodge this judicial power to define rights. But he does not appreciate that states *do* establish facts.

He is correct that a single state, citing only its own authority, can't change SCOTUS' understanding of abortion. *Roe* ruled as much. But the consensus of 38 states, dozens of juries, thousands of expert witnesses, Congress, and several individual judges, can certainly establish a fact!

For Forsythe's complete statement and my interleaved response to it as well as to others of his articles, see "AUL Missing Opportunity". (https://tinyurl.com/y4qwgy8e)

Although defense attorneys always submit evidence and argument beyond what legislatures include in their findings, surely *findings of facts* have more force in court when a legislature says them, than when an attorney in court merely claims that the legislature thinks them.

When Texas Attorney General Wade told SCOTUS that babies are people, *Roe* reported the argument as if it were the position of the whole state of Texas, even though the legislature had enacted no such finding. ("...Texas urges that a fetus is entitled to Fourteenth Amendment protection as a person..." - Footnote 54) But had the legislature explicitly made that finding, perhaps *Roe* would have hesitated a little more before saying "the unborn have never been recognized in the law as persons in the whole sense." *Roe v. Wade*, 410 U.S. 113, 162 (1973)

Just a theory.

I am grateful for the hope given me by the Chief Counsel for Alabama's Foundation for Moral Law, that the defense this time will indeed include evidence from other states. He emailed me on August 23:

> "You make some good points, one of which is that we need to rely upon more than just the Alabama Legislature's Findings of Fact to uphold this law. Fortunately, in establishing a basis for the law, we are not limited to the Legislature's Findings, and we will fight to articulate others' evidence of the personhood of the pre-born child. As we get closer to briefing time, we will carefully consider the points you make in your message and also on your website, ipatriot.com. We appreciate your continued prayerful support. Godspeed." - John A. Eidsmoe, Colonel(MS), Mississippi State Guard, Senior Counsel, Foundation for Moral Law, Pastor, Association of Free Lutheran Congregations

Which issue should prolifers place before courts:

* "All unborn babies are humans (persons)"? That was the issue brought by Rhode Island in 1973 and by Alabama May 16. Or...

* "Abortionists need to murder humanely, clean their murder rooms, show girls who they are about to murder, and murder before they can hear a heartbeat – but it certainly isn't our purpose to reduce abortions"? That's the issue placed before courts by every state abortion restriction in between.

What a difference, legally as well as Biblically, between Alabama's 2015 prolife law, which said that before a baby is torn limb from limb, he must be killed in a way that causes less pain, and this year's law! The premise of Alabama's dismemberment law was that murder ought to be humane. The premise of the current Alabama law is that murder ought to be outlawed.

Which kind of case appears most likely to focus judges on the evidence which *Roe* said would "of course" spell the end of legal abortion?

Why courts ignore evidence

SCOTUS has *never* ruled evidence of "when life begins" "irrelevant". In fact, SCOTUS has never *taken* any case that would have made them address that issue.

But thousands of judges *below* SCOTUS have written that SCOTUS did indeed rule "when life begins" "irrelevant" "as a matter of law".

The only evidence of Life that should be irrelevant to a prolife court defense is evidence outside court.

Evidence outside a court case doesn't count. All the scientific evidence in the world that human life begins at fertilization, presented *outside court,* is unlikely to move any judge to rule against abortion. In fact it is a principle of judicial "impartiality" that judges should disregard evidence they encounter outside the courtroom where the opposing side has no opportunity to refute it.

> Rule 2.9: Ex Parte Communications (A) A judge shall not initiate, permit, or consider ex parte communications, or consider other communications made to the judge outside the presence of the parties or their lawyers, concerning a pending* or impending matter,* ...." - Model Code of Judicial Conduct

Evidence has to be presented in court for it to count. To present it in court, there has to be a case. Cases must be either "criminal" or "civil": you either have to break a law and be arrested, or you have to sue somebody, or be sued.

Or pass a law, if you are a state, and be sued.

The *abnormal* rationale for ignoring evidence.

Normally, judges accept the testimony of expert witnesses. Normally, the testimony of thousands of expert witnesses that abortion in fact murders people, never contradicted, would have ended legal abortion decades ago.

It was not normal at all for all that expert testimony (in trials of prolifers who sat in front of abortionists' doors to prevent abortion) to be kept from juries on the ground that *the fact that abortion is murder is irrelevant to whether it is OK to prevent it.* Yet dozens of appeals courts said *Roe v Wade* ruled *"as a matter of law"* that the unborn are not persons, making irrelevant the *fact* that abortion is murder!

That is the opposite of what *Roe* or any later case said, but that is why judges below SCOTUS ignore evidence. But neither has SCOTUS ever addressed the snowballing evidence.

The confusion from Roe that judges had to slog through. Think of the legal confusion judges faced. If the *Roe* justices thought about the kind of case that would bring evidence before them to "establish" "when life begins", they gave no hint of it. They probably assumed society would be "unable to speculate" for generations, since it is as hard for Democrats today to look at such a tiny person and grasp that he or she is a person, as it was for Democrats two centuries earlier looking at black slaves.

The ink on *Roe* was barely dry before Rhode Island said "So you can't tell if a baby of a human is a human because state laws didn't spell it out for you? OK, here's a state law that spells it out clearly enough for a *judge* to understand." Were the *Roe* justices prepared for that? They wouldn't hear the case after a circuit court judge said *Roe* said what *Roe* clearly did not say. (Details in Part Two.)

Then the "Rescues" started. "Rescuers" sat in front of abortionists' doors so mothers couldn't get in to kill their babies. Although the movement began spontaneously, Operation Rescue (OR) was formed by Randall Terry to help organize some of the major events. Proverbs 24:10-12 was on their masthead: "Rescue those who are perishing, who are being led away to slaughter." OR gave the number of arrests at 60,000 when the movement was still strong.

In court their defense was that they were saving human lives. In the earliest cases, juries – finders of facts – acquitted after understanding that defense. (See the *Cincinnati Law Review* excerpt, p. 15-16, Part Two.) This happened as late as 1991 when I was arrested with 134 others in Iowa City, Iowa. The jury, told about the Necessity Defense, acquitted all of us.

Was *any* judge prepared for that? Judges were scrambling, as proved by what they did next, and the tortured logic they employed to pull it off.

But confusion wasn't the only pressure on them.

Political/social pressure on judges to ignore Life

Put yourself in judges' shoes. Judges never had to rule rationally on "when life begins", because they were under pressure to *not* rule rationally, by almost everybody including most prolifers. By contrast, the cases with strong prolife support didn't require judges to address the issue.

That's because "when life begins" case law was created by criminal cases. Criminals are never popular, so no defense that justifies them is popular. Not even when it is so strong that it can't be attacked without first recasting it as something easier to ridicule. (Part 2 gives examples.)

The defense prolifers mostly raised goes by different names in different states. It excuses a "lesser harm", like blocking someone's door, when that is "necessary" to prevent a "greater harm", like the person behind the door murdering people. One of the "elements" of the defense, therefore, is that people's lives were saved by the action being prosecuted. Which, in an abortion case, invites evidence that babies of people are people.

In the earliest abortion prevention cases, juries, upon hearing the defense explained, acquitted.

So judges, to the applause of almost everybody, invented the rationale that juries should not even be allowed to know that "we saved lives" was the defense of the defendants, even when (1) that was the only defense, (2) it was supposedly a "trial by *jury*", not a trial where the *judge* decides the only contested issue, and (3) "when life begins" is a fact issue, treated by *Roe* as a fact issue, and juries are "triers of facts", leaving judges without any lawful jurisdiction to rule on facts in jury trials.

The judges' rationale for not letting juries (the "judges of the facts") *hear* the evidence that the defendants' actions saved many lives was that babies are *not* "lives" "as a matter of law", and *judges* are the "judges of the *law*".

In fact, such trials became a contest of wits between the defendant and the judge, the defendant trying to slip to the jury some hint of what his only defense was before the judge could silence him or jail him for contempt!

The majority of prolifers didn't mind that those rulings were irrational, lawless, contrary to *Roe,* contrary to the Bible, an affront to God, and enablers of infanticide. Those defendants were *lawbreakers* defying Romans 13, "Two wrongs don't make a right", and "The ends never justify the means!" Proverbs 24:10-12 didn't count because that's in the Old Testament.

Newspapers quoted Planned Barrenhood calling those defendants "fanatics", and quoted prolife leaders distancing themselves from the defendants. Those defendants embarrassed everybody. They lost jobs, business if they were self employed, and any future in politics.

Law abiding prolife leaders who had long before accepted a cut in their political and social prospects had another reason to distance themselves from "lawbreakers". They were working hard to persuade lawmakers to restrict abortion, and lawmakers are leery of lawbreakers. They were under pressure by news reporters to disassociate themselves from those "lawbreakers" or suffer labels that damaged the "credibility" they needed to lobby lawmakers.

Prolifers weren't even a clear or consistent majority of Republicans. These leaders were forced to choose between supporting their lawbreaking friends and getting legislation passed. They saw more hope of saving lives through legislation.

Unfortunately the necessary "distance from lawbreakers" required meritless accusations not just against the "lawbreakers", but also against the legal defenses which justified them. Not that their defenses were refuted. Rather, their conclusions were condemned, without addressing their legal arguments. Some conclusions are so unacceptable, that it becomes irrelevant whether they are correct.

The lawbreakers' Bible studies about saving lives, ie. http://theroadtoemmaus.org/RdLb/21PbAr/LifHlth/Abrt/PaulHl.htm received similar treatment. Their conclusions were treated as a disgrace, without addressing their verses and logic.

Which left judges with almost unanimous pressure to convict, whatever the cost to reason, law, justice, or Life.

In 1993, Congress passed the Freedom of Access to Clinic Entrances (FACE) act, which created federal penalties that were as high, for sitting in front of a door thrice, as for shooting an abortionist. Door blocking mostly ended. A series of about seven shootings of abortionists, over the next two decades, began. Those defendants raised the same Necessity Defense. Prolifers had even *less* desire for abortion to end through one of *their* cases!

The point of this short history is not to blame anybody, but to explain, as accurately as possible, why judges ruled the way they did, creating the case law we must overcome today.

Even in 1776, only a bare majority of the people had the Biblical understanding of civil disobedience needed to support rebellion against King George. There is a lot less enthusiasm for the tactic now. It's just facing reality, that a case capable of forcing judges to address Life will not have majority prolife support if it arises from "lawbreaking". And without majority prolife support, judges will continue to feel intense pressure to rule *against* Life. A different kind of case will be necessary to end legal abortion.

Why a case now should draw prolife support. Rhode Island pioneered such a case: a review not of law breaking, but of law *making*. This proposal is a case like theirs except we have personhood findings of not just one state, but of states, juries, expert witnesses, and Congress.

No case after 1973 that invoked this evidence had strong prolife support. No case with strong prolife support invoked this evidence or was even about "when life begins".

Missouri came close, in 1989. But Missouri promised to not use its personhood law to restrict abortion, so SCOTUS said it is premature to review a restriction before there is a restriction to review. See Part 2, p. 30. Ohio, in 1992, didn't come close. Ohio regulated abortion, without making SCOTUS address the growing evidence that abortion kills humans. So SCOTUS didn't. See Part 2, p. 31.

Not even the partial birth rulings, in which *all* the justices described the "procedure" as barbaric – something one would not say of how we treat tumors – touched the question whether those babies are human. See Part 2, p. 33.

Will prolifers resist arguing in court, today, that all categories of court-recognized fact-finders have said what *Roe* ruled must finally end legal abortion, because "lawbreaking" created the precedents that supplied two of those categories (juries and expert witnesses)?

It is thanks to criminal cases that juries can complete our list of court-recognized categories of fact finders who affirm unborn personhood. Courts won't let a jury review the constitutionality of a law, since that is primarily a legal question, not one of guilt or innocence. But the consensus of juries that were shown the evidence, and the demonstrated expectation of judges that most juries would join that consensus if allowed, (Part 2, p. 11) is strong relevant evidence which can help defend a law against abortion.

Many sacrificed much to generate that evidence.

Why Courts ignore Personhood Laws that lack specific penalties for abortion

There have been personhood bills which don't specify abortion and don't explicitly assign penalties for performing abortions. They say murder of the unborn should be prosecuted the same as murder of anyone else.

But without prosecution guidelines for situations unique to abortion, how would prosecutors know how to proceed?

Murder [of adults] laws lack prosecution tools for murder of the unborn: (1) there is often no body to prove anyone died, (2) the woman who contracts the murder is often not culpable, being pressured by parents, and misled by our whole culture – even by courts and churches, (3) RU 486 and contraceptives can be mailed from other countries.

Accessories to murder: With murder of adults, anyone can be prosecuted who "harbors" the murderer or helps in any way. Can those laws be applied to abortion without appropriate modification? Should there be any limit to the prosecution of "accessories" to abortion? The landlord? Secretary? Parents of the abortion customer? Lawmakers who fund it? Voters who installed those lawmakers? These decisions need to be clear in laws.

In *Webster v. Reproductive Health Services* (492 U.S. 490), 1989, the Court found no "concrete way" in which Missouri's Personhood law affected abortion, because the law applied no penalties to abortion to make it clear that abortionists would be prosecuted, or if so, how. The Court said it is premature to rule on whether a law is "the least restrictive means of achieving a compelling government interest", before a restriction exists.

The ruling did *not* say, as many today allege, that should any state dare to apply its personhood law to outlaw abortion, the law would certainly be found unconstitutional. The ruling said the opposite just might happen.

About the Author

Dave Leach is actually listed in Marquis' "Who's Who in America", since about 1995. (This is to balance the other stuff you've heard.)

He is grateful, but marvels that he would be considered qualified.

He is not qualified to do hardly anything he does.

He wrote a book presenting a theology of Hell unlike any other – "Eternal Hell: Heaven's Loving Purpose" - [available at Amazon.com] although he never went through seminary except on his way from the music hall to the football field when it was raining.

He wrote another book, "The Prehistoric Angel Diary", [also at Amazon], supposedly the diary of an angel from before creation thru Noah's flood - "a fictitious angel, but an angel nonetheless" - although he has never even *seen* an angel. *He has not even seen a fictitious angel!*

He has published hundreds of articles about immigration even though he is a citizen.

He ran for statehouse seven times even though he never studied Political Science.

His college major was in music education; his major instrument was trumpet; and he isn't even that good on his trumpet. And yet at the age of 73, he still practices it, as if he can't kill his hope that if he keeps at it, maybe someday he will be good.

And now he writes a book showing lawmakers how any one of them can start a snowball rolling down Heaven's hills that will grow so big that when it reaches its target, Hell's outreach post in Abortionland *really will* freeze over.

This, to top off the five (count 'em – FIVE!) appeals he has written to the U.S. Supreme Court about abortion – the first two for himself and the last three for others – and he isn't even a lawyer!

And after all that, he is tired of writing in third person.

Hey, when you are as lacking in official credentials as I am, you appreciate endorsements people give you over the years. I can't be sure those good folks didn't change their minds afterwards, but the fact that they at least once thought those kind things keeps me going over the years of having my research unreceived by almost everybody else.

This book is the result of addressing much criticism. It is what is left after serious criticisms died away, leaving only personal attacks, being ignored, or having nice talks with prolifers whom I never hear from again after I give them more than a page to read.

The few responses I have had from people who actually did review my material and get back to me are encouraging enough for me to be afraid to give up. What if this opportunity really is of God, and I give up after years of offering the opportunity to people praying for such a solution but who will not analyze it or even bother to refute it, and then I die and Jesus tells me "why did you quit? Just a little longer and those millions of lives you wanted to save would be alive now instead of waiting up here for you!"?

No, I am afraid to quit. Until someone takes the trouble to explain to me why this strategy really won't work. Something I always appreciate because either it will alert me to a weakness which I can repair, or it will free me to quit and watch TV like normal people of retirement age.

So here are the few beacons of endorsements, bobbing on a sea of rejection: (being rejected has become a habit)

Two (count 'em) TWO 60-day extensions of time were requested by the U.S. Justice Department headed by Attorney General Janet Reno to respond to the pro-se Supreme Court brief I wrote with Regina Dinwiddie in 1995.

Regina was the first person charged under FACE

(Freedom of Access to Clinic Entrances). It was over an injunction against her to stop talking into her bullhorn (portable microphone and amplifier) outside murder offices, which she used because abortionists had fences that kept her about 100 feet from their patients.

I kid you not! After abortionists persuaded Congress to pass a law enabling them to give draconian penalties for people who blocked their doors, their first prosecution under the law was for someone talking!

The brief is posted at www.Saltshaker.US/American Issues/Life/DD-1.htm.

When the Justice Department, headed by the notorious Janet "Waco" Reno, finally submitted their response brief, it was remarkably unremarkable. I wrote a response brief for Regina.

The U.S. Justice Department response?

Before SCOTUS was scheduled to decide whether to take the case, the Justice Department dropped the charges against Regina, to make the appeal "moot", so that there remained no case for the Supreme Court to take!

"...your brief...appears to be good...You do a good job of setting forth the law", Bill Kurth emailed me in 2002. Kurth, of Carroll, Iowa, now deceased, was an attorney who used to grade bar exams, and who once headed up an Iowa arm of the Rutherford Institute.

He was responding to my explanation of how the Iowa legislature could end legal abortion and survive a court challenge, by amending Iowa's version of the Necessity Defense, called "compulsion" in Iowa, Iowa Code 704.10.

The plan is at www.Saltshaker.US/AmericanIssues/ Life/Compulsion%20Amendment.htm I published Kurth's endorsement in my campaign newspaper; I was an Iowa statehouse candidate.

Iowa's "compulsion" law already says it's not against the law to save a life or to prevent "serious injury" even when that requires what would otherwise be a violation of a less important law. My amendment would specify that abortion counts as a "serious injury". It would stop arrests and prosecution of door blockers by state or local police under Iowa law, but would not stop action by federal marshals.

"If this passes, it could facilitate the closing of every abortion clinic in Iowa." That was the response to the same plan, of Chuck Hurley, a home schooling, Bible-quoting lawyer who founded and headed the Iowa Family Policy Center, (now called the Family Leader), Iowa's branch of James Dobson's Focus on the Family, and who previously headed the Iowa House Judiciary Committee.

"This initiative to spell out the necessity defense is valuable even before it is passed." The same initiative got this response from Joe Scheidler, who heads Prolife Action League in Chicago, and was a defendant in the 16-years-long *NOW vs Scheidler* case before the Supreme Court as of 2002:

"There's a private swimming pool not far from our office with a 'no trespassing' sign on it. But if I saw a toddler thrashing around in the water, I'd jump the fence and try to save him.

"That's the necessity defense. It sets aside the letter of the law for the spirit of the law.

"In any other situation besides abortion, the necessity of trespassing to save lives would be accepted in a flash. But the so called 'right to privacy' has blinded our judges. But if you present the facts of the humanity of a child to a jury, they are much more likely to accept the reality of the defense.

*"The Necessity defense was our legal ace in the hole from the earliest days of clinic blockades. One of the major reasons we allowed ourselves to be arrested was to try the necessity defense. It is still law, **which presents a fact issue to the juries.** Anything that makes that clear will be a powerful tool.*

"We should have kept our focus on this defense, but we haven't, so today most lawyers laugh if you bring it up. But a lot of water has gone over the dam since then, from cloning to the sale of baby body parts. The public may be ready to see the defense tried now. Public education on the child's humanity is crucial.

"That is why this initiative to spell out the necessity defense is valuable even before it is passed. It won't work if you don't try, and I am willing to help."

Chet Gallagher, PersonhoodUSA board member. Chet began his prolife career when, as a motorcycle cop in Las Vegas ordered to arrest protesting prolifers, he laid down his motorcycle and badge and joined the protesters.

He was on the board of PersonhoodUSA when he gave this endorsement, for my campaign for Iowa Senate against Matt McCoy, a sodomite.

This video does not mention my legal arguments about abortion, but he gave it after I talked to him for about an hour about the opportunity I see, an opportunity not realized by the Personhood movement of which he was a leader, because a Personhood law appeals to no greater consensus of fact finders than itself. It cites no other states.

He gave this endorsement months after I was every reporter's favorite target for writing a brief for Scott Roeder.

He described me as a "moral conservative" with a "Christian foundation" who is a Republican, but has crossed party lines over principles. "If we are not one nation under God, we will be one nation gone under, and it's a man like Dave Leach who can keep that from happening....he is accountable to a higher law, and will honor Jesus Christ with all that he has." See https://tinyurl.com/y5k2lxf6

"Incredibly elaborate well thought out document" was the description of my legal brief by criminal trial author Stephen Singular, talking to the anchors of "In Session" (successor to "Court TV").

He was talking about my pro-se trial brief written for and submitted to the Court by high profile prolife defendant Scott Roeder, who shot and killed the infamous late term abortionst George Tiller, of Wichita, Kansas, whose website had boasted of 60,000 notches on his scalpel.

Tiller even hired a Methodist preacher to mix "holy water" with amniotic fluid to "baptize" Tiller's victims, and to give "Christian" burials – a remarkable degree of compassion for mere "blobs of tissue", even if those services cost the mothers several hundred dollars each.

(Singular's statement is at http://youtu.be/EMNHhayn22c The brief itself is at www.Saltshaker.US/Scott-Roeder-Resources/Brief4Roeder.pdf)

Singular attended Roeder's trial to write a book about it which was published the next year. A few pages from the book, about me, are reprinted with my comments, at the end of this section.

"The judge allowed the Voluntary Manslaughter defense because of your brief", *In Session* anchor Jean Casarez told me personally at Roeder's 2010 Wichita trial. Casarez seemed surprisingly exuberant about the defense being allowed thanks to my brief.

The following excerpt from Singular's book agrees with that conclusion. That conclusion is also supported by the fact that according to the transcript of the hearing right after Roeder submitted it, Judge Wilbert said he had stayed up all night reading the 104-page brief, and the fact that at that hearing, he was more open to the defense than at the previous hearing.

(See the brief: www.Saltshaker.US/Scott-Roeder-Resources. That site also links to a series of entertaining videos I made to explain the denial of the right to trial by jury. See all the rest of the trial documents, including the appeal briefs I wrote for Scott to the Kansas Supreme Court and the U.S. Supreme Court, at www.Saltshaker.US/Roeder.)

"You make some good points, one of which is that we need to rely upon more than just the Alabama

Legislature's Findings of Fact to uphold this law....As we get closer to briefing time, we will carefully consider the points you make in your message and also on your website...." - John A. Eidsmoe in an email August 23, 2019. Colonel(MS), Mississippi State Guard; Senior Counsel, Foundation for Moral Law; Pastor, Association of Free Lutheran Congregations

"You make some fair points." - Martin Cannon, Thomas More Society, who defended Iowa's Heartbeat Law.

Now, about that "other stuff you've heard":

Unfortunately all books must have an "about the author" section. I wish at this point that I were someone else, about whom media had not lied for the past 30 years, so that my public reputation would not be an obstacle to using this vital information.

But I am not, so I must address it. In doing so I respond to an article partly about me, which is typical of the hundreds of articles about me over the years. It was published, while I was in my last few days of finishing this manuscript, by Judy Thomas of the Kansas City Star.

I also include a few pages from Stephen Singular's book about the 2010 Scott Roeder trial, published 2011, which are about me, with my comments. Some of what he wrote is quite flattering. Other things are half true and cry out for context. All of it is very interesting. He writes well.

The one thing Singular did which I don't know if any other reporter did, was actually read my legal arguments. Most found that unnecessary. After all, once they know my legal arguments point out elements of American law which favor Scott's defense, why, everyone "knows" they cannot possibly be true. Actually READING them would only be redundant.

I'm an equal opportunity target. I have been trashed by liberal and conservative reporters equally.

By liberals, because they reject my fundamental premise that God's laws are supreme and all humans are created by God in the Image of God, and merit rights demanded by God.

By conservatives who share my premises, by no logic that I can quite follow, apparently because as Paul reported, "only lest they should suffer persecution for the cross of Christ." Galatians 6:2. While I am in the mud spray, who wants to stand beside me? I have learned that:

> Some accusations are so serious, that it becomes irrelevant whether they are true.

The habit of news reporters of execrating legal arguments they have not read is well illustrated by the time reporters heard I wrote a legal brief for Scott Roeder which he submitted in January, 2010, pro se [which means by his own choice, in his own name, for which he assumed full responsibility, without the involvement of an attorney even though he was helped by two court-appointed attorneys].

Some of the reporters asked law professors what they thought of the Necessity Defense, a small part of the brief. They said it was ridiculous because Courts reject it.

Later on in the articles they conceded that they hadn't actually read my brief. But they hardly needed to; if it defended Roeder, it was *ipso facto* false.

But those were the more enlightened articles. Most news articles about the conclusions of my legal analyses and Bible studies never mention that I have ever written even a single legal brief. Or that I have ever read the Bible.

I don't know if any reporter, other than Singular and *In Sessions* reporter Jean Casarez, ever read either my legal briefs or my Bible studies. If they did, they certainly didn't betray themselves in their articles about me.

Proverbs 18:13 He that answereth a matter before he heareth it, it is folly and shame unto him.

So what is left of an article about my analysis of what law and Scripture say about stopping a killer, stripped of any hint that my conclusions are based on either law or Scripture?

This is what is left: "Dave Leach [personally] advocates shooting abortion doctors."

What I personally advocate is helping persuade legislatures to create the kind of court case that will finally outlaw abortion, so that no one will *have* to break any law to save babies.

No, I don't like shooting. But when one abortionist takes thousands of lives, our laws, and God's laws, provides for those thousands. That's not my personal idea. I didn't pass those laws, and I didn't write those verses. I just read them and report them, and marvel at the disinterest in them of my fellow citizens and Christians.

Are we allowed any perspective? It's 10 million times safer to be an abortionist, than it is to be a baby. Seven shootings of abortionists, I think. 70 million babies slain, just here in America, not counting the infanticide that spread from here to Europe, Russia, and China.

An example of this kind of reporting came while I was finishing up this book. Judy Thomas, reporter for the Kansas City Star, called me on election day, 2018. She wrote about Shelley Shannon who was released from a halfway house the next day. Shelley had just served 24 years from shooting the same George Tiller in each arm, at point blank range, in the hope that she could prevent him from doing any more abortions without having to kill him. (It didn't work. He testified at the trial that he was back killing babies the very next day.)

I am "another advocate of the 'justifiable homicide' position", eh? I wonder what Judy thinks it means? I can imagine what her readers must think it means: a doctrine made up by terrorists to justify murdering people who don't agree with you, in order to earn a nice mansion in Heaven with 72 virgins. The term by itself suggests no association with saving lives.

I wonder if Judy knows that "justifiable homicide" is a legal name of a self defense law in a few states like Florida, and a name used generically to describe the similar laws enacted in most states?

Florida 782.02 Justifiable use of deadly force. — The use of deadly force is justifiable when a person is resisting any attempt to murder such person or to commit any felony upon him or her or upon or in any dwelling house in which such person shall be.

The law changed in 2005. Before, it applied only in your own home; outside your home, you had a "duty to retreat" from a threat. A little hard when someone robs you at gunpoint. In 2005 it was amended to allow you to defend yourself, or others, anywhere, when you have a right to be where you are, doing what you are doing, and are threatened.

So do I "advocate" the laws of most states? I confess.

But Judy jams this unexplained term into an article about abortion. What does the law have to do with abortion?

Especially since Judy doesn't report that I speak in legal terms, though my primary involvement in the prolife movement has been in analyzing and reporting about law and legal and legislative strategy, including writing briefs for myself and others.

I hope I use terms more correctly than she reports. Because her term is from Florida law, I used the term while I reported on the Paul Hill trial, which was in Florida, because that was the defense he raised. I don't mention the term in the context of a Kansas case, like Shelley's, where the equivalent law is called "Defense of Others". Neither should Judy.

Of course, "Defense of Others" sounds a lot more supportable than "Justifiable Homicide", even without explaining its elements, which could explain Judy's choice of terms.

"The Necessity Defense" is the most common name states use for their self defense laws like what Kansas calls "Defense of Others" and Florida calls "Justifiable Homicide".

I can't imagine how any reader could get a clear picture of what I "support", legally, without at the very least explaining the elements of the law, and that they apply to the saving of human lives where some action is necessary that otherwise would be prohibited, so that applied to abortion the issue is not *whether one may save human lives*, which no one disputes, but *who is human.*

I am trying to remember if any reporter, of hundreds over 25 years, ever explained even that much.

Not only do I "advocate" American law – I even appeal to *Roe v. Wade;* my argument is with lower courts which say *Roe* said what *Roe* obviously did not say, as I thoroughly explain in the preceding legal brief.

Judy's article: www.kansascity.com/news/local/crime/article221194600.html

The fact that I wrote that first pro se trial brief which Scott submitted in January, 2010, was reported by nearly every newspaper in the world, but none other than *In Session* said enough about the brief's reasoning to give any sense of whether the brief had legal merit. Only that it was for Scott. Which led most readers to assume, "well of course if it defended Scott Roeder, it was irrational."

In 2010, I begged Judy Thomas, and AP reporter Roxanne Hegeman, (each of whom spent hours on the phone interviewing me over several months), to mention the brief's complaint that judges in abortion prevention trials generally do not allow the jury — which judges call "triers of facts" — to judge, or even know about, the only contested issue of the trial, which is the fact question: "were those lives the defendant saved, human?"

In ordinary murder trials the defense is that the accused didn't do it, but I encouraged Scott to not contest that, but to freely admit doing it, as prolifers in thousands of other trials had done, in order to save days of testimony proving he "did it" which diverts jury attention from the only *contested* fact question of the trial: "when life begins".

The tactic made a small difference in news coverage. At least people learned that Scott believed in what he did. But it didn't embarrass Judge Wilbert into allowing the jury to know the legal defense which Scott's court-appointed attorneys wanted to explain to the jury.

Judy knew all these things. We had many long conversations during Scott's trial and for months afterward. I begged her to report these details. I am no longer hopeful.

A Singular Answer

Excerpts from *A Death in Wichita: Abortion Doctor George Tiller and the New American Civil War* by Stephen Singular
With comments and perspective by Dave Leach

Page 312: Awaiting trial, Roeder had deepened his relationship with the anti-abortionist Dave Leach of Des Moines, Iowa. If Randall Terry had for decades represented the flamboyant, media-grabbing wing of the pro-life movement, the aging Leach was less intrusive and more scholarly, but every bit as committed to stopping abortion.

> *[Hmm. "...the aging Leach..." Who isn't "aging"? That is the condition of all humans/persons from fertilization. "More scholarly" than Randall Terry. I think I like receiving more credit than I deserve, than less. There is definitely an art to "grabbing" liberal media when you are a conservative, and Terry is a master. At one point In Session's Jean Casaras had scheduled an interview with me, which she later canceled to give the time slot to Terry.]*

With his wife, he ran a music store in Des Moines and instructed children on various instruments, but nowadays he needed Social Security to keep up with his bills.

He was curious and a good listener, **[presumably an allusion to the half hour conversation Singular and I had during the trial]** but his extremism regarding abortion wasn't far below the surface.

> *[I wonder how long it will be reported as "extremism", to raise a legal argument that relies on what every category of court-recognized fact-finders has ruled unanimously? However, that point had not entered my writing by 2010. I noted then, only that Congress had "established" the fact 6 years before.]*

Once Tiller was dead, Leach had begun studying how to use the killing as a vehicle to bring the necessity defense into the courtroom in a serious way, during a high-profile case, in order to get crucial issues in front of a judge, a jury, and the national press. He wanted the Roeder trial to become a publicized legal forum on abortion.

> *Actually, getting the facts in the news is important to me only indirectly. The biggest reason I think it is important that the general public correctly understand the law, is so that when judges sidestep the defense, the public will know and will hold judges accountable to squarely address the issues.*

While not an attorney himself, he was a dedicated student of the law and had finished his 104-page motion, written on behalf of Roeder and submitted to Judge Wilbert in the weeks preceding jury selection.

Like others in his movement, Leach drew parallels between the fight to stop abortion at the start of the twenty-first century and the battle to end slavery in the years leading up to the start of the Civil War in 1861. The anti-abortionists liked to cite the infamous 1857 Dred Scott U.S. Supreme Court decision, which ruled that people of African descent imported into the United States and held as slaves —and their descendants—were not protected by the Constitution and could never become American citizens. Further, Congress could not prohibit slavery in federal territories, slaves could not sue in court, and they could not be removed from their owners without due process. The failure of the legal system to remedy slavery had fed the momentum that created the War Between the States.

When abortion opponents brought up the Dred Scott decision, one implication was that because the U.S. Supreme Court had made abortion legal under Roe v. Wade, the only option left to prevent the killing of the unborn was violence against abortion providers.

Did other "abortion opponents" draw that conclusion? I

With Roeder having sacrificed his freedom in order to make this point, Leach saw his chance to have an impact on the trial and possibly on setting legal precedents. He'd taken the writing of his motion very solemnly, citing case law and quoting the Bible, but then presented the document as if Roeder had penned it himself.

[Singular leaves the impression for the legally uneducated that I was trying to trick people. But the law requires this process. Because I am not a lawyer, I am not allowed to sign my own name to a document I write for a

207

defendant. But I can write a document for a defendant, and IF the defendant is willing, he can then sign his own name to it and submit it to the court, taking full legal responsibility for it himself. The evidence that this process is legal is that I never went to jail for it, even though hundreds of top Planned Barrenhood lawyers want me there.]

"Every defendant," the motion began, "has the right to present his theory of his defense..." While Roeder appreciated the efforts of his attorneys, Steve Osburn and Mark Rudy, the letter said, "they have publicly given mixed signals about their willingness to represent me on the central theory of my defense, which is the *only* reason I maintain my innocence and demand a trial by jury, and is the *only* reason I took the action which got me here... American justice embodies the vision of the freedom of defendants to at least raise their defense high enough to be shot down in a public forum after all sides are heard...The facts and arguments motivating defendant are not the exclusive fabrications of wild-eyed fringe kook radical fanatics, but are established by American leaders who include Congressmen, presidents, and Supreme Court justices..." As the document unfolded **under the guise of the defendant,** ...

[Again, the insinuation that I was trying to trick people. The fact is I was articulating, as well as I could, and as every lawyer is supposed to attempt, what I understood were Scott's feelings and reasons. We talked much, to help me be sure, and I sent him a draft in advance of the final copy that he read and submitted, and encouraged him to hand-write any changes he wanted. He made no changes.]

...Leach delivered his own...

[My own? Millions of prolifers through thousands of articles share my frustration that courts fail to address some of the most basic and obvious issues. Threats? Threats? "Warning", of what I myself am powerless to accomplish, yes; "threat" means stating a harm which I intend to accomplish.]

...subtle warnings and threats: "Courts simply have failed to squarely address questions about the legality of abortion to the satisfaction of even a majority of Americans. This case presents the court an opportunity to resolve these lingering disputes and heal America, which will end the violence. It is America Herself which will suffer, if Courts gloss over these unanswered questions one more time.

"Conscience's cry for justice will continue to press for satisfaction outside legal channels, as long as legitimate questions cannot be addressed through legal channels...

"Defendant desires the violence to stop. On both sides. Defendant offers the rest of his life for the lives of the unborn whose murders he prevented...Kansas law will not help a hero who saves thousands of lives if the cruel and unusual slaying of these human souls is legal..."

> *[Singular skips what followed in my brief, a quote from Kansas law: "21-3211(a) A person is justified in the use of force against another when and to the extent it appears to such person and such person reasonably believes that such force is necessary to defend such person or a third person against such other's imminent use of unlawful force."]*

(Singular's quote of the brief, continued:) "what really made me despair [was] the law could not or would not touch him [Dr. Tiller]."

To support his argument, Leach mentioned another famous American criminal trial: hadn't the deceased unborn Connor Peterson been legally regarded as a person and a homicide victim, along with his mother, Laci, in the notorious 2005 Scott Peterson double murder case?

> *[Singular passes on my mistake. Actually the murder was December 24, 2002. In my brief I said the legislation was passed in 2005, the date which Singular repeats, but actually it was April 1, 2004.]*

Therefore, shouldn't all unborn fetuses be viewed the same way in the courtroom?

[My argument was not that all unborn fetuses should be viewed the same way as born children because the infant Connor was regarded as a person in the murder case, but because all unborn human babies are declared humans/persons by Congress, whose findings of facts are in ordinary cases highly regarded by the Supreme Court.]

Since 2005, Leach wrote, the "entire legality of abortion has been reversed," even though this may not yet appear to be true because of current inconsistencies in case law.

"The only mechanism for resolving this is a case that requires those inconsistencies to be resolved. This is that case."

[This summary does not explain well the process by which court precedents are updated according to newly established facts. It leaves out a sentence which I think is needed for it to make sense. Besides that, Singular's quote gets a word wrong. Here is my statement:

[Referring to the 2004 law which establishes all unborn babies as humans/persons:] "Up until such time as courts declare laws unconstitutional, courts must conform their rulings to them. No court has declared this law unconstitutional, so Roe v. Wade, and the entire legality of abortion, has been reversed since 2005. It may not appear so now, but that is only because inconsistencies between law and case law are not resolved instantly; the only mechanism for resolving them is a case that requires those inconsistencies to be resolved. This is that case.

Leach ended with a flourish, evoking the cultural war that had pervaded the United States since the 1960s. Woven into his words was the same impassioned rhetoric about a changed and changing America used by the men in the Order a quarter century earlier.

[Huh? What "Order"? Searching the book, I find on page 5 that Singular is talking about "a small band of neo-Nazis from the Northwest, called the Order, who'd committed nearly 250 other crimes."

[Well, I don't know anything about "The Order". Never

heard of it. But American conversation is more productive when each idea is judged on its own merits, rather than by some imagined loose association or similarity to some other idea that has already been successfully shot down, eliminating the need to waste a separate bullet shooting this new one down.

[Certainly "impassioned rhetoric" is no measure of the correctness of an idea, since the most successful liars are masters of it. It is a distraction – I hope not a deliberate one – from the duty of honest men to evaluate whether the information I have given is actually true. Unfortunately I see no such scrutiny here – only a dismissal of it as "impassioned rhetoric" like that of a few criminal loonies.]

(Continuing description of "The Order":) They'd hated what their country had become and saw no alternative but to blame others for the massiveness and complexity of that change.

[Huh? I don't regard "blaming others" as much of a solution! And I don't think showing courts the specific legally correct way forward from their alleged "inability to speculate" about "when life begins", and devoting years of my life to getting that solution where it will be considered, quite matches the tenor of the idiom "blaming others".]

"I pray," Leach wrote, "along with God's spiritual army that the terrible natural consequences prophesied for crimes so great as America's need not fall any harder than they already have. I pray America will turn from kicking the roses barefooted (Acts 9:5) to cradling the bruised but still fragrant roses, allowing the bloodshed to stop on all sides.

"What suffering has been the natural consequences of hearts hard enough to slay 50 million of our own offspring! Unfaithfulness. Divorce. Domestic violence. Child abuse. Crime. An economic black hole at hand, created by political corruption added to a depleted work force from abortion and the turning away of immigrant labor. Are we bloody enough yet to stop kicking?

"It is not my vision that America's judiciary will walk still in the dark footsteps of Dred Scott until reversed by a civil war, carrying this scar until America ceases as a nation, but that this time courts will reverse the evil which they initiated and lead our nation in righteousness.

"[signed] Scott Roeder."

The motion claimed that the trial would be a "charade" unless the defendant could argue that his actions were needed to save unborn children. "This is not," Judge Wilbert had said, "going to become a trial over the abortion issue. It will be limited to his [Roeder's] beliefs and how he came to form those beliefs..."

> [Just as I wish this book had treated whether what I wrote was true, by offering some scrutiny to either affirm or refute it, I wish this book had scrutinized this determination of Judge Wilbert that "this is not going to become a trial over abortion", a vow he repeated frequently from the pretrial hearings through the jury deliberations through the trial.
>
> [What else was the trial about? About "his beliefs and how he came to form those beliefs"? Seriously? "Insanity" was not one of the defenses raised. The "Defense of Others" and "Voluntary Manslaughter" defenses required a determination of whether those 60,000 babies Tiller murdered – according to his own website – were humans/persons. Wilbert refused to rule on that fact issue, and refused to allow the jury, the "triers of facts" as he called them, to even know that fact issue, THE ONLY CONTESTED ISSUE OF THE TRIAL, even existed.
>
> [Only by not allowing the defendant to present his only defense, and by not allowing the triers of facts to know the only contested fact issue of the trial, could he fulfill his vow to keep the trial from being "about abortion."
>
> [God had something to say about Wilbert's belligerent, lawless, reason-defying vow. Quite outside Wilbert's power, and certainly contrary to his will, the first day of the trial fell on the 37th Deathday of Roe v. Wade. Every newspaper in the nation, it seemed, noted the irony on their front pages.
>
> [Wilbert had limited control over that. He had to start the trial after jury selection was over. Jury selection is unpredictable, and was made more so by Wilbert's decision to

exclude the press from jury selection, which the press instantly appealed to the Kansas Supreme Court, which ruled against Wilbert the same day. Once open to the press, jury selection was over in another day.

[It is hard for me to imagine writing a book about the trial and omitting that teensy detail. Especially since God underlined it with a jury deliberation that lasted 37 minutes, as newspapers across the globe reported in wonder, though this time without mentioning that those 37 minutes were the conclusion of a trial that began on Roe's 37th birthday.

[There were about a dozen other God-grade "coincidences" about that trial of which I became aware, which I put in a song I named "If you love infanticide", and posted at https://tinyurl.com/y357b3au.

[I must mention another series of "coincidences" which were obviously, emphatically not the will of those who said this: during Scott's trial, there were slips of the tongue, calling Tiller "Killer", by Judge Wilbert, by one of Scott's prosecutors, and by attorney Jean Casarez, lead reporter for In Session. I asked Jean about it in the Wichita courtroom hallway. She was quite embarrassed that I had noticed, and was hopeful that it would be forgotten. But who but God made it happen? It wasn't Jean's fault.

[At the trial, I distinctly heard Wilbert articulate "Killer" when he intended to state his name, "Tiller". When I got a complete digital copy of the transcript I searched for that "slip of the tongue". But the court reporter had dutifully "corrected" it. I would love to get an audio copy of Thursday's trial.

[Before Tiller was shot, he was widely dubbed "Tiller the Killer" by prolifers; although after he was shot, even Operation Rescue's Troy Newman publicly condemned Scott for shooting him. Scott told me he did not expect that, from his many conversations with Newman before.]

After the judge had received the 104 pages, he cracked open still more legal doors on January 8, saying that he could imagine "the very real possibility evidence could come from the defendant alone that would give me a duty to instruct the jury on voluntary manslaughter."

[This is published confirmation of what "In Session" reporter Jean Casarez told me privately, that the brief is

what persuaded the judge to consider a Voluntary Manslaughter defense.]

And that one instruction could change the entire course of the trial, and its verdict. This handful of words angered abortion rights supporters across the country, and by sundown of the eighth, Katherine Spillar, executive vice president of the Feminist Majority Foundation, prepared a statement in response to Judge Wilbert's ruling. "Today's perplexing decision," she said, "is effectively back-door permission for admitted killer Scott Roeder to use a 'justifiable homicide' defense that is both unjustifiable and unconscionable. Allowing an argument that this cold-blooded, premeditated murder could be voluntary manslaughter will embolden anti-abortion extremists and could result in 'open season' on doctors across the country..."

*[**The "Extremist" Label.** See how Singular prejudices the credibility of the legal argument of myself and even of Scott's attorneys who were appointed by Judge Wilbert, by helping a killer lob the label "extremists" over the defendants we help? Singular's following paragraph likewise labels as "extremists" the group trying to find an attorney to help with Scott's legal defense, which included myself.*

[The same label dominated the many articles during Scott's trials, mostly by Judy Thomas and AP reporter Roxanne Hegeman. In Thomas' recent article about Shelley Shannon's release from prison for shooting both arms of late term abortionist George Tiller in 1993, Thomas wrote "[Don Spitz] said Shannon told him she will likely be prohibited from communicating with anti-abortion extremists for some time. ...Spitz said 'So I won't be able to speak to her again once she leaves the halfway house for 2½ years.'"

["Extremists" wasn't Don's label for those on Shannon's no-contact list. That was Thomas's label. Neither Thomas nor Singular nor Hegeman ever applied the label to people who personally execute tens of thousands of babies, or to leaders of the political Party of Murder. It doesn't enter their minds that one must be a Fanatic to take pride in such a career!

Baby killers act with the full blessing of American law,

but certainly not with the blessing of God's Laws. Heaven is where people love and help each other, or at least are willing to let God heal their hearts. How hard is such a heart? Will such a murderer come to Heaven's portals and say "if destroying people isn't allowed here, I'm going there"?

[Next excerpt, from page 264:] "While Operation Rescue, Kansans for Life, and other anti-abortion groups had immediately distanced themselves from Roeder, the extremists in the movement rallied around the inmate. They were still talking about pooling their funds and hiring a private attorney for the defendant to fight the first-degree murder charge with a legal strategy called the 'necessity defense' or 'defending those who cannot defend themselves.' One was justified in committing a murder, went this argument, in order to stop a greater evil. The tack had been tried before in the case of Paul Hill, and it had failed."

[Well now that you mention that case, how about a note about WHY it "failed"? As it turns out, Florida's version of what other states call the "Necessity Defense" is called "Justifiable Homicide", because that Florida law specifically justifies even killing someone, if that is the only way to save lives. So obviously that would be Paul Hill's defense.

[But Paul's judge, as usual, would not allow the jury to even know the defense existed, much less rule on it, even though (1) it is essentially a fact issue, (2) juries are supposed to be "judges of the facts", and (3) it was supposed to be a "trial by jury"!

[Not only did the judge refuse to let Hill explain his only defense, a fact issue, to the jury, the triers of facts, but the judge would not even allow Hill to choose his own attorney! Hill's choice was Michael Hirsch, a graduate of Regent University Law School, founded by Pat Robertson, founder of Christian Broadcasting Network. Hirsh's J.D. thesis was even about the Necessity Defense in relation to abortion, a fact noted in prolife media at the time. Hirsch lived out of state, but it would have been a simple routine matter for the judge to arrange for him to speak for Hill on the legal coat-tails of a Florida attorney. The judge refused.

[To not allow a man to present his defense, or to engage

his own lawyer, or to let the jury (triers of facts) know about, much less judge, the only contested issue of the trial – a fact issue, doesn't sound to me like a failure of the defense, but a huge failure of American justice.

[Small wonder the jury sent Hill to death row, where he was executed years later, just days after he was able to finish his book, "Mix My Blood With the Blood of the Unborn: The Writings of Paul Jennings Hill" – January 10, 2008, available at Amazon. As much as the judge stacked the case against Hill, as if he was afraid of the jury acquitting, it is a miracle the jury didn't lynch him before the trial was over.

[Incidentally, Michael Hirsch was one of the attorneys our small group approached about defending Roeder, but he required, if I remember correctly, $80,000, while our group had little over $20,000.]

"Donald Spitz, the sponsor of the Army of God Web site, sent Roeder seven anti-abortion pamphlets, which the prisoner distributed to others through the mail. He got more support from two anti-abortionists in the Kansas City area, Anthony Leake and Eugene Frye, and Leake in particular saw him as a new hero of their movement. Roeder had the backing of the activist Michael Bray, author of *A Time to Kill,* and of Dave Leach of Des Moines, Iowa.

"In 1996, Leach had interviewed Roeder for his Uncle Ed Show on Des Moines's public access cable, giving Roeder the chance to explain his Freeman philosophy."

[Which, by the way, was a lot less controversial than saving lives with a gun. I still don't relate to Freeman ideas or methods, but it made an interesting show. The show is posted at https://www.youtube.com/watch?v=izXJHdnHStc]

"In the mid-1990s, Roeder had visited Shelley Shannon in a Topeka jail, and she now sent him money from her cell in Minnesota, where she was still serving time for her anti-abortion crimes. Bray, Leach, and Spitz had all signed the 1993 declaration advocating the use of force against abortion providers, distributed by Paul Hill before he'd killed Dr. John Britton.

"Following Tiller's murder, Leach created a homemade video, available on the Internet."

> *[See www.Saltshaker.us/Scott-Roeder-Resources.htm. The girls were 10 years old. They played the role of news anchors for Pee Wee TV. I played three roles: myself, a prolife lawyer, and an abortionist gangster.*
>
> *["Homemade?" Well, I suppose most Youtube videos, produced by people who don't own major television networks, could be called "homemade". But I must say the editing, acting, and scripts, not to mention the grasp of law presented, were on the high end of "homemade".*
>
> *[Referring to Tiller's death as a "murder" shows the prejudice of Singular against babies. Had Roeder shot Tiller to keep him from murdering any more criminal trial authors after he had already murdered 60,000, Singular wouldn't refer to Tiller's killing as a "murder". Neither our laws, nor does common sense, call it "murder" to kill a murderer in the act of murdering – unless no human beings were being murdered.]*

"It featured two very young girls, one black and one white, who stood next to some stuffed animals and posed questions. "Can a pro-lifer," the white girl asked, "shoot an abortionist and still get a trial...by jury?" Leach answered this by saying that "most lawyers" did not expect Roeder to get "what average citizens would call a trial by jury. I'm trying to help him get one."

"To this end, Leach began composing a detailed and legally sophisticated motion that would run to more than a hundred pages and eventually be submitted to the judge in Roeder's case.

"Leach would emerge as the defendant's most significant anti-abortion ally and his document would play a role in the upcoming trial—a role that some found outrageous."

> *["...a role that ONLY SOME found outrageous"? Wow! That's generous.]*

[Excerpt beginning p. 324:] "The only thing perhaps more

unusual than the tension in the gallery was Roeder's legal position. He was not disputing that he'd 'killed' Dr. Tiller. The defendant not only agreed with nearly every aspect of the state's case against him, but was about to provide some new details that made him look even guiltier of the premeditated destruction of the physician. He revealed, for example, that he'd thought about cutting off Tiller's hands."

[That sounds pretty barbaric, doesn't it? Singular leaves it at barbaric, omitting the context which mitigates it at least somewhat. Roeder's reasoning, he explained, was that he wanted to end Tiller's violence against babies with the least possible violence to Tiller that would succeed in ending Tiller's killing spree. But remember, years before, Shelley Shannon had shot Tiller in both arms with the same goal, but Tiller was back to "work" the very next day.]

"Roeder's goal, like Leach's and Terry's, was to make the trial about abortion and to give the jury the opportunity to consider his beliefs and motives in killing the doctor.

"If just one juror among the eight men and four women agreed with his views and felt that he'd stopped a greater evil in Wichita, he or she might vote for his acquittal. If the judge gave the jury the instruction that they could find the defendant guilty of voluntary manslaughter, instead of murder, this might make casting that vote much easier."

[Just to clarify: our focus was not what happened to Scott. It obviously wasn't his focus either. He offered his life, not knowing if he would be shot on site, or executed later, or spend life in prison; his was pressuring the judge to squarely address the only contested issue of the trial and allow the jury to do its job, which would have legally "established" that abortion is legally recognizable as murder and cannot remain legal. The slaughter would have ended.]

"By ten a.m., the judge had instructed the jurors about the charges and sent them off to deliberate. In the lobby, crowded with cops and full of activity, Dave Leach stood by himself taking in the movement around him, as the spectators clustered in their usual groups and talked on cell phones. He was joined by Randall Terry, who'd been loitering nearby. Throughout the morning, Terry had been passing out a three-page flyer about what was wrong with the anti-abortion movement and how it needed to make a stronger commitment to its goals and take bolder steps.

"Seizing the opportunity to talk with Leach, because he was now accompanied by a journalist, Terry strode up in his striking alligator boots and introduced himself to the reporter."

> *[I don't think Singular is very impressed with Randall Terry. Actually he sings Terry's number pretty much right on key, although possibly the details here call for clarification.*
>
> *[I suspect the unidentified "journalist" in this memoroid is Singular himself. I did have a nice conversation with Singular for several minutes; it was ending as Terry came.*
>
> *[In fairness Terry did not talk to me only to cut into a conversation with a reporter. At another time we talked for a good half hour together. And we had several other short conversations. And months later when he came to Des Moines to protest something, he called me up and invited me to join him.*
>
> *[I appreciated the time with the hero of the Operation Rescue movement. I made notes afterward about the meeting. I'll add them to the end of these Singular excerpts.]*

"The conversation had only begun when a uniformed deputy approached. 'You better get up to the ninth floor,' he said. 'The verdict is already in?' He nodded. 'Get up there.' The trio went to the bay of elevators and stepped into an open one, Terry complaining that he couldn't believe that less than forty-five minutes (thirty-seven, actually) had passed since the judge had given the case to the jury. Leach was silent, but a little smile played around the corner of his mouth, as it often did, his purpose never as obvious as Terry's.

"The day before, Leach had said that bringing

national attention to the Roeder trial, and getting the public to think about violence being justified to stop an abortion doctor, and motivating a judge to consider the necessity defense and the voluntary-manslaughter charge in these circumstances were all victories. He didn't seem to take the situation nearly as personally as Terry.

" 'This case can be the start of a new process,' he had said. 'And no matter what anyone says, the trial was about abortion.'

"From her own cell in Minnesota, Shelley Shannon commented on the jury's decision in an e-mail to Dave Leach. Her message, which found its way to the Associated Press, was that because of the trial's outcome, America could expect more violence. 'Abortionists are killed,' she wrote, 'because they are serial murderers of innocent children who must be stopped, and they will continue to be stopped, even though Scott didn't get a fair trial. May God bless Scott for his faithfulness and brave actions on stand.'

[Excerpt p. 344:] "A few days later, Dave Leach recorded a long prison interview with Roeder via telephone and put it up on YouTube. He gave the inmate the time and opportunity to say for the public all the graphic things about abortion that the judge had not allowed him to say in court. He reemphasized his lack of sympathy for Jeanne Tiller and again compared her to a woman who'd been married to a hit man. [https://www.youtube.com/watch?v=JkIw_fqmC1k]

[Excerpt beginning p. 7:] "Did Roeder realize that back in the 1990s Kansas had reinstated capital punishment and if convicted he could have faced lethal injection? 'That never crossed my mind,' he said.

"'What Tiller was doing was wrong, even though it wasn't illegal. When something is morally wrong, even if it's legal, it violates God's law. God's law is always more important than man's law.'

"He paused, made eye contact with me through the glass, and forcefully stated, 'I stopped abortion in Wichita.'

"It took a few moments for the full weight of those five words to sink in, given the history of the city's involvement with the issue since the mid-1970s.

"'I've heard,' he went on, 'that since this happened three women have changed their minds and decided not to get an abortion, because Tiller isn't around anymore.'

"He smiled and said, 'Wichita is no longer the abortion capital of the world.'

"He conveyed no emotion at all about Dr. Tiller's death—a void where one might have expected rage or anxiety or fear about his legal fate. Nothing was there, and that was the most unsettling thing about him. He seemed to have released his own personal stress over the abortion issue, and could at last relax.

"I asked if this was true. 'Yes,' he said. 'I'm more relaxed now and so is Wichita.'"

Interaction with Randall Terry

"Why are you putting this in your book?" I ask myself.

"Well, it's kind of interesting to me", I answer.

"But to anybody else?"

"Maybe not so much."

"Is it relevant to stopping abortion?"

No answer.

The best excuse I can come up with is that it graphically explains, and then links with Scripture, our temptation to acknowledge only part of the truth, which we justify for "strategic" reasons, but then when others do it, to blame them for their "weak faith".

Perhaps this can help us understand the pressures on prolife leaders. Perhaps this can help us understand our own fears, and put them in the context of the Word of God.

I recorded these notes from memory, two months after my conversations with Terry:

During Scott's trial, Terry came to give press conferences and observe the trial. He was certainly a media draw! Not only did he get about a dozen reporters behind his rope when he scheduled his meeting, while only one reporter (NPR) interviewed me and later did not air the interview, but *In Session* had scheduled an interview with me, but canceled it to give Terry my spot, and then never rescheduled mine!

Not that my view of Terry is colored by this, but I am giving you a view of the far greater public draw he has than mine, and therefore the far greater public scrutiny of him than what I suffer.

Terry, on Wednesday of the trial, (January 27, 2010) showed me an advance copy of what he was going to talk about at his press conference. It was a vision of what is wrong with the prolife movement.

It was actually very good at stating the problem, but it offered no solution. One problem was the surrender of rhetoric; he listed great movements of the past – prohibition, slavery, etc. and said their powerful rhetoric gave their movements power. Another problem was leaders who do not say what they know is true, in order to succeed.

I stood out of camera range to take in much of his press conference. I was grateful that he eloquently made the case that Scott Roeder is not getting a fair trial – the facts about infanticide are not getting a fair hearing – and *although he personally condemns Scott's action,* Scott deserves a real trial.

He personally condemns Scott's action? His Operation Rescue website used to have Proverbs 24:10-12 on its masthead: "Rescue those who are perishing, who are being led away to slaughter." It was removed after the first shooting, in 1993. He used to preach, "If you believe the unborn are humans/persons, ACT like they are humans/persons."

So I was curious: by what logic did he "personally condemn" Scott? And yet want a fair trial for infanticide? When abortion is legally recognized by courts as infanticide, won't that make Scott look a little more heroic for stopping the most notorious chunk of it?

I remarked to Terry afterwards that his point was like a point I have made: that even if you can't stand Scott, stand for his right to present his only defense, because if that is allowed, abortion will end! But why would Terry "personally condemn" Scott?

I approached him in the cafeteria to tell him the paper was very good, but what is the solution he proposes? He said the solution is to understand the problem.

So I proposed my solution: I talked about the legal arguments I had discovered that legally authorize lawmakers to outlaw infanticide *already*. I talked about how these arguments are in the Roeder trial record, and by affirming them, prolifers can ride them to end infanticide.

I don't remember the exact order in the conversation, but I asked him about some Operation Rescue history. I asked if I remembered correctly that the masthead of Operation Rescue included Proverbs 24:10-12, from whence Operation Rescue got its name; along with the slogan, "If you believe it's murder, act like it's murder!" but that verse, and that slogan, disappeared from the masthead after the first shooting.

I can't remember if he positively affirmed that detail, except to confide in me, that "morally", he agrees with me about the justice of Scott's action!

In other words, what he told the press about "personally condemning" Scott, was a strategic lie! (Now why did I write that? Aren't all lies strategic?)

But then he described how much scrutiny he is under; he has to be careful, he has to watch what he says, etc.

I asked, but isn't holding back from all you know to be true, for strategic reasons, precisely what you accuse prolife leaders of in your press release?

He answered, "Good point."

I had a second opportunity a couple of days later to talk with him again at some length. He was still considering my point, it appeared.

I marveled at his intellectual integrity, to concede so vital a point to anybody, much less a nobody like me. Furthermore I respect his position, even though I criticized it. Technically, I can say it shows a blindness springing from lack of courage: but that is like criticizing Peter for sinking in doubt after only walking on water a few yards, while I have not even taken a single step on water! When I accomplish as much with my whole life as Randall Terry has accomplished for a few years, then I will decide if I want to call him a coward!

Back at the cafeteria, at some point he became alarmed at my linkage between the opportunity I described to stop infanticide, and Scott's action. When I said something that sounded to him like I was going to endorse violence, his eyes widened and he warned me that was exactly the kind of thing I needed to be careful of because the place was crawling with Feds who would be happy for a reason to prosecute me.

I responded by explaining that my vision is of stopping abortion without firing another shot. I explained how it would work, a theme I developed in my video series "Trial by Jury".

Once Necessity is uncensored, through precedents being considered in this trial, so that people can block infanticidist doors without fear of arrest, abortion will end peacefully; and in fact anyone who shoots, after the opportunity to sit is created, would have no defense in court because shooting would not be the least violent way to effectively stop infanticide. [Which is one of the conditions of the Necessity Defense.] My explanation took the steam out his objection.

Back to Peter: this giant who walked on water, who named Jesus as the Christ, did the same thing I accused Randall Terry of, which Terry had accused prolife leaders of: he held back from proclaiming all he knew to be true, for strategic reasons:

> Galatians 2:11 But when Peter was come to Antioch, I withstood him to the face, because he was to be blamed. 12 For before that certain came from James, he did eat with the Gentiles: but when they were come, he withdrew and separated himself, fearing them which were of the circumcision. 13 And the other Jews dissembled likewise with him; insomuch that Barnabas also was carried away with their dissimulation. 14 But when I saw that they walked not uprightly according to the truth of the gospel, I said unto Peter before them all, If thou, being a Jew, livest after the manner of Gentiles, and not as do the Jews, why compellest thou the Gentiles to live as do the Jews?

But what was remarkable about Randall Terry was the same thing that was remarkable about Peter: when corrected, he did not put up a wall, or fume, or attack, but he received it, acknowledged it, and considered it. How many will do that?

Here is where Peter showed what he was made of, writing about Paul many years later, surely aware of what Paul had written about him to the Galatians, if not still burning from the memory of when the incident happened:

> 2 Peter 3:15 And account that the longsuffering of our Lord is salvation; even as our beloved brother Paul also according to the wisdom given unto him hath written unto you; 16 As also in all his epistles, speaking in them of these things; in which are some things hard to be understood, which they that are unlearned and unstable wrest, as they do also the other scriptures, unto their own destruction.

Conclusion

There is something obviously wrong and yet ingeniously obscured about courts insisting the Constitution protects the right of mothers to murder their very own babies. When I begin to explain, as I do in this book, people frequently interrupt me as if "finishing my sentence", with some point that has impressed them about what is absurdly wrong about legal abortion.

Like "they protect eagle eggs but they won't recognize the baby of a human as a human." Or Scriptures like Psalm 139 which describes "me" from before "I" had limbs, or Luke 2 which describes a 6-month-old womb baby leaping with joy at the sound of a righteous voice. Or a video of an ultrasound.

Sometimes that "finishing of my sentence" seems to dampen any further interest in the subject. Like "why are telling me about this? I already know how dumb it is to blame genocide on the Constitution. You can't persuade me that it is dumber than I already know it is."

Yet this widespread grasp of how dumb abortion's legality is seems unable to answer the objection raised by abortion supporters: "but it's legal." (My answer: abortion is legally recognizable as murder, by criteria established in Roe v. Wade.)

More importantly, this grasp has proven impotent to interject itself into court rulings that keep abortion "legal".

Most ironically and pathetically: the very people who tell me the humanity of the unborn is so obvious that it merits no further discussion, say they don't have the intelligence, or the "legal mind", to help me get prolifers and lawmakers behind a strategy for interjecting the obvious into court rulings in a way that will end legal abortion. Even lawyers have told me they can't process this opportunity because that is not their specialty in law – which is the situation of virtually all lawyers, since defending impoverished prolifers from a "stacked deck" against even explaining your only defense to the jury is not the financial base upon which to build a legal specialty.

This article, and my book, are about how to get the obvious – what Roe itself called the "of course" – into court cases in a language judges understand. And with legal arguments so irrefutable that it will be impossible for judges to squarely address them and keep abortion legal. And in at atmosphere of political pressure so well informed that judges will not be able to get away with not addressing them.

Ezekiel 3:18-20 warns "When I say unto the wicked, Thou shalt surely die; and thou givest him not warning, nor speakest to warn the wicked from his wicked way, to save his life; the same wicked man shall die in his iniquity; but his blood will I require at thine hand."

Do we escape this judgment by telling *each other* how obviously evil abortion is? No. We must tell *the wicked*. In this case, we must especially tell those "at the point of the spear" of perpetuation of this evil. Judges. Not that they are the whole "spear"! But they started the madness and they can stop it.

Judges only listen to us through court cases. This article, and my book, are about what we, together, can do to to get the obvious before them.

Dave Leach
Family Music Center
4110 SW 9th Street
Des Moines IA 50315
Store and cell: 515-244-3711

Websites:
www.Saltshaker.us Bible studies about shining Bible light
www.SaveTheWorld.Saltshaker.us A wiki
www.Talk2me.Saltshaker.us A wordpress blog

Video channels:
Biblewizard2
FamilyBandChannel

Books at Amazon.com:

[This book:] "How States can Outlaw Abortion in a Way that Survives Courts" Court recognized fact finders have unanimously established what Roe said would end legal abortion. (Free PDF: www.saltshaker.us/SLIC/HowStates CanOutlawAbortion InAWayThatSurvivesCourts.pdf)

"The Prehistoric Angel Diary" Book 1: From Beelzebub's Fall thru Adam's Fall – the diary of an Angel! (A fictitious angel, but an angel nonetheless!)

"Eternal Hell: Heaven's Loving Purpose" Hell's aim: Heaven's Love - a treasure hunt through the Word of God